D1832427

ARCHAEOLOGICAL SURVEY OF INDIA NEW IMPERIAL SERIES, VOL. XXXVIII.

ANTIQUITIES OF INDIAN TIBET

BY

A. H. FRANCKE, Ph.D.
OF THE MORAVIAN MISSION

PART I
PERSONAL NARRATIVE

WITH MAP, 45 PLATES AND 4 TEXT-ILLUSTRATIONS

Edited under the authority of the Government of India

GYAN

Published by

Gyan Publishing House
5, Ansari Road
Daryaganj, New Delhi-110002
Phone: 011-47034999, 9811692060
E-mail: books@gyanbooks.com

Distribution Network
gyanbooks.com
India, USA, Canada, UK, Australia, France

© Publisher

All rights reserved. No part of this work may be reproduced, stored, adapted, or transmitted in any form or by any means, electronic, mechanical, photocopying, micro-filming, recording or otherwise, or translated in any language, without the prior written permission of the copyright owner and the publisher.

ISBN : 978-81-212-2223-5 (Set)
ISBN : 978-81-212-2123-8 (HB)
First Published, 1914

2nd Impression 2021

Printed at: Gyan Press, Delhi.

The book is sold subject to the condition that it shall not, by way of trade or otherwise, be lent, resold, hired out, or otherwise circulated without the prior publisher's written consent.

Antiquities of Indian Tibet, Part I
Author: A. H. Francke

ARCHAEOLOGICAL SURVEY OF INDIA, NEW IMPERIAL SERIES, VOL. XXXVIII.

Antiquities of Indian Tibet

BY

A. H. FRANCKE, Ph.D.,

OF THE MORAVIAN MISSION

PART I
PERSONAL NARRATIVE

WITH MAP, 45 PLATES AND 4 TEXT-ILLUSTRATIONS

Edited under the authority of the Government of India

CALCUTTA
SUPERINTENDENT GOVERNMENT PRINTING, INDIA
1914

AGENTS FOR THE SALE OF BOOKS

PUBLISHED BY THE

Superintendent Government Printing, India, Calcutta.

IN THE UNITED KINGDOM.

Constable & Co., 10, Orange Street, Leicester Square, London, W.C.

P. S. King & Son, 2 & 4, Great Smith Street, Westminster, London, S.W.

H. S. King & Co., 65, Cornhill, and 9, Pall Mall, London, W.

Kegan Paul, Trench, Trübner & Co., 68—74, Carter Lane, London, E.C.

Grindlay & Co., 54, Parliament Street, London, S.W.

Bernard Quaritch, 11, Grafton Street, New Bond Street, London, W.

T. Fisher Unwin, 1, Adelphi Terrace, London, W.C.

W. Thacker & Co., 2, Creed Lane, London, E.C.

Luzac & Co., 46, Great Russell Street, London, W.C.

Deighton, Bell & Co., Cambridge.

B. H. Blackwell, 50 & 51, Broad Street, Oxford.

Oliver & Boyd, Tweeddale Court, Edinburgh.

E. Ponsonby, Ld., 116, Grafton Street, Dublin.

ON THE CONTINENT.

Martinus Nijhoff, The Hague, Holland.

Ernest Leroux, 28, Rue Bonaparte, Paris, France.

IN INDIA AND CEYLON.

Thacker, Spink & Co., Calcutta and Simla.

Newman & Co., Calcutta.

S. K. Lahiri & Co., Calcutta.

R. Cambray & Co., Calcutta.

B. Banerjee & Co., Calcutta.

The Calcutta School Book and Useful Literature Society, 309, Bow Bazar Street, Calcutta.

Butterworth & Co. (India), Ld., Calcutta.

The Weldon Library, 18-5, Chowringhee, Calcutta.

Rai M. C. Sircar Bahadur & Sons, 75-1-1, Harrison Road, Calcutta.

Higginbotham & Co., Madras.

V. Kalyanarama Iyer & Co., Madras.

G. A. Natesan & Co., Madras.

S. Murthy & Co., Madras.

Thompson & Co., Madras.

Temple & Co., Madras.

Combridge & Co., Madras.

P. R. Rama Iyer & Co., Madras.

Thacker & Co., Ld., Bombay.

A. J. Combridge & Co., Bombay.

D. B. Taraporevala, Sons & Co., Bombay.

Radhabai Atmaram Sagoon, Bombay.

Sunder Pandurang, Bombay.

Gopal Narayan & Co., Bombay.

Ram Chandra Govind & Son, Kalbadevi, Bombay.

N. B. Mathur, Superintendent, Nazir Kanun Hind Press, Allahabad.

A. Chand & Co., Lahore, Punjab.

Rai Sahib M. Gulab Singh and Sons, Mufid-i-Am Press, Lahore and Calcutta.

Superintendent, American Baptist Mission Press, Rangoon.

Babu S. C. Talukdar, Proprietor, Students and Co., Cooch Behar.

A. M. & J. Ferguson, Colombo, Ceylon.

EDITOR'S PREFACE.

It was on the strong recommendation of Dr. J. H. Marshall, C.I.E., Director-General of Archæology in India, that the Government of India applied to the Moravian Mission Board for the loan of the services of Dr. A. H. Francke with a view to his carrying out an archæological survey of the districts which once formed the kingdom of Western Tibet. These mountainous regions, now belonging to the Indian Empire and therefore here indicated as "Indian Tibet," had never been explored by any scholar combining a knowledge of local history and antiquities with a thorough acquaintance of Tibetan. These rare accomplishments Dr. Francke had acquired in the course of his many years' sojourn in Ladakh and Lahul, the fruits whereof had been made known to the learned world through a series of valuable publications, among which was his "History of Western Tibet." Dr. Francke was, therefore, singularly fitted for the proposed task, whilst his previous wanderings in the mountains of "Indian Tibet" had trained him to endure the severe privations and hardships which must always attend a journey through so inhospitable a country. We, therefore, owe a great debt of gratitude to Bishop B. La Trobe and the Moravian Mission Board for placing the services of so excellent an explorer at the disposal of the Government of India.

Starting from Simla on the 14th of June, 1909, he travelled up to Satluj Valley through the hill-state of Rāmpur-Bashahr, and by the Hang Pass (16,000 feet) reached Spiti. He then crossed the Pharang Pass (18,300 feet) and continued his journey through Rubshu along the wild shores of Lake Thsomo Riri. Two more mountain passes, the Phologongkha Pass (16,500 feet) and the Thaglang Pass (17,500 feet), had to be surmounted to enable the explorer to reach Ladakh, the real centre of the ancient realm of Western Tibet. After a brief stay at Leh, the ancient seat of the *rGyal-po* rulers of that country, Dr. Francke travelled westwards, and, after crossing the Photho La (14,000 feet), the Namika Pass (13,400 feet) and the Zoji La (11,300 feet), reached Śrīnagar on the 16th of October.

In the course of his four months' travel—it will be seen—Dr. Francke had to cross seven mountain passes of an average height equal to that of Mont-Blanc. In the valleys, also, the roads in these hill tracts are often of the most primitive description, while the crossing of rivers by rope bridges adds to the perils of the journey. Owing to the nature of the country to be traversed, the explorer had to march on foot most of the way from Simla to Śrīnagar, except where the rarified air compelled him to mount the yak —certainly not the most comfortable means of locomotion.

The journal, however, here published, bears ample evidence that the exceptional difficulties of the road had little effect on the spirits of the explorer, who was animated by the true enthusiasm of the scholar and who, moreover, was compensated in no small measure by the solemn grandeur of that mountain scenery so seldom seen by cultured eyes. The very important additions to our knowledge of the archæology and history of Indian Tibet are the best reward for labours so strenuous and so cheerfully borne.

As Dr. Marshall proceeded to England on leave in April 1910, and I was appointed to officiate during his absence, it fell to me to arrange for the publication of Dr. Francke's materials. No task could have been more welcome to me, since for several years I had found in Dr. Francke a fellow-scholar who had chosen a field of research bordering on that which it had been my good fortune to explore. Personal experience thus enabled me to appreciate the value of Dr. Francke's results as well as the exertions by which they had been attained.

The Government of India readily sanctioned our proposals which provided for the publication of Dr. Francke's results in two parts, one giving the personal narrative of his adventures and researches and the other containing all inscriptions and chronicles collected by him in the course of his tour. It has been our object in the present volume to illustrate Dr. Francke's account as fully as possible by means of the excellent photographs taken by Babu Pindi Lal of the Archæological Survey. The forty-five plates, each containing two photographic views, testify to the excellence of Pindi Lal's work, while Dr. Francke's narrative bears ample evidence that the explorer found in his photographer not only a useful assistant but also a cheerful companion who did his work successfully under very trying conditions. The reproduction of the plates was entrusted to the well-known lithographers, Messrs. W. Griggs & Sons, of Peckham, London.

The map showing Dr. Francke's route, which has been added to the present volume is an extract from Survey sheet No. 835-S. 1905. It has been especially prepared by Mr. H. Hargreaves, Superintendent, Archæological Survey *pro tempore*, who has marked on it several places not found on the original. Dr. Francke's route, as well as the places visited by him in the course of his tour, has been marked in red. The map has been reproduced at the Office of the Survey of India.

J. PH. VOGEL.

CONTENTS.

AUTHOR'S PREFACE.

In publishing my journal of an archæological tour in Indian Tibet, undertaken on behalf of the Indian Government, I wish in the first place to express my sincere thanks to Dr. J. H. Marshall, C.I.E., Director-General of Archæology, who made all necessary arrangements in connection with my deputation—no slight addition to the already heavy burden of his office—and who has followed my journey with the keenest interest. As in the spring of 1910 he went home on long leave, Dr. J. Ph. Vogel, while officiating for him, undertook to arrange for the publication of my materials. His proposals met with the approval of the Government of India in the Education Department, and it was decided that my report should consist of two volumes both fully illustrated : the first containing a personal narrative of my journey and the second dealing with the historical chronicles and inscriptions collected in the course of my tour. It is a matter of no small satisfaction that, thanks to the liberality of the Indian Government, my results will be made available in so excellent a form. Dr. Vogel's thorough revision of the whole text has in many ways greatly added to the value of the publication. To Mr. H. Hargreaves, Acting Superintendent in the Archæological Department, I am indebted for assistance in verifying references and preparing a map to illustrate my itinerary. Here I wish also to record my sincerest thanks to the following ladies and gentlemen who have been good enough to read through my first rough manuscript of the journal :—to Dr. John Hutchison of the Church of Scotland Mission in Chamba ; to Mrs. S. A. Becker-Chapman of Herrnhut ; and to Messrs. J. E. Wilkinson and J. Thom of Simla.

I owe my gratitude also to the Public Works Department for placing their resthouses in the Satluj Valley at my disposal. At Poo and Leh I was the guest of the Moravian Missionaries who did their utmost to assist me in my work. Of the greatest importance was my meeting Mr. G. C. L. Howell of the Indian Civil Service in Spiti, at a time when I was suffering from illness. His hospitality, knowledge of local conditions and ready help were of the greatest possible assistance in furthering my undertaking.

A. H. Francke.

ITINERARY.

I.—The Satluj Valley.

June 14. Simla—Kōṭgur (map Kotgaṛh).
„ 15—16. Halt Kōṭgur. Doum festival.
„ 17. Kōṭgur—Nirth.
„ 18. Nirth—Nirmaṇḍ.
„ 19(?) Nirmaṇḍ—Rāmpur (Bashahr State).
„ 22. Rāmpur—Gaura.
„ 23. Gaura—Sarāhan.
„ 24. Sarāhan—Taranda.
„ 25. Taranda—Paunda.
„ 26. Paunda—Urni, by Wangtu bridge
„ 27. Halt Urni.
„ 28. Urni—Chini.
„ 29. Chini—Rarang, by Pangi.
„ 30. Rarang—Kanam, by Jangi.
July 1. Kanam—Shasu (rope bridge).
„ 2. Shasu—Poo.
„ 3—5. Halt Poo.
„ 6. Poo—Namgya.
„ 7. Namgya—Shipke.
„ 8. Halt Shipke.
„ 9. Shipke—Namgya.
„ 10. Namgya—Poo.
„ 11—20. Halt Poo.

II.—From the Satluj to the Indus.

July 21. Poo—Tsuling, by Hang Pass; 16,000 feet.
„ 22. Tsuling—Li.
„ 23. Li—Nako.
„ 24. Nako—Chang (Bashahr State).
„ 25. Halt Chang.
„ 26—29. Chang—Tabo (Spiti).
„ 30. Tabo—Phog.
„ 31. Phog—Drangkhar (map Dankar).
August 1. Halt Drangkhar.
„ 2. Drangkhar—Kaze (map Kaja).
„ 3. Kaze—Kyibar (by way of Ki.)
„ 4. Halt Kyibar.
„ 5. Kyibar—Lhanartsa
„ 6. Lhanartsa—Jugda.
„ 7. Jugda—Drathang, by Pharang Pass; 18,300 feet.

August 8. Drathang—Umna.
„ 9. Umna—Nemo-ringmo.
„ 10. Nemo-ringmo—dKor-rdzod (map Karzok), along Lake Thsomo Riri.
„ 11. Halt dKor-rdzod.
„ 12. dKor-rdzod—Lake mThso-kyag.
„ 13. dThso-kyag—Raldrong.
„ 14. Raldrong—Nyoma (map Nima).
„ 15. Halt Nyoma.
„ 16—18. Nyoma—Lake mThso-dkar, by Phologongkha Pass; 16,500 feet.

III.—The Indus Valley.

„ 19. Lake mThso-dkar—rGya (Ladakh), by Ṫhaglang Pass; 17,500 feet.
„ 20. rGya—Martselang, by Meru.
„ 21. Halt Martselang.
„ 22. Martselang—Leh.
„ 22—September 20. Halt Leh.

IV.—From the Indus to the Jehlam.

September 21. Leh—sNyemo (map Snemo).
„ 22. sNyemo—Saspola, by Basgo and Likir.
„ 23. Visit Alchi.
„ 24. Saspola—sGyera.
„ 25. sGyera—Khalatse.
„ 26—29. Halt Khalatse.
„ 30. Khalatse—Lamayuru.
October 1. Lamayuru—Kharbu, by Phothola Pass; 14,000 feet.
„ 2. Visit Chigtan.
„ 4. Kharbu—Mulbe, by Namika Pass; 13,400 feet.
„ 5. Mulbe—Kargil, by Shargola.
„ 6. Kargil—Shimsha-Kharbu, by Dongga.
„ 7. Shimsha-Kharbu—Dras (or Hembabs).
Dras—Sonamarg (Kashmir), by Zoji La; 11,300 feet.
„ 16. Arrival Śrīnagar.

LIST OF PLATES.

TEXT ILLUSTRATIONS.

BIBLIOGRAPHY.

BAILEY, T. G., A brief grammar of the Kanauri language. *Z. D.M. G.*, vol. LXIII, p. 661.

CONWAY, W. M., Climbing and exploration in the Kārakorum.

CUNNINGHAM, A., Ladak physical, statistical, and historical. London, 1854.

DAS, SARAT CHANDRA, Indian Pandits in the Land of Snow. Calcutta, 1893.

„ , dPag-bsam-ljon-bzang, Tibetan Text and Glossary. Calcutta, 1908.

„ , 'aDzam-gling-ye-shes, English translation. *J. A. S. B.*, 1887.

„ , Journey to Lhasa.

„ , Various historical articles, in *J. A. S. B.*, 1882-1910.

DIACK, A. H., Gazetteer of the Kangra District, Parts II to IV, Kulu, Lahoul and Spiti. Lahore, 1889-1897.

„ , The Kulu dialect of Hindi. Some notes on its grammatical structure, etc. Lahore, 1896.

DUKA, Life of Csoma de Körös.

DUNCAN, JANE E., A summer ride through Western Tibet. London, 1906.

DREW, F., The Jummoo and Kashmir territories, A geographical account. London, 1875.

ELIAS, N. and ROSS, E. DENISON, The Tarikh-i-Rashidi of Mirza Muhammad Haidar Dughlát. A history of the Moghuls of Central Asia. London, 1895.

FLEET, J. F., Corpus Inscriptionum Indicarum, vol. III. Inscriptions of the early Gupta kings and their successors. Calcutta, 1888.

FERGUSSON, JAMES, History of Indian and Eastern Architecture.

FORBES, G., Simla to Shipke in Tibet. Simla.

FRANCKE, A. H., A history of Western Tibet. London, 1907.

„ , Historische und mythologische Erinnerungen der Lahouler. Kyelang 1907.

„ , Musikalische Studien in West Tibet. *Z. D. M. G.*, vol. LIX.

„ , Historische Dokumente von Khalatse. *Z. D. M. G.*, vol. LXI, pp. 583 ff.

„ , The kingdom of gNya-khri-btsan-po, *J. A. S. B.*, vol. VI, pp. 93 ff.

„ , The eighteen songs of the Bononā festival. Dard text, translation, vocabulary. *Ind. Ant.*, vol. XXXIV, pp. 93 ff.

„ , Archæological notes on sBa-lu-mkhar. *Ind. Ant.*, vol. XXXIV, pp. 203 ff.

„ , Archæology in West Tibet. *Ind. Ant.*, vol. XXXV, pp. 237 ff, vol. XXXVI, pp. 85, 148 ff.

„ , First and second collection of Tibetan historical inscriptions. Leh, 1906 and 1907.

„ , Tibetan inscription in front of the Ta-chao-ssu Temple at Lhasa. *Ep. Ind.*, vol. X, pp. 89 ff.

„ A Lower Ladakhi version of the Kesar Saga, *Bibliotheca Indica*, N. S., Nos. 1134, 1150, 1164, 1218.

„ , The rock-inscriptions at Mulbe. *Ind. Ant.*, vol. XXXV, pp. 72 ff.

„ , and PANDIT DAYA RAM SAHNI, References to the Bhoṭas in the Rājataraṅgini of Kashmir. *Ind. Ant.*, vol. XXXVII, p. 181.

GERARD, A., A vocabulary of the Kunawar language. *J. A. S. B.*, vol. XI, part II, pp. 479 ff.

„ , Account of Koonawar. Ed. by G. Lloyd, London, 1841.

GRIERSON, G. A., Linguistic Survey of India, vol. III, part I. Calcutta. 1909.

GRÜNWEDEL, A., Mythologie des Buddhismus in Tibet und der Mongolei. Leipzig, 1900.

HARCOURT, A. T. P., Himalayan districts of Kooloo, Lahoul, and Spiti. London, 1871.

HEDIN, SVEN, Transhimalaya. Leipzig, 1909.

HIUEN-TSIANG., Si-yu-ki. Buddhist Records of the Western World, translated by S. Beal. London, 1884.

HOFFMEISTER, W., Briefe aus Indien. Braunschweig, 1847.

HUTCHISON, J., Chamba State Gazetteer. Lahore, 1910.

IBBETSON, D. C. I., Gazetteer of the Kangra District, vol. II, Kulu, Lahul, and Spiti. Lahore, 1897, 1899.

JÄSCHKE, H. A., Tibetan-English dictionary. London. 1881.

KONOW, STEN, On some facts connected with the Tibeto-Burman dialect, spoken in Kanawar, *Z. D. M. G.*, vol. LIX, pp. 117 ff.

LAWRENCE, W. R., The Valley of Kashmir. London, 1895.

MARX, K., Three documents relating to the history of Ladakh. *J. A. S. B.*, part I., vol. LX, pp. 97 ff; vol. LXIII, pp. 94 ff; vol. LXIX, pp. 21 ff.

MEEBOLD, A., Indien. München, 1908.

MOORCROFT, W., and TREBECK G. Travels in the Himalayan Provinces of Hindustan and the Panjab, etc., Edited by H. H. Wilson. London, 1841.

PUINI, C, Il Tibet, secondo la relazione del viaggio del P. I. Desideri. *Società Geografica Italiana*, vol. X. Roma. 1904.

SCHLAGINTWEIT. E. VON., Könige v. Tibet, *Abhandlungen der K. bayer. Akademie der Wissenschaften*, vol. X.

" , Tibetan Buddhism.

VIGNE, G. T., Travels in Kashmir, Ladak, Iskardo, etc., Second edition. London, 1842.

VOGEL, J. PH., Triloknāth. *J. A. S. B.*, vol. LXX, pp. 35 ff.

" , The Rāṇas of the Panjab Hills. *J. R. A. S.*, 1908.

" , Antiquities of Chamba State. Calcutta, 1911.

WADDELL, L. A., Ancient historical edicts at Lhasa. *J. R. A. S.*, 1909, 1910.

WALDEMAR, PRINZ., Reise des Prinzen Waldemar von Preussen. Berlin, 1853

ABBREVIATIONS.

A. S. R. Archæological Survey Report.

Ep. Ind. Epigraphia Indica.

Ind. Ant. Indian Antiquary.

J. A. S. B. Journal Asiatic Society of Bengal.

J. R. A. S. Journal Royal Asiatic Society.

Z. D. M. G. Zeitschrift der Deutschen Morgenländischen Gesellschaft.

INTRODUCTION.

Towards the end of April 1909, I received a telegram from the Indian Government asking me to enter their archæological service for a period of eighteen months, from the 1st June of that year. I arrived in Simla on the 30th May and from the 1st to the 14th June, Dr. J. H. Marshall, C.I.E., Director-General of Archæology, sacrificed a great deal of his time in drawing up a plan for my journey and discussing with me various matters connected therewith. Thanks to his energy, all preparations were finished on the 12th June, and on Monday the 14th June, our caravan started for the frontier districts.

As regards our plans, it was determined to cover as much ground as possible and to spend a considerable portion of the summer months within the limits of the Jammu and Kashmīr State. For within its territory are known to exist several interesting relics of Tibetan antiquity which have not yet been properly examined. Putting aside the ordinary routes, the Kashmīr State can be entered from two parts of Indian Tibet, from Lahul and from Spiti. As Lahul had already been investigated by Dr. Vogel,[1] the course to be taken by me was to enter the Kashmīr State from the Spiti side. Spiti was one of the countries of Indian Tibet which I had not yet seen. As the road to Spiti took me high up in the Satluj valley, I proposed to pay a short visit to Tholing and Tsaparang beyond the frontier. These places interested me particularly on account of their connection with Atīśa and d'Andrada. This proposal was, however, not sanctioned by the Supreme Government, and I was advised to remain within the Indian Frontier.

Our party was to consist of a Government Photographer, Babu Pindi Lal of the Archæological Survey, who also knew how to take impressions of inscriptions, and a Khalasi who had to be engaged in the interior. In addition to these there were two men whom I engaged privately, a bearer and cook in one person, and a Tibetan who assisted me in the reading and copying of inscriptions and documents. Dr. Marshall was very fortunate in his choice of the photographer; for in the case of an expedition like ours, an ordinary proficiency in photography would not have sufficed; what was wanted was a man ready to endure hardship, and one who was prepared to carry on his work under adverse circumstances. Pindi Lal has amply justified Dr. Marshall in his choice.

[1] *Cf.* his *Trilōknāth*, *J. A. S. B.*, Vol. LXX (1902), Part I, pp. 35 ff.

CHAPTER I.

The Satluj Valley.

We left Simla on the 14th June and reached Kōṭgur (map Kotgarh) on the 16th at noon. At Kōṭgur I enjoyed the hospitality of the C. M. S. missionary, the Rev. Mr. Beutel, who is an authority on the language, customs and geography of his district. On the rocks near Kōṭgur are found carvings in the shape of a *Yōnī*. This is Mr. Beutel's explanation at least, and it agrees exactly with the interpretation I have given of many similar carvings found all over Kuḷū and Lahul. This symbol is found even in Ladakh, but it is rarer there. I am convinced that this symbol is intended to remind the worshipper of deities of the Kālī type, as we find them all over the hills, under various names. These goddesses, together with gods of the Śiva type, represent the creative principle which is the main feature in the religion of all the Western Himalayan tribes.

During our short stay at Kōṭgur, Pindi Lal witnessed the Doum festival which is celebrated annually. The Doum is a tablet with silver and gold masks fixed to it. As Mr. Beutel told me, such masks are dedicated to the temple by the ruling chiefs of Kōṭgur and neighbourhood, on the occasion of deaths in their families. But whether these masks are supposed to be portraits of the deceased persons or not, I have not been able to ascertain. We find the same custom all over Kuḷū,[1] and also at Trilōknâth in Chambā-Lahul. The spirit (of the deceased ?) is supposed to enter a man set apart for this cult, who performs a sword-dance and thrusts needles through his cheeks. When he is in a trance, he is asked questions and acts as an oracle. Pindi Lal placed his apparatus carefully in front of the mask board and was on the point of snapping, when he was suddenly assailed by the priests, who said that they could not allow him to photograph these objects of sanctity. Pindi Lal, snapping off his apparatus, calmly said: "Well, if you will not allow me to take a photo, I can do without it," and carried his treasure home (Plate I, a).

That there is a possible connection between these masks and those used for the devil-dances of Ladakh and Tibet, is made apparent by the following passage by Dr. Vogel,[2] who speaks of two miniature *śikhara* temples at Trilōknāth in which a number of wooden masks are preserved. "At the death of a member of the Rāṇā's family, such a mask is prepared and placed in the temple, whence it is on no account to be removed. An exception is made for three masks which are used at the *Chār* or Spring festival, and are said to represent a man, a woman and a demon, called in the local dialect *gāmi*, *mēzmi* and *kulīnza*. The main substance of the *Chār* festival is a performance symbolizing the advent of Spring and the defeat of Winter. The latter, personified as an evil demon, is represented by the bearer of the *kulīnza* mask, who is

---

[1] *A. S. R.* for 1907-8, pp. 270 ff., plates LXXIV and LXXV.

[2] *Chamba Gazetteer*, p. 44.

a. Gold and silver masks. Doum festival at Kotgur.

b. Sculpture near the Kothi, Nirmand.

chased by the joint villagers and pelted with snow-balls till he retires from the village and drops his mask, after which he joins in a dance with the *gāmi* and *mēzmi* mask-bearers."

Most of the devil dances of Indian Tibet are held during the time of the winter solstice, and in my opinion originally symbolised the struggle between the benevolent gods of spring or summer, and the demons of winter. Lamaism later on converted these performances into a struggle between the elevating elements of Buddhism and its fierce enemies representative of the pre-Buddhist religion.[1]

The greatest enemy of Lamaism, Langdarma, had to take the part originally played by the winter, and it is his tragic end and his torments in hell which are now-a-days celebrated in the mask dances. Side by side with the Lamaist mask dances the ancient ceremonies of chasing out the evil spirits of the winter were continued, and a manuscript describing the festival of the winter solstice at Khalatse and a photo of the interesting Dosmoche performance, at Leh, is among our collections. At the monastery of Nako, we even acquired a very ancient wooden mask which had once done service in the mask dances. This mask was found in a godown and sold to us for one rupee. At Leh we had an opportunity to buy implements and a trumpet made of a human thighbone, used on the occasion of devil dances. (Plate XXIX, b).

As I had the intention of spending Sunday the 20th at Kōtgur, on my return from Nirmaṇḍ, Mr. Beutel advised me to leave Kōtgur on the same day and to cross the rope bridge to Nirmaṇḍ early next morning. The caravan under Pindi Lal was to follow later on. I arrived on the Satluj late at night on the 16th and spent the night in Mr. Beutel's garden house. Early on the 17th I marched with my Khansaman to Nirth and beyond this village to the rope bridge. In the vicinity of Nirth, we searched for the cave inscriptions discovered by Dr. Marshall in 1908, but could not find them. The rope bridge did not look at all inviting, but I thought that I ought to try it, in particular, because we should have to cross several more of them in the course of our journey. So we shouted for the people in the next village who work it. They brought a wooden saddle to which were attached several ropes and led us down the *khud* to the starting place, a rock not much over a yard square, 30 or 40 feet above the river. Before and behind, the rock was perpendicular. From this pedestal one was expected to seize the saddle which dangled above one, and to put his legs through two slings of rope which were attached thereto. While seizing the saddle I jumped up in the direction of the slings, but unfortunately knocked off my hat against the wall of rock behind me. It disappeared at once in the river and was not seen again. I knew that it would not be advisable to continue my journey under a tropical sun without a hat. Therefore, I renounced all further gymnastics on that day and went back to Nirth to write to Mr. Beutel that I had not succeeded in reaching Nirmaṇḍ on the fixed day and had to alter my programme. Early next morning a messenger from Mr. Beutel made his appearance with the latter's *sola topi* and a letter urging me to try again. I must

[1] Luther, in a similar manner, changed the song: Nun treiben wir den Winter aus! into a song celebrating the turning out of the Pope: Nun treiben wir den Pabst hinaus

confess that I felt ashamed that I a young man, should not venture to do what old Mr. Beutel had done so often. The Khansaman and myself, therefore, made a fresh effort, got safely into the sling and across the river and reached Nirmaṇḍ on the same evening, after a long and trying climb.

Pindi Lal marched with the caravan to Rāmpur, but kept himself in readiness to come to Nirmaṇḍ with his apparatus, as soon as he should be wanted. Nirmaṇḍ, the Kāśī of the mountains, as it is called, was perfectly inaccessible in the days of the brothers Gerard (1817) who wished to see it, but were not allowed to enter it. Later on, it was opened to visitors, and Capt. Harcourt (1871) witnessed here the curious ceremony of the swinging rope. A young man is fed at the public expense for a year, during which time he has to plait a rope of considerable length. On the day of the *Mela*, this rope is stretched from the top of a precipice and he has to slide down on it. This custom which is also practised at Lhasa and at Śrīnagar of Gaṛhwāl is, as Dr. Vogel says, probably a survival of human sacrifice, the prevalence of which in former times in these districts is indicated by popular tradition.[1] "But in this peculiar case the victim, instead of being actually killed, had to undergo a risk which endangered his life. An offering was thus made to the deity who might decline or accept the sacrifice according to her divine pleasure. In 1856 the man was killed, and since then the practice has been prohibited."

At Kōṭgur, the tree under which the human sacrifices took place is still shown. Until quite recently several iron links, the last remains of chains, could be seen there. Regarding the abolition of human sacrifices, at Kōṭgur, Mr. Beutel told me the following tale: A young virgin had to be sacrificed every year. Once it was a poor widow's turn to offer up her only daughter. The widow cried and asked the oracle below Hatti if there was not a way out of her difficulty. The oracle answered that on the day of the execution there would be a thunderstorm of unusual force, and the rain would carry off even men, and this would be the end of human sacrifices. When on the day of execution the heavy storm actually broke forth, the frightened Brahmans declared that the divinity was angry and did not wish to accept any more human sacrifices.

The story of the Rākshasa Bamburaha at Kōṭgur, also told by Mr. Beutel, is not very different. This Rākshasa devoured the breasts of women, and from time to time he demanded a woman to eat up altogether. He was blinded by the bird Karaita who thrust pollen of the cedar into his eyes. Then he was killed by armed men. This had also been announced by the Hatti oracle.

Although Nirmaṇḍ is nowadays open to visitors, the inhabitants do their best to make a stay there as unpleasant to the stranger as possible. The town, being a holy place, is inhabited chiefly by Brahmans, who dress in white. Besides them, there are only two other castes represented, the Sōnārs or goldsmiths, and the Kōlīs or peasants (aboriginal population). Wherever one goes, one finds Brahmans on both sides who

---

[1] *J. A.. S. B,* Vol. LXX, Part 1, No. 1, 1902, p. 35.

suddenly stop one and demand a turn to the right or left, or even prohibit one's further advance. In spite of all its sanctity, Nirmaṇḍ is poor in inscriptions and other written records. People showed me the copper plate grant of the 7th century by king Samudra-sēna which has been published by Dr. Fleet,[1] and a very obliterated inscription on a rock in front of the *Dharmaśālā*. We took an impression, but were not quite successful. The script seems to be a late type of Śāradā. As the names of Samudra-sēna's father, grandfather and great-grandfather, which occur on the copper plate, have not yet been discovered in the Bansaulīs of Kuḷū or Bashahr, I hoped to find them among the ancestors of the present Ṭhākur of Nirmaṇḍ. This man, however, did not possess a family record of any kind.

Proof of the great age of Nirmaṇḍ is the fact that all the principal temples are of the hill type. They are built of layers of rubble masonry, alternating with beams of cedar wood. The roofs are sloping and slightly concave on either side of the central beam and laid with slates or wooden shingles. None of these buildings seem to be of a very great age. But, as they were always repaired in the same style, the temples of Nirmaṇḍ of two or three thousand years ago probably did not look different from these extant.

This refers only to the chief temples. By the side of most of them, we find numerous stone temples of the *śikhara* type. (Plate III). They are, however, never in prominent positions. This style of architecture has been fully described by Fergusson.[2] It was introduced into Nirmaṇḍ probably between the 7th and 11th century and many specimens may go back to those times, although there are no written records. The many tablets with religious sculptures which are scattered all over the place in great numbers, may also date from those times. It appears that the original cult of Nirmaṇḍ was entirely Śivaist. Most of the temples are dedicated to Siva or Kālī, or to deities of a similar type. Perhaps about the same time when Vishnuism became powerful in Chambā (tenth or eleventh century), this form of worship was also introduced in Nirmaṇḍ, without, however, doing much harm to Śivaism.

Originally the town consisted, it is said, of five main streets with a great temple in each of them. Cholera and small-pox have decimated the population, and the town has become very much reduced in size. Its situation is sublime, on a high practically level plateau with a magnificent view of apparently endless mountain ridges.

I made the following notes on the principal buildings. The Ambikā temple (Plate II, a) is below the village, and a flight of 184 steps leads up towards it, and continues from the back of the temple towards the village. This temple is said to be the oldest in the place, and Ambikā (probably a form of Kālī) is the chief deity of Nirmaṇḍ. According to Pindi Lal, the Dēvī image is in a standing posture and about two feet high. Her face is black, and her clothes covered with gold. Whoever approaches her (only Brahmans are allowed to do so) has to take off his trousers. In this temple is kept the copper-plate grant of King Samudra-sēna of the 7th century mentioned above

---

[1] *Gupta Inscriptions*, p. 286.

[2] *History of Indian and Eastern Architecture*, Vol. I, p. 322.

In front of Ambikā's temple there is an ancient stone figure buried in the ground up to the shoulders.

The Kōṭhī is a large building of the hill type, with stags' and antelopes' horns fixed over the door. Old sculptures are inserted in the walls, for instance, a head on a stand adored by two kneeling figures (Plate I, b). This may have been suggested by the well-known Buddhist sculptures of relics with two worshippers. The head is probably that of Śiva, as we find it on so many temples at Nirmaṇḍ, carved above the entrance. On the right corner of the house, there is a very rude figure of Hanumān riding on a rather diminutive horse. Inside, there are stone figures of Kālī, and a bronze figure of Paraśurāma. The latter is exhibited only every twelfth year when two naked men have to carry it out of its prison. When the image is brought back to the temple, a glass, filled with water, is placed in front of it. This is not removed until twelve years have elapsed, and the water is found as fresh as it was originally. In front of the Kōṭhī is a large round stone seat with sculptures on its circumference, for instance, *makaras* swallowing men (?). An apparently modern cave is in the vicinity.

The *Dharmaśālā* we were not allowed to enter. It is a court formed by houses of the ordinary hill type situated in the middle of the village. On a rock in front there is an inscription in a late type of Śāradā characters much obliterated.

The temple of Chaṇḍī Dēvī is close to the wells from which the people fetch their drinking water. There are several small water tanks of dressed stones below it, and a great number of sculptured slabs are inserted in the masonry of the tank (Plate II, b). Stone figures of Nandi are also conspicuous. One of the sculptures, a head with three faces, is said to look like Paraśurāma in the Kōṭhī.

The temple of Śiva situated above the village, is said to contain a *liṅgam*. Over the door is a sculptured head and a figure of Gaṇēśa. In front of it, there are water tanks with stone reliefs and a figure of Nandi.

The temple of Śiva and the Pāṇḍavas is situated in the middle of the village. It was shown only to Pindi Lal who says that it contains many images in little niches.

The Ṭhākur's temple found in the middle of the village is small and neat, but in bad preservation. The interior was shown to Pindi Lal only, in whose opinion the image was the finest sculpture in the place. Unfortunately he could not photograph it. It represents a man and a woman seated, and another woman lying on the ground. There is an elaborate halo round the three figures.

The doors of all the houses of the goldsmiths are distinguished by well-carved door-posts of stone with the figure of Gaṇēśa in the centre.

In conclusion I may say that we did not find any traces of Buddhism at Nirmaṇḍ.

From Nirmaṇḍ we marched to Rāmpur, the capital of the Bashahr State, beautifully situated on the left bank of the Satluj. The descent was steep, but the road well shaded by luxuriant vegetation. The Hindu temples of the city with their very primitive, though not ancient, sculptures did not appear of any interest. Rāmpur is the first place on the road up the Satluj valley where Lamaist buildings may be seen. The

a. Temple of the goddess Ambika, Nirmand.

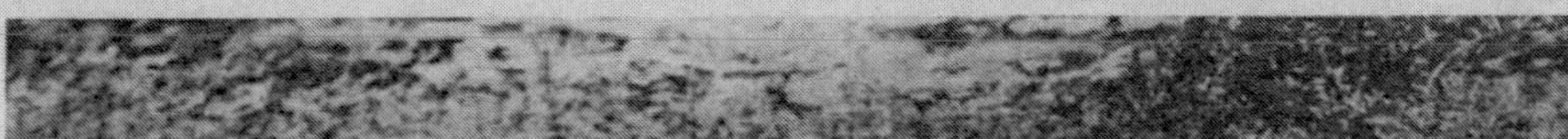

b. Sculptures at the watertank, Nirmand.

PLATE III.

a. Sikhara shrine near the temple of Chandi Devi, Nirmand.

b. Sikhara shrine near watertank, Nirmand.

Lamaist temple is a recent structure and is said to be only twelve or thirteen years old. Its style is not different from that of the ordinary dwelling-houses of Rāmpur: this temple, therefore, differs from the common Tibetan temples, especially on account of its sloping roof. It contains modern frescoes and a huge prayer wheel.

In one of the Rājā's garden-houses, we found more Lamaist frescoes. One of them interested me in particular, for it evidently represents a historical scene. (Plate IV, a). When we met His Highness Ṣhamsher Singh, a few days later, he told us that the picture was a copy of a picture in the palace of Lhasa. The fresco evidently represents the treaty between Tibet and Bashahr concluded about 1650 A.D., when Bashahr was supported by the Mughal emperor. The figure in the middle of the picture is apparently the Mughal emperor, surrounded by his soldiers. The elephant procession which approaches from the left is either the retinue of the Mughal, or of the Bashahr king, Kēhari Singh.[1] A party of Bashahr people, distinguished by their black round hats, are placed in front of the Mughal, while the embassy from Tibet is shown on the right side of the painting. This treaty, which is mentioned in the chronicles of Bashahr, was of great importance to the State. The Tibetans who had been beaten by the Mughal army at Basgo, near Leh, had to cede a portion of Guge, *viz.*, the Satluj valley down to the Wangtu bridge, to the Bashahr State. We had the good fortune, in the course of our expedition, to discover two versions of this treaty, concluded in 1650, in original documents.

At Rāmpur we inspected also the royal palaces, gardens and guest-houses, but nothing appeared to be of particular interest. Unfortunately the Rājā and his party were not present. Here we engaged a Khalasi called Sâdhu, to accompany us on our further travels. Although this man had hardly seen any place beyond Rāmpur, he proved useful and was always ready to work even under difficulties.

The road up the Satluj valley, from Rāmpur to Chini, is on the whole very pleasant. The mountains are wooded in many parts, and the rocks and hills which rise abruptly from the narrow valley form charming pictures. The road continually ascends and descends, and for this reason the traveller passes through ever-varying temperatures. Often we started from a bungalow five or six thousand feet above the Satluj in a cool morning breeze. Then the road took us down almost to the valley with its blazing heat, and it was rather hard to begin the ascent again under the scorching rays of a tropical midday sun.

We arrived at Gaura, a little village above Rāmpur, on the 22nd June. The people were holding their "Festival of prayers for a good harvest," and for that reason we could not sleep much. They sang without a break through the whole of the night. It would have been very pleasant to listen to them in the day-time, but before the sun was up they had all disappeared. They had always two choirs, one for the line with the lower notes, the other for the line with the higher notes. I took down one of their tunes which is based on the Chinese scale. Others of their tunes were based on different scales. Each

---

[1] For genealogical list of Bashahr Rājās see beneath Appendix D.

party held out the last note of their melody for a time, whilst the other party started theirs.[1]

On the following day we reached Sarāhan. It is the ancient capital of the Bashahr State, and the palace here is by far superior to that at Rāmpur. Here we found the Rājā residing. Shamsher Singh, a man of seventy years of age, is the last of a long line of a hundred and twenty Rājās, enumerated in the *Rajowari* of Bashahr, which was first brought to light through Mr. H. A. Rose's exertions. The dynasty claims to have come from Kāñchanapurī (*i.e.*, Conjeevaram) in the Deccan, and to be of Brahman caste Once the throne of Bashahr being vacant, it was prophesied that the Brahman who should enter the palace-gate first, was the destined king. The younger one of two Brahman brothers, Pradyumna, who came from Kāñchanapurī, entered the palace-gate first, and was accordingly made king. The descendants of the elder brother became family priests and are said to be still in office. It is very difficult to believe that the pedigree with its 120 members can be genuine in its more ancient parts. All the Rājās are called by the dynastical name *Singh* (Sanskrit *Siṁha*), but there is no instance of any ancient Indian family which makes use of that name earlier than the 15th century. The family of the Bashahr Rājās, as Mr. Howell, Assistant Commissioner of Kuḷu, tells me, is recognised all over northern India as very ancient and the other rājās are desirous of receiving their caste-mark from the Bashahr Rājā, even if the latter condescends only to put it on their foreheads with his toe.

Shamsher Singh is very favourably inclined to Europeans and wishes to make friends with all of them. Shortly after our arrival, therefore, he announced his intention to have tea with me. He was carried in a litter by several of his subjects, and a small crowd was gathered together near the bungalow to receive him with shouts, "Ho! Mahārāj." His state is of considerable extent, but thinly populated, and has a future before it. The Rājā asked us first to take a photo of himself, and then to go to the other side of his palace and take a general view of it from there. (Plates IV, b and V, a). The palace presented itself at its best from the mountain side, where it showed all its symmetrical beauty. It is one of the finest specimens of hill architecture I have ever seen. Although there are no written records about it, it is evidently of considerable age. The Rājās ought to be urged to keep it in good repair, but not to make any structural alterations. Like all buildings of the hill-type it is built of layers of rubble masonry and beams of cedar wood. The roofs are slanting and slightly concave like those of the Chinese. In the walls of the court, several carved stone images of very rude execution have been inserted. I was told that they represent Kālī and Bhairava.

There is also an ancient Kālī temple connected with the palace which is not accessible to Europeans. It is said to contain a deep pit. There are rumours that human sacrifices were offered here every tenth year, and that they are still continued secretly.[2] The victim is thrown into the pit. If a human sacrifice be not forthcoming at the

---

[1] A description of this style of music is found in my article, "*Musikalische Studien in West Tibet*, Z. D. M. G., Vol. LX, pp 91 ff.

[2] *Cf.* Gerard, *Account of Koonawar*, p. 86.

PLATE IV.

a. Fresco in the palace, Rampur.

b. Raja Shamsher Singh of Bashahr.

appointed time, a terrible voice is heard calling from the depth of the pit. We received a full written statement about these practices from a native of the place.

We travelled from Sarāhan to Taranda on the 24th June. In the pass above the village and bungalow, there is an ancient deserted Dēvatā temple of the ordinary hill type with slanting but straight roof, in ruins It contained two beautifully carved columns and other wood sculptures. In front of it, there are several stone slabs with rude carvings of human figures. They look exactly like the slabs put up in commemoration of the dead in Manchad (Lahul) or like very ancient *Satī*-stones in Kuḷū. I was informed that here also, they were erected in commemoration of the dead.

We proceeded to Paunda on the 25th June. Below the village, on the road to Taranda, we saw the first Tibetan *maṇi* wall, *i.e.* a stone wall covered with inscribed slabs of stone, bearing the inscription *Oṁ maṇi padme Hūṁ.* The characters employed here were mostly Lañthsa. Near the wall was a gate with modern Lamaist frescoes on the ceiling and a prayer flag on the top. These signs of Lamaism do not, however, indicate that the population of this district are believers in Lamaism. In fact, in spite of many inquiries, I could not ascertain that there were any Buddhists round about. I believe that these Buddhist structures were erected by Tibetan travellers on their way to the Rāmpur market.

On the 26th June, we marched from Paunda to Urni. Between Paunda and Nachar is the village of Sungra, a little below the road. It is famous for its ancient wooden Mahēśura (Mahēśvara) temple (Plate VI, a). It is a fine specimen of hill architecture, and reminds one of the famous temple of Hiḍimbā at Manālī in Kuḷū which was built by King Bahādur Siṅgh in the 16th century.[1] While the temples of Nirmaṇḍ have the shape of an ordinary rectangular house with a single gable roof, the temple at Sungra has a square ground-plan and three slanting roofs, one above the other, the lower one being the largest, and the top one the smallest of the three. While the two lower ones are square, the top one is round, of the shape of a funnel. The four corner beams of the lowest roof end in wooden figures of walking lions, almost life-size (Plate VI, b). The temple contains a *liṅgam*. There are no inscriptions round about. In the temple yard we saw two very rude specimens of *śikhara* stone temples.

On the road from Sungra to Nachar we noticed the first Lamaist *mchod-rten* (*stūpa*). It was only about 6 feet high, and contained some dried apricots and a leaf or two of a modern Tibetan printed book with a text half Tibetan, half Sanskrit.

The temple of Nachar has also a certain fame on account of its wood carvings. We did not, however, visit it.

From Nachar the road took us down to the Satluj by a long descent, and at Wangtu we crossed the river by a beautiful modern bridge. There was already a wooden bridge in this place when Gerard travelled here in 1817.[2] This bridge is an important

---

[1] *Cf. A. S. R.*1905-96, p. 26. There are three temples of this kind in Kuḷū ; that of Hiḍimbā (or Hiṛmā) Dēvī at Dhungrī Manālī, near that of Tripura-sundarī Dēvī at Nagar, the ancient capital, and that of Tiryug Nārāyaṇa at Dhār opposite Bajaurā.

[2] It was destroyed by the Gurkhas in 1819 and replaced by a rope bridge.

feature in the Bashahr State; for it marks the ancient boundary between Bashahr and Tibet. In fact, the West Tibetan Empire reached as far as Wangtu up to 1650 A. D., when the Satluj valley from Wangtu to Namgya was made over to Bashahr. Although Tibetan is not yet spoken for several marches up the Satluj, the former Tibetan influence makes itself felt in the frequency of personal Tibetan names. We could not escape making this observation, because we had to jot down on our vouchers the names of all the coolies in our employ.

We are now outside the area of the Pahāṛī dialects of the Satluj valley and have entered that of the Kanāwarī language. This language was noticed as early as 1817 by Gerard, who published a vocabulary of it.[1] Mr. Diack made a beginning in the study of its grammar; but the true nature of this language was not recognised, until the Rev. J. Bruske, of the Moravian Mission, began to study the language thoroughly and made a translation of the gospel of St. Mark into it. It was then recognised, as pointed out by Dr. Sten Konow,[2] that the grammar of this language shows close affinities to Muṇḍārī (spoken in Chota Nagpur), and that in very early times in these mountain valleys an amalgamation must have taken place between Muṇḍā aboriginal tribes and Tibetans. Within the fifty miles of road between Chini and Poo, one meets with several more languages of probably a similar type which have not yet been properly studied, although notes on them can be found in various books of travel. The study of the folk-lore literature of the Kanāwarī language has been taken up by Mr. H. A. Rose, who is also compiling a dictionary of this language. Mr. Rose's collection contains historical as well as lyrical pieces. With regard to the former it is strange to note that they all refer to very modern times only. In the course of our journey we heard a song about the Kyahar castle, but it also contained the name of a very modern personage, that of the Ṭikā Sāhib of Bashahr, who died a few years ago. One of the most interesting of Mr. Bruske's collection is the song on Mr. Minniken, forest officer of Bashahr. This officer is praised in this song as the ideal master of the woods who gives the petitioner as much wood as he wants to get. As regards metre and parallelism, these songs are of the same character as the Tibetan songs.

The result of the blending of the Muṇḍā and Tibetan population with a superficial sprinkling of Indian Aryans is not at all bad, and many of our coolie women were of very attractive appearance. I must add a few words with regard to the latter. Among the population of these mountain valleys the cooly caste is not very numerous, and for this reason the villagers, also those of good caste, have to take up cooly work. This kind of forced labour is felt as humiliating by most of the people, and for this reason the male population will not participate in it. They press it on the women of their families, and do not see that they disgrace themselves even more by this arrangement. Our transport therefore was for the greater part of our journey to Poo the work of women carriers. This has its great advantages, as has been observed also by other travellers, for these women are pleasant to deal with, they never grumble, and do their utmost to please the

[1] *J. A. S. B.*, Vol. XI, part I, 1842, pp. 479, ff. *Linguistic Survey*, Vol. III, part I.

[2] *Imperial Gazetteer of India*, New Edition. Oxford 1907. Vol. I, pp, 306 ff.

PLATE V.

a. Raja's palace, Sarahan.

b. Lamaist gateway, Rarang.

sahib. It is also true that many among them are quite athletic and carry heavy loads over great distances. What I disliked, however, was the injustice done to the female population of a little village when a large caravan like ours demanded the service of practically all the women between twelve and fifty years of age. Then the claims of their babies were left quite out of consideration, and the poor mothers had to see what arrangements they could make with regard to their offspring for a full day or so. Our box which contained the photographic plates was the heaviest of all, and it was always the last taken up. The first comers took hold of the lighter loads and darted off as soon as possible. When we were at Chogan on our way to Urni, this box with the plates did not arrive, and Pindi Lal volunteered to stay behind and wait for it. He caught me up at Urni when it was quite dark. The heavy box had fallen to the lot of a child of fourteen years of age who was absolutely unequal to the task. This girl, therefore, asked three of her friends to assist her in the hard work she had to perform, and so Pindi Lal received the box out of the hands of four girls 'all very young and very beautiful' as he said. They were, of course, all of high caste, and the way they took leave of the Babu and wished him a good journey was quite charming. The system of the Tibetans is quite different from that of the Bashahr State. In Tibet the men come first, and they are ready to do the hardest work themselves. The women who offer to do cooly work are such as can be spared from their homes.

I hope that the chivalrous chief of the Bashahr State will undertake to teach his male subjects a little more chivalry.

The bridge of Wangtu is evidently in a place where there has been a bridge from time immemorial, as is made probable by ancient carvings on the rocks. One of them shows a man with a sword in his left hand, and a club in his right. In the rocks there are many caves used by travellers, and on the rocks about them I saw many Tibetan inscriptions in charcoal and red chalk, one of them reading: *Sa-kya-pa-mkhyen-no*, "Take notice of this (or 'of me') O Sakya-man!" In one of the caves, there were many tablets of burnt clay, just like those which are made of clay and the ashes of the dead. They have generally the figure of a Buddhist saint printed on them and are deposited in *mchod-rten* or caves. Here, however, they were quite plain. A dead lama was probably cremated here in ancient times, and a mould not being at hand, the clay-tablets were formed without it.

Sunday, the 27th June, was spent at Urni. In the afternoon I went to see the *mandirs* or temples. The 'old temple' is of the square tower type, like so many of Kuḷū, and has a wooden verandah running round below the slanting gable roof. It was almost without any carvings, and people said that the *dēvata* had left the place. The 'new temple,' not far from the old one, was thoroughly renovated, as people say, about twenty years ago. There are many wood-carvings dating from that time, for instance hunting-scenes: a man shooting a leopard with a rifle. They were all very primitive. There was also a carving of a cock, and what I took for a hen with chickens, eating a snake. But people said it was a peacock. (Garuḍa devouring Nāgas?). The villagers showed us also several obscene representations of a man and a woman, and said that it was always a grand moment, when these pictures were shown to the girls on the occasion of a *Mela*. This will serve to show what a religion which worships the creative powers leads to. The slanting gable beams of the temple had again representations of walking lions, like those at Sungra.

As regards the houses of the ordinary peasants, here at Urni, and in other places since we passed the Wangtu bridge, the Tibetan flat roof is becoming prominent. Here at Urni village most of the roofs exhibit the Tibetan style. But the *mandirs* still show the old slanting roof of the Indian hill tribes. The first temple with a flat roof I saw at Rogi on the 28th. It is of the square tower type and has wood carvings on the beams.

We spent the night of the 28th and the 29th June at Chini, in the Moravian Mission house. The view from Chini towards the snow mountains on the other side of the river is one of the grandest imaginable. The local name of these glaciers is Kailāsa and a certain pinnacle is called Śiva by the people.[1]

Looking down from the Mission house, there is a large mound to the left of the village (Plate VII, a). This is said to be the site of a castle of an ancient Ṭhākur who came here from the 'Upper Country' (apparently Tibet). Mr. Bruske, who used to reside here as a Moravian missionary, was told that there exists a song which treats of the exploits of this Ṭhākur. But it has not yet been reduced to writing. On the site, many fragments of hand-made pottery can be found, but, people assured me, never any coins. The site is now occupied by small Lamaist buildings, a square tower and an enshrined *mchod-rten*. The fact that Lamaism has taken possession of the site, speaks in favour of the alleged Tibetan origin of the Ṭhākur.

Mr. Bruske informs me that there is another mound below the village where many red bricks can be found. This is held to have been the principal (perhaps winter) residence of the same Ṭhākur. At both sites excavations might prove successful. The most interesting feature in connection with this ancient chief is, as Mr. Bruske tells me, that traces of his aqueducts are met with from time to time by people when digging. They consist of earthenware pipes, and the water was conducted in them for miles.

Above the door over the staircase which leads up to the mound, there is a stone lion, which looks very old indeed. People told me, however, that it was made only a few years ago. Older are the carved slabs of stone on the mound, near the Lamaist temple. They show lines similar to those on a chessboard. On these ancient slabs, the Tibetan game of *mig-mang* was probably played.

Mr. Bruske tells me that stories of Ṭhākurs are told also of other ruined sites on the way from Chini to Poo. These Ṭhākurs, although independent in a way, probably acknowledged the supremacy of the Tibetan chiefs of Guge, before the country came under Bashahr.

The Kālī temple of Chini is situated below the village. No stranger is allowed to enter it. It has been the scene of human sacrifices, and there is a rumour that such

[1] The earliest picture of Chini and the Kailāsa is found in '*Reise des Prinzen Waldemar von Preussen*,' 1845, Plate XVI.

PLATE VI.

a. Temple of Mahesvara, Sungra.

b. Roof beams with lion figures, Sungra.

sacrifices are still carried on secretly. The following has been observed by a European, whose name I am not allowed to mention. At the *Mela* at this Kālī temple, the object of the sacrifice is carried down to the temple by a person who must not be met by anybody. In fact, the rumour is spread that every person who meets that man will die before a year is passed. The European quite unexpectedly made his appearance before the priest who cursed him. However, he is of opinion that what the priest carried wrapped up in his bundle looked very much like human limbs. The prohibition of the Brahmans, that nobody must meet the priest on his way to the Kālī temple, has its origin in the wish to keep eye-witnesses away from this ghastly sacrifice.

On the road from Chini to Pangi, not far from Chini, below the road, there is a ruined house which is known as the house of the first European who settled in the country. He was married to a Kanāwarī woman by jungle rites. He has become the hero of a song in Kanāwarī, discovered by Mr. Bruske at Chini, in which the complexion of the European is praised as having been like butter. Like most of the Kanāwarī songs, this one has also a personal touch. These songs treat of prominent people who have become known to the Kanāwarīs. The fact that all the heroes of their songs are modern men, could be explained in this way. The songs were composed in early times in honour of kings or heroes whose names have been entirely forgotten. When a new king, or a new hero arises, the words of the old songs are left unchanged, whilst the personalities are exchanged for new ones. We have very similar cases in Tibetan folklore.[1]

On the 29th June, we passed through Pangi. In the vicinity of the village, there is one of those Lamaist gates built across the road, such as are frequently met with in these parts. (Plate V, b.) In Ladakh there are many similar ones. They all have a *mchod-rten* on the roof, and frescoes on the ceiling. Here in the Kanāwarī country these are distinguished by their elegant wooden roofs which are built over the *mchod-rten*, to protect it from rain. The roof is covered, and, therefore, has somewhat the appearance of a Chinese roof. Gerard believed all this kind of architecture to be influenced by the Chinese style of building, which he believed to exist immediately on the other side of the Tibeto-Chinese frontier. However, we should have to travel thousands of miles, before we should meet with the first representatives of Chinese architecture. These doors are here known by the name of *kang-ga-ni*, a name which is given in Ladakh only to the most ancient specimens.

Close to the door, there are two large erect stones, perhaps rude specimens of *liṅgams*. They have carvings on them, which I copied. One of the carvings I take for a kind of sun-symbol. It was very distinct on one of the stones. On the other stone was carved a *stūpa* and what appears to be a repetition of the sun-symbol.

At Pangi, I met Mr. Bruske and his wife, who were encamped there. I spent a few pleasant hours with them, and received much valuable information from them.

We spent the night of the 29th and the 30th June at Rarang. In the evening, we visited the Lamaist temple, which is built somewhat in the style of the wooden hill

---

[1] See my Introduction to Ladakhi Songs, *Ind. Ant.* Vol. XXXI. 1902. pp. 87 ff.

architecture, at least in regard to its roof. It is said to be only about twenty-five years old. In the courtyard, we found cremation tablets with figures of Avalōkitēśvara represented with four arms and a lotus, and *Mi-akhrugs-pa* (Akshōbya). Although they were also said to be of recent date, the mould from which they were cast must be decidedly old. It was possibly brought here from Kanam monastery, which claims to be old. The tablets were furnished with Tibetan inscriptions, but these were so indistinct that nothing could be read. It was just possible to see that the characters employed were Tibetan.

Above the village of Rarang, on the road, there is an old hut which is known as the most ancient *mandir* of Rarang. (Plate VII, b.) It is rectangular, and has a slanting roof. The door beams are furnished with wood carvings. On the lintel, the figure of an elephant carrying a human being can be distinguished. This is possibly a representation of Indra. Of particular interest is the gable-roof which ends in the carving of a ram's head, and thus reminds us strongly of the *dēvatā*-huts in the Manchad valley (Lahul). In its general appearance also, this *mandir* resembles the *dēvatā*-huts of the Manchad valley and goes to prove that the religion of the Kanāwarīs was similar to that of the Manchad people, who are closely related to them by lingual and ethnic characteristics. As this hut is practically the last specimen of Indian hill architecture on the road (not taking into account a ' gate of blessing ' at Poo, which is furnished with a roof in Kanāwarī style), it will be well to review all the observations we have made with regard to this architecture. Under hill architecture are comprised all the structures which are composed of rubble masonry and beams of cedar wood. Of an entirely different character are the structures of the Tibetans, which consist of sun-dried bricks. The former have slanting, and the latter flat roofs. On the frontier between the Tibetan and Kanāwarī peoples there are also some intermediate forms. There are houses built of rubble masonry with flat roofs, for instance the temple at Rogi, and houses built of sun-burnt bricks with a slanting roof, for instance the temple at Rarang.

The most elementary form of hill architecture is represented by the ancient *mandir* of Rarang, which consists of a one-roomed house with a rectangular ground-plan and a slanting roof. Later on, the roof assumed a concave appearance, and was often supported by a covered verandah. This type of house is much in evidence as the ordinary peasant's dwelling on the Satluj up to the Wangtu bridge, and the Nirmaṇḍ temples are of this type. It was then modified in the following way. The ground plan was made square and the walls were raised. This is the type of the Kuḷū castle towers which were introduced even into Lahul, and of the shrine of the old *mandir* at Urni. A beautiful combination of this rectangular house and square tower is found in the ancient palace of Sarāhan. The Kanāwarī gates of blessing have another extraordinary feature in addition to the concave roof, in that they have also the front and back walls widening out towards the gable beam. Thus the walls are further apart at the top than they are at ground level.

On the square ground plan was developed also the pyramid type of roof with four slanting sides. This we find in its simplest form in the modern temple of Urni, and in

Plate VII.

a. Site of Thakur's castle, Chini.

b. Shrine of Devi, Rarang.

one of the old temples of Sungra. Then there arose the custom of building with superimposed pyramidal roofs one on the top of another, the upper ones decreasing in size ; the whole structures reminding us of Burmese Pagodas. Such temples we have at Sungra, Manālī in Kuḷū, and probably also at Nachar.[1]

The religious buildings of the Hill-type are distinguished by their wood carvings. Mention has been made of the almost life size figures of lions on the beams of the roof. The most prominent figure among the ornaments, is the full-blown lotus (*padma*) with leaves arranged radially. This ornament was believed by Captain Harcourt to be of Buddhist origin. As has been shown by Professor Grünwedel, however, the wheel and the lotus are by no means purely Buddhist emblems. The same must be said with regard to the snake and bird ornaments which are frequently met with. The continual warfare between Garuḍas and Nāgas was a favourite topic among the hill tribes long before the rise of Buddhism. Representations of the human figure are also of frequent occurrence among these wood carvings. But they are by far inferior to the representations of animals and look very much like the effigies of men on ancient rock carvings. The types are stiff and conventionalised, as if on the way to become pictographs. The wooden eaves-boards which are often seen on the edges of roofs, form a very pretty kind of ornament. Many of the roofs or gable beams end in dragon heads with open mouths. Of the rams' heads at the end of such beams mention has been made.

We passed through Jangi on the 30th June. Tibetan *maṇi* walls are now becoming frequent, but up to this place they contained nothing beyond endless repetitions of the *Ōṁ maṇi padme hūṁ.* Here I found for the first time on our expedition a *maṇi* wall with a votive tablet on one end. This shows that the knowledge of the Tibetan language is more general here than in the previous villages. The tablet was, however, so much worn that I could not read much beyond the words *Khungs-btsun-ga-ga-che*, "the great nobleman of excellent origin." Neither this nor any of the preceding *maṇi* walls look as if they were of great antiquity. In the district between Chini and Poo Lamaism has made progress in outward show during the last thirty years or so without, however, ousting Hinduism.

Opposite Jangi lies the village of Kinam with a fine castle on a rock above the river. It was built, it is said, by the Rājā of Bashahr.

After Jangi, the country begins to show a Tibetan character. Vegetation becomes very scarce, and only a kind of Juniper, generally known by the name of Pencil Cedar (the holy tree of the pre-Buddhist religion of Tibet) makes us realize that we are not travelling on the moon. The pencil cedar never forms forests, but at best dots a hillside with a tree to every 500 square yards or so. Also the road, which up to this had done great credit to the Public Works Department (to which I am indebted in particular for the hospitality of their bungalows), becomes more and more uncivilised, and reminds one of the days of hardships when Gerard travelled here almost a century ago. After this

[1] As I said before, I did not get to see the Nachar temple, but in Gordon Forbes' book *Simla to Shipki in Tibet*, the Nachar temple is compared to Burmese temples. Similar temples in the vicinity of Simla and Kōṭgur were not examined on our tour.

experience of desert travelling it is very pleasant in the evening to branch off from the Satluj valley into a side valley which is irrigated by the glacial stream of Kanam: The green waving fields, the many willow, poplar, and apricot trees refresh the eye of the traveller and invite to a short rest in their midst.

We spent the night between the 30th June and 1st July at Kanam. Although Tibetan is very well understood here, it is not yet spoken among the peasants themselves. They speak a language of the Kanāwarī type. But the village as well as the monastery presents a purely Tibetan appearance. This monastery (Plate VIII) was the first on the road which by the natives themselves was asserted to be of ancient origin. It is said to go back to the days of Lotsaba Rin-chen-bzang-po (Ratna-bhadra) 964—1054 A.D. No relic of these ancient days, however, remains. The monastery consists of three separate halls situated in different parts of the village.

The uppermost of them is called *dGon-pa* or monastery proper. It is a building of the ordinary Tibetan type, constructed of undried bricks with a flat roof. It contains the cells of the lamas who belong to the Ge-lug-pa sect, and an insignificant temple. In the latter is found an image of Buddha, gilt bronze with blue hair of the pin-head type. This image was brought from bKra-shis-lhun-po (*vulgo* Trashi lunpo) about seventy years ago, so I was told. The wooden garlands which are behind this image of Buddha as well as behind some other images, may be older. The chief attraction of the Kanam monastery lies in the fact that the pioneer of Tibetan studies, the Hungarian Csoma de Körös spent several years in it, studying the Tibetan language. According to Duka's *Life of Csoma de Körös*, he lived here from August 1827 to October 1830[1]. In 1829, Csoma was visited at Kanam (spelt Kanum in his report) by Dr. Gerard, who gives a very interesting account of the Hungarian's life and work in this out of the way place. Let me quote a few passages from his account—

"I found him at the village of Kanum, in his small but romantic hamlet, surrounded by books, and in the best health......The cold is very intense, and all last winter he sat at his desk wrapped up in woollens from head to foot, and from morning to night, without an interval of recreation or warmth, except that of his frugal meals which are one universal routine of greasy tea; but the winters at Kanum dwindle to insignificance compared with the severity of those at the monastery of Yangla (in Zangskar) where Mr. Csoma passed a whole year......There he sat (at Yangla) enveloped in a sheep-skin cloak, with his arms folded, and in this situation he read from morning till evening without fire, or light after dusk, the ground to sleep on, and the bare walls of the building for protection against the rigours of the climate.

"The cold was so intense as to make it a task of severity to extricate the hands from their fleecy resort to turn over the pages,............he is poor, humbly clad, and reserved, unless stimulated to animation by some temporary interest."

The chief attraction of the little village of Kanam, for Csoma, rested in the fact that the monastery contains complete copies of the *bkā-ugyur* and *bstan-ugyur*, the great

---

[1] See Duka, *Life of Csoma*, pp. 82 ff.

a. Kangyur Monastery, Kanam.

b. Lotsabai Monastery, Kanam.

encyclopædias of Lamaism. It was here that he was enabled to study these gigantic collections of Tibetan literature, and to write his still invaluable 'Analysis of the Kanjur and Stanjur.' The library is kept in a separate building called *bkā-ngyur* some distance below the monastery. Gerard who inspected this library on the occasion of his visit to Csoma in Kanam, has the following note on it: "The edition of the Kahgyur and Stangyur at Kanum was sent from Teshi lhunpo (bKra-shis-lhun-po) only about 9 years ago (*i.e.* in 1820); the printing bears a date of ninety years, yet the ink and type look as perfect and fresh as ever. No insects attack them, though the climate here is varying in summer. The book cases being made of cedar are indestructible......The works, being distinct, are arranged in separate places. These resemble large chests or cisterns, standing on end, and partitioned into cells, each containing a volume, which is carefully wrapped within many folds, laced with cord, and bound tightly between boards of cypress or cedar......Some of the volumes were opened before me, and I gazed with a sort of reverential feeling upon such gigantic compilations yet unfolded to the world, and thought of the humble individual in the hamlet who was occupied in illustrating their unexplored contents."

There is yet a third Lamaist building in the place. It is called *Lhabrang* and is situated between the village and the fields. It is said to be of not much later date than the *dGon-pa.* No ancient relic has been preserved in it. It contains a modern stucco statue of Maitrēya. Another small stucco statue represents the white Tārā and is believed to be of some antiquity. It is a really good piece of workmanship, and the face shows expressive features, more spiritual than usual.

Above the *dGon-pa,* there is a long row of white quadrangular buildings which are said to be crematories. In most villages, a single such incinerator has to suffice for many people. Here one once used for a high lama, is apparently not used again. It is converted into a kind of quadrangular *mchod-rten.*

Although no ancient remains can be found at Kanam, it is quite possible that, as asserted, a Lamaist monastery was built here in the 11th century. The present buildings were probably erected on the sites of still more ancient ones. The monastery may have been ransacked several times; for the last time by the Gurkhas. When Gerard was on his expedition in the Satluj valley, he met with continual reports of the devastations by the Gurkhas from Kōṭgur to the Tibetan frontier.

On the 1st of July we marched from Kanam to the Shasu rope bridge. I arrived at the bridge at 11 A.M., but did not reach the opposite bank of the river, a tributary to the Satluj, before 5 P.M. When I arrived at the site of the bridge, nothing could be seen but a steel rope. We had sent intimation of our intention to cross the bridge to the next village, but there was no response. I found only a single old man on our bank of the river, who had a one-wheeled trolley without any ropes at hand. When all our coolies had come up and enjoyed a little rest, the ropes which they had used for carrying our bags and boxes, were tied together and fastened to the trolley, and after much experimenting it was found possible to work it, and our boxes one after another were slowly pulled across.

Then one of the ropes broke, just as one of the bags was right in the middle of the steel rope, and we spent a very exciting time in watching two daring youths who waded through the strong current, up to their chins, until they found the broken end of the rope. Having finally reached the other bank, it was night, and there being no time nor room to pitch tents, we had our beds in the open air and slept very comfortably.

We arrived at Poo on the 2nd of July, after a tiring march over a horrible road of very rugged and unstable foundation mostly along the face of the precipice. There were hardly any more Pencil cedar trees (*Juniperus excelsa*) on the road. The scenery was now quite Tibetan in character. Bad as the road was, the Missionary at Poo told me that it was excellent compared to what it had been only five years ago. Honour to the brave Mission ladies who have travelled on it in its old state! The rocks are dangerous, even to the natives.

About an hour before reaching Poo, the valley widens a little, and it is a relief to be able to walk here without continually looking out for a safe foothold. Poo is situated on a plain on the right bank of the Satluj and looks very pretty with its green fields, apricot and apple tree gardens. Its elevation is about 9,500 feet, and it is the first village on our road, the language of which is entirely Tibetan. It looks as if it was entirely closed in by steep bare mountains.

When approaching the village, we passed by a great number of *maṇi* walls, and as I noticed votive tablets on several of them, I began to study them. None of them seemed to be very ancient. The inscriptions consisted generally of four parts. The first part may be called devotional, the second part consisted of a eulogy of the country of which the village of Poo (spelled *sPu* in the inscriptions) was the centre, the third part praised the Rājâ of Bashahr who was reigning at the time, and the fourth part contained the account of the building of the wall, and stated for whose religious benefit it was meant. As regards the names of Bashahr Rājās on the tablets, only the following four have been traced through Mr. Schnabel's and our own combined efforts: Rudar (in Tibetan *Lurdur*) Siṅgh; Ugar (in Tibetan *Urku*) Siṅgh; Mahindar (in Tibetan *Metar*) Siṅgh; Shamshēr (in Tibetan *bSam-gser* 'golden thought') Siṅgh. These names cover about the last century. But there are some more *maṇi* walls with votive tablets which, instead of giving the proper name of a chief simply speak of 'the great king' at Sarāhaṇ (*So-ra-rang* in Tibetan). This shows that the personal names of the rulers of Bashahr previous to Rudar Siṅgh, were not known to the Tibetans. As regards the geographical part (the eulogy of the country) of these inscriptions, it contained many references to places beyond the border, thus showing that in the minds of the people, Guge and Poo were not yet separated. Of particular interest are the clan names occurring in these inscriptions. One of them is *Thogar*. It is found in two inscriptions and points to the Tokhar origin of part of the Poo population.

During our stay at Poo, we enjoyed the hospitality of the Rev. R. and Mrs. Schnabel of the Moravian Mission, who took great pains to make me comfortable and to show me the sights of the place. Their intimate knowledge of the customs and traditions of the people were of the greatest value in the pursuit of our researches.

I was told that there was an inscribed stone in the village of dKor, below Poo, and went to examine it. Although the stone was generally known, nobody, not even the lamas, had tried to read it. The village of dKor is situated on the right bank of the little brook of Poo. The stone was found in a field belonging to a lama called *bKā-rgyud* It is about six feet high. The upper half of the sculpture shows a well executed representation of a *stūpa*, the lower half that of a human being. This part of the stone is in very bad preservation and most of it underground. The human figure wears a three-pointed hat. On the reverse of the stone is a Tibetan inscription of eleven lines. Only the first two lines are in fair preservation ; of all the other lines only the beginning and end have been preserved, whilst the middle part of those lines has been obliterated. While we were examining the stone, a Christian Tibetan who was with us, began to read the first lines : *dPal-lha-btsan-po-Lha-bla-ma-Ye-shes*............When he had got so far, I suddenly remembered that I had heard of a person whose name began *Lha-bla-ma-Ye-shes.* But what was the syllable following after *Ye-shes*? It suddenly flashed on me, that it was *'od*, and that *Lha-bla-ma-Ye-shes-'od* was the name of the royal priest, the early king of Guge, who had tried in vain to draw the famous Buddhist monk Atīśa to his kingdom. Did the inscription really contain his name— a name which has not yet been traced anywhere ? We all went close to the stone, and looked at it from all sides, even from below. And lo, it was so. The stone contained the full name of this famous personage of Tibetan history (c. 1025 A.D.) and the words following the name were *sku-ring-la*, meaning 'in his life time.' I was so overjoyed at the discovery of this important record that I could not help jumping about in the field, and then embraced the lama who was just on the point of becoming displeased with my treatment of his crop.

The story of King Ye-shes-'od is found in the second part of the Tibetan historical work *dPag-bsam-ljon-bzang*, and a translation has been published by Sarat Chandra Das.[1] Up to the present, nobody had known whether the story contained in those works was really true and whether the persons mentioned in it had actually lived or not. This inscription of King Ye-shes-'od is the first record which can be brought forward to confirm the statements of the Tibetan historians. Fragmentary though it is, it contains some interesting information. We learn from it that in the days of the priest-king Ye-shes-'od the villages of *sPu* (Poo) and *dKor* both existed, that Poo even possessed a palace (*pho-brang*). *dKor* is called *dKor-khang*, house of *dKor*. There were ten princes according to the inscription, and all of them were sent to Poo. What was their object in this place, cannot be said with perfect certainty, but from the frequent occurrence of the words *lha-chos* (religion of the *lha*), and *sngar-chos* (former religion) it appears that they were sent here for the propagation of Buddhism. In the end we read that they erected something. This was probably the first Buddhist temple at Poo of which local tradition asserts that it was erected in the place where now-a-days the inscribed stone is found. This site is lower than most of the houses of Poo, and as an object of sanctity could not be suffered to stand on a lower elevation than ordinary houses, a new temple was built higher up, in the centre of Poo, and embellished with the furnishings of the old one.

[1] *Indian Pandits in the Land of Snow*, pp. 51 ff.

This temple, the oldest of the existing temples of Poo, is called *Lo-tsa-bai-Lha-khang* and is asserted to have been built by Lo-tsa-ba Rin-chen-bzang-po (Ratna-bhadra), the spiritual adviser of King Ye-shes-'od. It contains a stucco statue of a seated Buddha, and two standing images of his disciples Sāriputra and Maudgalyāyana, locally known as *Shar-gyi-Bu* (son of the East) and *Mi-yong-gal*. In front of these large images are three small ones, representing Padma-sambhava, Vajra-pāṇi, and Buddha. (Plate IX, a). Besides these images, the temple contains books, musical instruments, and masks. Neither the books nor any of the images are very ancient ; there is nothing that can claim to date from the time of Ye-shes-'od. As this temple was the successor to the ancient temple of dKor, all the traditions connected with the latter were probably transferred to the former.

About a mile below the village of dKor, on a hill above the river, there exist the extensive ruins of an ancient fort called Kalagtrung or Kalag Koṭ. It is supposed, once to have been the seat of a Ṭhākur. The Lambardār of Poo tells me that iron arrow-heads have often been found in the vicinity. Such articles are ultimately converted into nails or knives by the people, and therefore I could not obtain any of them. It is interesting that the site of the present summer house of the mission, high above the castle on the hillside, is also called Kalagtrung. It seems to have been part of the same settlement as the castle, in earlier days. We visited the site of the castle on the 14th July. Of ancient remains we found only sherds of hand-shaped pottery, sometimes with linear ornaments impressed on them. Only very little could be seen of ancient walls. The site was covered all over with large undressed stones, such as people still use for building purposes. In a few cases, the site of a former room could be seen, in still rarer cases that of a door. Part of an ancient staircase was in rather good preservation.

Opposite the castle, on the other side of the trade road, were the ruined terraces of deserted fields, abandoned long ago. My impression is that the site does not only contain the ruins of a chief's castle, but that of a whole village. This part of the country was formerly under Guge and Ladakh, and, as in Ladakh, people were here also compelled to live in fortified places on hilltops round their chief's stronghold.

The deserted fields are locally known by the name *Khola-ring*. The word *ring* seems to be the same as Bunan *rig*, 'field.' The name would then mean 'fields of the Khola.' Khola is very likely the same as *Koli*, the name of a low caste all over the Panjāb hills and possibly the tribal name of the aboriginal population of these districts.

High up on the hill-side, above Kalagtrung, there is a locality called "the old place of the Shar-rgan festival." It is a comparatively large plateau which was left vacant in ancient times, as it was used for dancing. At present there have been built on it several enclosures for sheep and cattle, two *maṇi* walls, and some small stone huts. One of the *maṇi* walls contained an inscribed slab in Sanskrit and Tibetan, instead of the ordinary votive tablet. I made an eye copy of it. The inscription contains a passage apparently taken from the *Prajñāpāramitā*, addressed to the Yum-chen-po, the 'great mother.' This great mother is Tārā, the wife of Śiva, and at the same time the goddess of learning. It is not remarkable that we should find here a prayer addressed to the wife of Śiva, for the festival of Shar-rgan which was distinguished by a human sacrifice, was apparently celebrated in her honour.[1] A little above the old dancing place, the remains of a pit into which the victims were thrown, are shown to the traveller. The pit is said to have been of considerable depth, but now-a-days it is only a yard or so deep. Every year a child of eight years of age was thus sacrificed. Now-a-days a goat is offered instead. This happens at the new Shar-rgan place. Old people in the village say that their own grand-mothers were witnesses of human sacrifices in their young days. Behind the pit, there are several terraces, on which people used to sit on the occasion of such sacrifices. The Shar-rgan festival, Mr. Schnabel tells me, as celebrated now-a-days, is a kind of thank-offering by those parents who have been blessed with a son during the past year.

On the occasion of the festival, 'songs of the Shar-rgan festival,' are sung. I discovered a manuscript containing these songs in the village, and had it copied. Although their meaning is not yet intelligible to me in every part, I can see that they are of great importance, with regard to the study of the pre-Buddhist religion of Kanāwar as well as of Tibet in general. The first songs of the collection remind me strongly of songs of the pre-Buddhist religion, as we find them in Ladakh, the *Ling-glu* and the 'Marriage ritual,' some of which have been published by me. It is of great importance that the religion they represent is spoken of as *Lha-chos* and *Bon-chos* in the Poo songs.[2] I have all along been of opinion that in the gLing-chos we have remnants of the earliest type of the Bon-chos, called *Jo-la-Bon* in the *Grub-mtha-shel-gyi-me-long.* This has been ridiculed by men like Dr. B. Laufer who know the Bon religion only from its latest productions, when it took sides with various forms of Hinduism, in antagonism to Buddhism. Literary productions like the "Songs of the Shar-rgan festival" go far to prove that the gLing-chos as brought to light by my efforts, is precisely the Jo-la-Bon religion of Tibet. But the songs of the Shar-rgan festival do not only speak of deities of the Bon religion, Gung-sngon-snyan-lha, the god of heaven, sPang-dmar-lha, the god of the red meadow, the earth, Bya-rgod, the sun, King Ke-sar, etc., but make also mention of new deities, the *pho-lha* and the *mo-lha*, the deities of the 'male and female creative principle.'[2] These are unmistakably the Tibetan names of Śiva and Kālī, the gods of the pre-Tibetan population of the Satluj valley. And it is very probable that the human sacrifices which used to form part of the Shar-rgan festival, belong to the religion of this aboriginal population, and not to the

---

[1] The following proverb, discovered by Rev. R. Schnabel, refers to the former custom of human sacrifices at Poo :

Dang-po-nga-rgya-gar-nas-yong-tsa-na,
glang-phrug-lo-gsum-byis-pa-lo-brgyad.

Translation :—When I (Tārā) came here from India,
[I used to receive] a calf, three years old, and a child of eight years of age.

[2] A class of deity which is of great fame at Poo and surrounding districts are the *dGra-lha* who are also mentioned in the *Shar-rgan* songs. As Mr. Schnabel tells me, there are nine *dGra-lha* of different names said to exist in nine villages of Upper Kanāwar. They are the following : *Khro-mo-min*, at Poo ; *Chags-drul* at Kanam ; *Pal-lim-bzang-mo* at Dabling ; *Chos-lha bzang-rig-pa*, at Dobbaling ; *Tsa-khang* at Lid or Sarkhung ; *Klu 'abrug bkra-shis*, at Shasu ; *Ju-ti-dung-mo*, at Khab ; *gSer-jen-chen-po*, at Namgya ; *dMag-gi-dpon-po*, at Hang. Six of them are of the male, and three of them, those at Poo, Dabling, and Khab, are of the female sex.

Tibetans. The Tibetans practised human sacrifices, but for different motives from what we have observed in the Satluj valley. Oaths at important treaties were emphasised by human as well as animal sacrifices. New houses were inaugurated by immuring human beings and a person was killed when a house was first inhabited.[1] Thus, at the village of Poo, a lama had only recently beheaded his own father while asleep, to make the new house he had built, properly habitable.

The Shar-rgan sacrifices as well as the human sacrifices in the Satluj valley and in Lahul are of a very different character. To understand them, it is necessary to investigate the character of the deities in whose honour they are celebrated. Śiva and Kālī, as we find them in the Himālayas, are personifications of the creative powers; they do not only produce the harvest of the fields, but also bless the women with children, especially sons. In this respect, the principal deities of the pre-Buddhist religion of the Tibetans, in particular Ke-sar and 'aBru-gu-ma, resemble Śiva and Kālī. For as I have shown previously,[2] Ke-sar and 'aBru-gu-ma were both invoked by the people to grant children. This explains the union which was formed between the Tibetan pre-Buddhist and the aboriginal Śiva-Kālī religion, as we find it represented in the Shar-rgan hymnal. (The word *shar-rgan* means "young and old".) But Ke-sar and 'aBru-gu-ma were not of the fierce character of Śiva and Kālī. The latter were only ready to grant a blessing, when a portion of what they had given, was returned to them. Hence not only a portion of the harvest of the fields, or some of the lambs of the flock had to be returned to them in sacrifice, but they also claimed some of the children with whom they had blessed the village. Almost invariably the traditions speak of children who were sacrificed. Here at Poo, the sacrifice had to be made on the occasion of a festival which is still now-a-days recognised as a festival or thanksgiving for the blessing of offspring. In Lahul, the prayer on the occasion of such sacrifices was apparently intended more as a thanksgiving for a good harvest in the fields.

The old Shar-rgan place is exactly above the site of the ancient castle of Kalagtrung and probably belonged to it. The new Shar-rgan place is situated a little above the road from Poo to Rizhing. At the latter place, there are a few old pencil-cedars, and a number of rough altars, furnished with horns of goats and wild antelopes, and pencil-cedar twigs. They look exactly like the *lha-tho* of Ladakh. A third place which is connected with the same festival is found in the middle of the village of Poo, and is called Dralang (*sGra-lang* (?) 'raising the voice'). It is used for dancing and has a pole in the middle. On two sides of the place, there are *lha-tho* like those on the new Shar-rgan place, and two perpendicular stones, one showing traces of an inscription seemingly *Oṁ-a-huṁ*. The other plain one is probably a rude kind of *liṅgam*, like those in Manchad. Not far from it, there are holes or pits where again children used to be sacrificed. (Plate IX, b).

The people of Poo although they are Buddhists, do not always cremate their dead, but bury them in certain cases. There are two burial places outside the village, one for

[1] The Dard Bridge, see my *History of Western Tibet*.

[2] *Z. D. M. G.*, Vol. LXI, pp. 583 ff.

a. Interior of Lotsabai Lha-khang, Poo.

b. Dralang, dancing-place, Poo.

more respectable people, as Mr. Schnabel informed me, the other one for poor people and such as die of infectious diseases. The graves consist of rocks and stones above the ground. Some corpses are even thrown into the river, especially those of people who die of dropsy. Do the people of Poo believe that the accumulation of water in the body of a sick person is a sign that the Nāgas (*Klu*) claim the body?

Before leaving Poo, I consider it necessary to write a short note about the line of kings who reigned here in former days. As has already been stated, King Ye-shes-'od, whose inscription we discovered at Poo, reigned at mTho-lding, the old capital of Guge, in the days of the great teacher Atiśa. Now a king of the same name is mentioned among the descendants of the first king of Zangskar, and closer research reveals the fact that the Zangskar kings actually reigned at mTho-lding in Guge. How is this to be accounted for? My explanation is this: King Nyi-ma-mgon of Western Tibet divided his empire among his three sons. The eldest received Ladakh, the second received Guge and Purang with mTho-lding as his capital, the third one's portion was Zangskar. The historical accounts of the Tibetans relate of descendants of the first and third sons, but they do not give any names of descendants of the second son. There were apparently none. The king of Guge and Purang died without issue. Then his country was seized by the king of Zangskar, whose sway thereby extended over Zangskar, Guge and Purang, and whose glory almost eclipsed that of the kings of Leh. Ye-shes-'od is a member of the important line of kings who reigned over the three countries mentioned above and whose capital was at mTho-lding.

We left Poo on the 6th July on our way to Shipke. At first our road took us down to the rocky banks of the Satluj where we had to cross a rope bridge. The place of this bridge is called mTho-rang, or 'Height itself.' From inscriptions on both banks of the river, it becomes evident that there has been a bridge in this place from ancient times. The oldest inscription is in Gupta characters, and too much effaced to allow of reading more than *sya*, the termination of the genitive case, at the end of the line. Several of the Tibetan inscriptions seem to be almost a thousand years of age, judging by the form of their characters. It is interesting to note that two of them, one on each bank of the river, give the following advice to the person who intends crossing: *Ma-ṇi-grongs-shig*! "Do not forget the *maṇi* (the *Ōṁ maṇi padmē hūṁ*) [when crossing]"! This was very appropriate advice, for unpleasant as this bridge is now-a-days, it was far more unpleasant in the old days when the traveller had to entrust his life to three rotten ropes plaited of willow twigs at an altitude of about 100 feet above a broad and violent stream. No wonder, people called the bridge 'Height itself.' At the present day, the bridge consists of a strong steel cable provided by the Public Works Department; and the usual trolley being broken, a wooden saddle with two rope slings attached to it, has to do service instead. As Mr. Schnabel informs me, hardly a year passes by without accidents on this bridge, and even a battered traveller like Sven Hedin who had to cross it ten months before us, clothed his feelings in the words: "This bridge is a proper place for people desirous of committing suicide!"

We arrived at the village of Namgya (spelt *sNam-rgya* in an historical document) on the 6th July, after a hot march over very uneven ground.[1] Soon after our arrival, the village chief, called Hira, made his appearance and entered into conversation with me. He said, he was a descendant of a Tibetan family of *blon-po*, ministers, who had formerly been in charge of this district, and indeed, he had quite the bearing of a gentleman. In the course of our conversation he exhibited an extraordinary knowledge of things historical, in particular with regard to the battle of Basgo in 1646-47 A.D[2]. When I expressed my astonishment at such wisdom, he said that he was in possession of a document of ancient times. After much persuasion he produced it, and it turned out to be a copy of the treaty between Rājā Kēhari Siṅgh (*Kyeris Sing* in Tibetan) of Bashahr and the Lhasa Government, headed by Galdan Thsang (Thse-dbang). This Galdan Thsang is the very general of the Tibeto-Mongolian army who had conducted the siege of Basgo. Of this most important document, I ordered a copy to be made at once and offered R1 for it. I said that I expected to get the copy on our way back from Shipke in a few days, to which the old gentleman consented. On our way back, I had to find out, however, that Hira was no longer a gentleman, as he would not hand over the copy, until he had extorted R2-8 from me. As our conversation on my return visit to Namgya was more heated than logical, it did not become quite plain from his talk, whether he had copied his paper from an old document in his possession, or from a copper-plate of the Rājā of Bashahr. If the latter be true, this would be the first copper-plate inscription in Tibetan, and the Rājā of Bashahr ought to be urged to open his archives to students of history. The manuscript gives a short account of the war between Ladakh and Lhasa in 1646-47 and contains a few, but important local names. The difficulty is to assign them their proper places on a map. That the document is not forged, is quite plain from its internal evidence.

The road between Namgya and Shipke is bad beyond description. I have had some experience of awkward roads during my thirteen years' residence in Indian Tibet, but I must say, the Namgya-Shipke road beats them all. Here we had not only to march by very unstable pathways along the face of the precipice, but had also from time to time to climb up and down pinnacles with almost no road under our feet. It reminded me of chimney climbing, sometimes inside sometimes outside a chimney. The continual ups and downs alone would have been quite sufficient to exhaust the strength of any traveller on an ordinary road.

The frontier of Tibet proper is marked by a little brook, where a meal is generally taken by travellers. Having passed the brook, the people of Namgya and Bashahr dismiss caste and, Mr. Schnabel tells me, are ready to eat and drink even with a European. On the Tibetan side of the frontier, people find a blue kind of zeolith embedded in the granite rock, which they call *rDo-khyu*, or *rDo-khyug*. This stone, according to their belief, possesses medical powers. They tie it over the eyes of sheep

---

[1] The earliest picture of Namgya (Namdja) is found in *Reise des Prinzen Waldemar von Preussen*, 1845, Plate, XIX.

[2] See my *History of Western Tibet*, p. 108.

a. Mount Purgyul from rNamgya.

b. Lamaist gateway near rNamgya.

and goats, when they are hurt, and even rub their own skins with it, when they are sore. Several weeks later, we found more of this stone between Nako and Chang and Pindi Lal bought a large quantity of it for two *paisa.* There we were told that in a pulverised state this stone could be used internally and externally, and would cure all diseases both real and imaginary.

Pindi Lal's treasure stood us in good stead in the course of our tour, for people continually approached us with the desire to be cured of all kinds of diseases. Government had granted us five rupees worth of Quinine and Castor Oil which had to serve as a cure for everything. The fame of my medical skill which was, however, without any foundation, spread far and wide. Once when travelling through the desert between Bashahr and Spiti, and far away from any human habitation, I met with a youth and an old woman, his mother, who said that they had travelled three days to meet me and get medicine to cure the old woman's eyes. As I was a Christian lama, it was my duty to render help, they said. All who have travelled in this country know how unpleasant it is to unload boxes in the middle of a stage, open them, and have them loaded again. In a case like the present there was, however, no escape, and I had to get at one of my boxes to find some ointment which would be, as I hoped, a little more efficacious than Castor Oil. Ordinarily Pindi Lal attended to the sick who were continually hovering about our camp and made them happy by handing over to them one or other of our blue stones with much genial advice.

The aspect of the village of Shipke is not different from that of the villages on the other side of the border, but the appearance of the inhabitants undoubtedly is. Not only does their dress show the genuine Tibetan cut, but also the pigtail is much in evidence here. I am sure that the people of Poo also were in the habit of wearing pigtails at an earlier date than 1650 A.D. But after they had become subjects of the Bashahr Raja, they assumed the fashions of that State. The people of Shipke try their best to extract as much money as possible from the few European travellers, they see. But as Mr. Schnabel said, there is some excuse, for tax-collecting is carried on in the most cruel way all over Tibet, and they have to part with all their few rupees, when the tax-collector comes. Only recently news was brought to Poo that an unfortunate wretch whose taxes had not been paid for the last three years was whipped to death at Shipke. No wonder, that most of the Tibetans would prefer to become British subjects.

There are three ruined castles at Shipke.[1] The oldest of them is situated rather high up above the village on the West. It is known by the name of *mKhar-gog* (broken castle), and is built in cyclopean style (Plate XI, a). Only portions of two walls are still in their original position. There are no traditions whatever current about this castle. We bought an ancient stone axe of the type of the Ladakhi *Kalam* which was asserted to have been found on the site of this stronghold. It is interesting that this kind of stone implement was in use here also.

---

[1] The earliest picture of Shipke with the Purgyul mountain is found in *Reise des Prinzen Waldemar von Preussen* 1845, Plate XXI.

The second of the ruined castles is called *Seng-ge-mKhar* (Plate XI, b). Its ruins are found below the mKhar-gog castle, on the left bank of the Satluj. Its lower part is built of large well fitted stones, and higher up the walls are of clay or sun-dried bricks, as is the case in the later Ladakhi buildings. I suppose that the castle was built by Seng-ge-rnam-rgyal of Ladakh, and called after him. Some of the walls are still standing. The building must have been of huge size. An inscription which I found on a *maṇi* wall just above the village of Shipke speaks of a king and his son who once resided 'at the castle.' No names are given. The kings of Western Tibet, or their vassal kings of Guge, may have resided here occasionally. A legend referring to this castle, was told by the Lambardār of Shipke, and taken down by Lobzang of Poo who accompanied me on this tour. According to it, the castle received its crooked ground plan through a race round its base executed in opposite directions by a poisonous snake and a scorpion.

The third castle of Shipke is situated on the road to the village of Khyug on the brook. It is called *sKyabs-mkhar* 'castle of refuge.' No walls are standing; only heaps of loose stones remain. No information of any kind regarding it was forthcoming, and I have no idea of what age it may be.

There are long rows of *maṇi* walls on the road from Shipke to Khyug. The Lambardār, Lobzang, and myself went there to examine them. The votive tablets on them were quite of the usual style, but in the place where the Ladakhi tablets give the name of the king, these contained the title of the Dalai Lama, and no personal name. For this reason it is impossible to assign a date to them or to the *maṇi* walls. Only this much can be said: they all date apparently from a time, not earlier than the second half of the seventeenth century. If earlier, they would have contained names of the kings of Ladakh, or of Guge. The tablets, however, generally contain versions of the eulogy of the country of Guge, a kind of national anthem, and for this reason I copied one of them, which I found in the village of Shipke. I am rather of opinion that after 1650 A.D., when Guge was made over to Lhasa, all those ancient tablets which contained the names of Ladakhi or Guge kings, were destroyed. It was in the interest of the Lhasa Government to make people forget their former masters.

This is one of their national anthems, as we find them in these inscriptions. It is taken from the only inscription which refers to a king.

> Jambudvipa of the south is a famous country among the ten directions of the world.
> There is the mountain Tise (Kailāsa) with its neck of ice, the dwelling place of those who have conquered all enemies (*arhats*).
> There is the turquoise lake Ma-spang (Manasarovar) the abode of the Nāga Ma-gros.
> On the right bank of the murmuring river which proceeded from an elephant's mouth (Satluj),
> There is the great castle sKu-mkhar, the abode of the king.
> In it there dwell the rulers of men, father and son. May you be always victorious!

a. Ruined castle, mKhar-gog, Shipke.

b. Ruined castle, Seng-ge-mKhar, Shipke.

Under the rule of this religious king, all the ten virtues were prominent, here in the capital of Hrib-skyes (Shipke).

This inscription contains, as we see, the name of the village of Shipke in its original Tibetan spelling. It reads *Hrib-skyes*, and means, 'arisen in a moment,' probably without the agency of man; it was built by fairies, like so many places in Tibet. The Nāga Ma-gros is one of the most famous Nāga kings, and figures in all the lists of Nāgas. His dwelling place is the Holy Lake of Tibet. The Kailāsa mentioned in this song, is the beautiful mountain group in the vicinity of the Holy Lake. As Hira of Namgya told me, the rKyang-drag monastery is situated in front of these mountains, and a glass window is provided just in front of the eyes of the image, so that it may always be enabled to enjoy the view.[1] As regards the Holy Lake, four different sects have their monasteries there, in five principal establishments. The oldest is the Byiu-dgon-pa (Sven Hedin's *Tschiu*) which belongs now-a-days to the Gelugpa sect; the same sect also owns the Dri-ri-dgon-pa (perhaps Sven Hedin's Diripu). The Glang-po-sna-dgon-pa, (Sven Hedin's Langbonan ?) belongs to the 'aBrugpa, and the bKa-rdzong-dgon-pa to the rNyingmapa sect. Besides these professedly Buddhist monasteries there is also a Bon monastery on the shores of the Lake. As stated by Graham Sandberg, the Manasarovar Lake was already known to Pliny and Ctesias who say that the natives collected pitch in a certain corner of it. As Dr. Longstaff informs me, there are certainly hot springs on the isthmus between the two lakes.

When I heard all this about the attractions of the forbidden land of Guge, and when the natives themselves invited me most cordially to proceed, it was certainly hard to turn back. But the promise given to the Indian Government, I had to keep. The Tibetans of Shipke did not understand my position, for they said: "If men like Sven Hedin, Sherring, Calvert, etc., are allowed to travel about in Tibet, why should not you ?" All these travellers had won the hearts of the Tibetans by their liberal payment for services rendered to them. The Tibetans were more than ready to serve me in the same way under similar conditions.

Opposite Shipke may be seen the Puri monastery. This, as well as the Ra-nyid monastery, a little north-east of Shipke, is asserted to have been founded by Ratnabhadra in the 11th century.

As I was not allowed to proceed to mTholding and Tsaparang myself, I asked Lobzang, a former pupil of the Poo mission school, to go there and copy any inscriptions he could find. Accordingly he went on alone from Shipke, and after twelve days he returned safely to Poo. He had, however, found no inscriptions of any antiquity at either of the two places. It is quite possible that none remain. Just as there are many inscriptions of the Dalai Lama's time at Shipke, but only one previous to 1650, the old inscriptions of mTholding and surroundings may have disappeared as well. Lobzang, however, did not return quite empty-handed. He brought me short descriptions in Tibetan of both places he had visited, and a copy of a written document which he had found in the

[1] As I see in Sven Hedin's *Transhimalaya*, Vol. II, p. 146, there is a similar window in the Gossul ('Gossul-gompa') monastery. An account of the monasteries on the holy lake and mountain is also found in Sandberg's *Tibet and the Tibetans*.

hands of the *rdzong-dpon* (castleward) of Tsaparang. This document turned out to be another version of the treaty between Bashahr and Tibet in 1650, and is of the greatest value for the study of this important treaty. By a comparison of the two documents (Namgya and Tsaparang), we may obtain a fairly reliable text of the treaty. His description of mTholding is a valuable supplement to Captain Rawling's description of the same place which, up to the present, is still the best account of it we have. According to Captain Rawling, mTholding consists of two settlements, one of which is situated on a practically inaccessible rock, and the other in the plain below. The town on the rock is the old capital, for the customs of Guge were not different from those of Ladakh. The king's castle being built on the top of the rock, the subjects had to build their houses below or around the castle on the same rock. One of Captain Rawling's sepoys climbed up to the old town with the assistance of some Tibetans and saw several of the gigantic old images in the midst of extensive ruins. Captain Rawling himself went to the famous temple of mTholding on the plain below and examined its contents. He is of opinion that it was built when the old town was deserted and that several of the valuable articles of furniture of the castle or temples were removed to this new sanctuary, for instance the wood-carved throne of the ancient kings of Guge. I am, however, of opinion that it is very likely that the famous temple of mTholding was built on the plain by Ratna-bhadra, and not on the rock. My reason is that a long study of temples of this period (1000—1050 A.D.) has shown me that these temples are invariably found on plains, and not on rocky heights. Of great importance is Lobzang's note that this temple is locally known by the name of *rNam-snang*, which is the abbreviated form of *rNam-par-snang-mdzad*(Vairōchana), and I am in a position to state that for the most part the temples erected by Ratna-bhadra are called by that name. Either the temple as a whole is called *rNam-par-snang-mdzad*, or one of the halls is so called. Schlagintweit has a note on this temple, to the effect that it was once burnt down and re-erected. If that be true, it would be difficult, indeed, to find here ancient records, and it is a very fortunate circumstance that other temples of the same age in Western Tibet have escaped destruction. d'Andrada, when speaking of Tsaparang in 1623-24 says that there are many symbols of Christianity in this place. I have not yet been able to make out what he means by this, whether he mistook Buddhist symbols (for instance *svastikas*) for Christian symbols, or whether there were actually crosses of a Christian type among the rock carvings of this place, like the Maltese crosses of Drangtse at the Pangkong lake. I had hoped that Lobzang would find it possible to clear up this question, but I was disappointed. Lobzang said that he had seen many rock sculptures (without inscriptions) at Tsaparang, but nothing to suggest the former presence of Christians in this place.

After we had almost completed our two days' march from Shipke back to Poo, we had once more to cross the rope bridge *mTho-rang*, 'Height itself.' To avoid unnecessary delay, I had told the Lambardār, on leaving Poo, to have everything in readiness for Saturday, for on that day I intended to reach Poo again. In spite of this precaution, however, nothing was in readiness when we arrived at the bridge on Saturday at noon. The people of Poo seem to be fond of practical joking and try to get as much fun out of their bridge as possible. They cannot think of anything more exhilarating than a person who wants to cross and cannot. I was told that they have kept old women waiting on the other bank for three days. What a grand idea to keep a European Sahib waiting and not move a finger to aid him! The banks of the Satluj are a trying place indeed for spending a long afternoon in midsummer. For miles around the bridge neither tree nor shrub is to be seen and nowhere is there a hollow in the rock to afford shelter from the merciless rays of the sun. How glad I was when I found a corner in the rocks to shade my face down to the nose as I lay stretched out on the ground. We did not at once understand that it was the obstinacy of the Poo people which kept us on the opposite bank, and thus we sent a man with a voice like a foghorn on to the top of a rock in the vicinity, to shout towards Poo, where people were seen working in the fields, and probably chuckling with delight. After this man had roared himself hoarse with shouting, we sent up another to continue the process. Whilst this man was thus engaged for the general benefit, we saw a man of Poo climbing about on the rocks of the Poo bank of the river. We asked him to go up to Poo for *bakhshish* and fetch the wooden saddle. "That is the last thing I would think of doing," was all he said, and with him our last ray of hope disappeared. Perhaps we should still be sitting on the other side of 'Height itself,' if Pindi Lal's craving for food had not been so imperative. He had had no food since a very early and hurried morning meal, and realized that he could not survive many more days in that barren spot. He therefore persuaded an athletic youth among our coolies to use one of his leather *chaplis* (sandals) in place of the wooden saddle, and ride across, making onward progress with his arms. So poor are these people that the youth was ready to undertake the daring experiment for two annas. It was a sight worthy of any circus to see the boy, suspended on a *chapli* 100 feet above the roaring torrent, draw himself slowly onward, often pausing to take a rest. At length he reached the opposite bank safely, and an hour later, he came back with the wooden saddle and ropes. The sun was just setting, when I crossed with my legs in the slings below the saddle. I had just reached the middle of the lofty passage, when I felt a knock on my back and was suddenly stopped. The rope behind me which had to be paid out whilst I was proceeding, had got knotted, and impeded further progress. The man who pulled me from the front did not understand the cause of my sudden halt, and believing that my weight had suddenly increased in a miraculous way, took the pulling rope over his shoulder, and marched off with full determination to drag me on by main force. As the knot, however, would not yield, I was pulled from the front as well as the back and all this at an unusual height above a roaring river. I managed, at last, to explain matters to the man who then took the rope off his shoulder, and I had to spend some trying minutes in sublime solitude, before the knot could be loosened, and I could proceed to the Poo bank of the river. I was not in my best humour when I met the Lambardār of Poo. He, however, pretended to have acted according to my instructions in posting a man on the bridge to report our arrival. It was this man's sense of humour which had kept him away. We punished him by making him pay the two annas *bakhshish* which had been more than earned by the brave *chapli* rider.[1]

On the way between Shipke and Poo, high above the Satluj, a monastery called bKra-shis-sgang may be seen. This is not the famous monastery of that name, erected by Seng-ge-rnam-rgyal of Ladakh. The latter is situated in Western Guge, and is generally called Byang-bKra-shis-sgang (Northern bKra-shis-sgang), to distinguish it from the monastery near Namgya.

CHAPTER II.

From the Satluj to the Indus.

We left Poo on the 21st July to travel through Spiti and Rubshu to Leh. This is a journey of about four weeks through the most uninhabitable country. Our outfit, as regards provisions and warm clothing, might certainly have been better. But the summers being short in these regions, we could not put in three more weeks of waiting at Poo, to let the required goods and means come up. The missionary at Poo kindly advanced me some money as well as tinned provisions, and we left with the determination to move on and be satisfied with the simplest fare.

On the first day we had to cross the steep Hang Pass, 16,000 feet high. It is a place which arouses painful memories in the minds of Mr. and Mrs. Schnabel; for when they had to cross it the last time with a child of only two years of age, the rarified air on the top of the pass proved to be too much for their baby which showed signs of suffocation. Only by taking up the child and hurrying down with it at a pace not at all in harmony with the awful condition of the road, was it possible to save its life. The eastern side of the pass is very bare and uninteresting, but on the western side alpine flowers of great beauty and scent greet the traveller, among them the wild purple aster and Aconitum moschatum. Before the village of Tsuling is reached on the western side, the road passes by the ruins of the old Gadgari monastery. Heaps of loose stones and some terraced ground is all that remains.

I could not discover anything of special interest in the little village of Tsuling. A small hut under a huge pencil-cedar tree is called Lhā-khang, "house of the gods," or "temple." It was quite empty with the exception of some drums which are kept in it. Some stones with the inscription *Ōṁ maṇi padmē hūṁ* were placed below the sacred pencil-cedar.

On the 22nd July we arrived at the village of Li which looks very beautiful with its many green fields and apricot trees in the midst of a chaos of bare rocky mountains. Li is very probably a place with a grander past than present. The Tibetan dictionaries and chronicles speak of two ancient places called *Li*, one in the north, the other in the south. The northern one has been correctly identified with Turkestan or a part of Turkestan. Of the Li of the South it is said that it is situated "near Nepal." I believe that the "Li of the South" is the Tibetan part of the present Bashahr State, the principal town of which was very possibly the present village of Li. On a steep rock on the bank of the river

[1] The earliest picture of this bridge is found in *Reise des Prinzen Waldemar von Preussen*, Plate XVIII. (Namtu Bridge.)

are the ruins of an ancient castle, *mkhar*. People told me that they had formerly to live on that rock (probably before 1650, when they came under Bashahr). They left the rock on account of many accidents in consequence of their getting drunk. I visited the site, but saw nothing beyond heaps of loose stones with fragments of rude pottery Some of the rooms can still be traced. The Tibetans of Li as well as of Kanāwar in general are distinguished from those of Spiti, Ladakh and Shipke by the fashion in which they wear their hair. The men of Kanāwar wear their hair like the people of Bashahr. No long pigtails are seen here. The same is the case in Lahul where also the long pigtail has disappeared. The Hindu rulers of Bashahr and Kuḷū were apparently against it.

The bKra-shis-lhun-grub monastery of Li is asserted to be of ancient origin. This may be true, for it belongs to the rNyingmapa sect, the most ancient order of monks in Tibet. This sect has not founded new settlements for a long time. The abbot told me that the Li monastery was founded by Padma-sambhava, which is quite probable, if it be not even older. As Sarat Chandra Das has shown, the rNyingmapa order has much of its literature in common with the Bonpos, the followers of the pre-Buddhist religion of Tibet.[1] Around Lhasa, the monks of the rNyingmapa order cannot be distinguished from other orders of the "red persuasion," as regards dress, but here in the west they can. Here the rNying-ma-pa monks grow long hair which is never combed, and gives them a savage appearance. The best specimens of this uncivilized order of saints can, however, be seen at Pyin in Spiti. Although I am convinced of the correctness of the assertion that the monastery is of remote origin, this statement cannot be confirmed by documentary evidence. The present building does not appear to be of many years' standing, nor the few idols contained in it. At the monastery, however, they have an ancient and beautiful wood carving of teak wood, representing Buddha surrounded by Bōdhisattvas. All the Bōdhisattvas are of the primitive and simple type. (Fig. 1).

Fig. 1.

Not far from the bKra-shis-lhun-grub monastery, a little above the line of cultivation, are the ruins of an old nunnery, called *Jo-moi dgon-pa*. It consists of three separate ruined houses, a *maṇi* wall covered with white pebbles and two *mchod-rten*. The nunnery was abandoned only a hundred years ago, so people told me.

[1] See *J. A. S. B.*, Vol. L, p 202.

The irrigation canals of Li are of some interest. In one case the water is conducted through a rock or mountain by a tunnel of considerable length. People here firmly believe that this tunnel was made by fairies (*mkha-'agro*) or gods (*lha*). In the West people would be proud of their clever ancestors.

In one of the *mchod-rten* at Li, on the road to Nako, I found a clay tablet representing Avalōkitēśvara with eleven heads and eight arms, an interesting stage in this divinity's development into a figure with a thousand arms.

On Friday the 23rd July, we marched to Nako. We had hardly left the village of Li, when our caravan had to cross the swollen Spiti river by a rope bridge. (Plate XII, a). I sincerely sympathised with Pindi Lal when he said "I am tired of these bridges." But we had a right to be tired of them, for it was, after all, the last one we had to cross in the course of our journey. After we had spent about three hours in transporting our luggage and ourselves across the foaming waves, we had to climb up a very steep and high mountain side with no shade and a scorching sun above us. When it seemed as if I had reached the ends of the earth with nothing beyond, the large emerald plateau of the village of Nako suddenly appeared before me. There were waving fields in which girls were working and singing merrily, and a picturesque town reflected in the mirror of a clear little lake.

We noticed at once the site of a great 'aBrugpa monastery, called Lo-tsa-bai Lha-khang (Plate XII, b). Four large temple halls are still standing and form a kind of court. South-east of them, there are many ruins of other buildings, probably the cells of monks. There are also plenty of more or less ruined *mchod-rten*. This great monastery is believed to have been founded by Lo-tsa-ba Rin-chen-bzang-po, in the days of king Ye-shes-'od of Guge, c. 1025 A.D., and I am convinced that this assertion is right. Here we are certainly on ancient ground. Let me now proceed to describe the different temples.

The western hall is called *Lha-khang-ched-po*. The principal figure in this hall is that of rNam-par-snang-mdzad (Vairōchana), the chief of the Dhyāni-buddhas of the five regions (Plate XIII, a). On his right we find Don-yod-grub-pa (Amōgha-siddha) and Rin-chen-byung-ldan (Ratna-sambhava); on his left sNang-ba-mtha-yas (Amitābha) and rDo-rje-sems-dpa (Vajra-sattva). Rin-chen-byung-ldan is represented once more on the same wall with a dragon frame, similar to that of the principal figure.[1] As regards the frescoes on the walls, they were arranged in circles, just as we find them at the Alchi monastery. However, their quantity being enormous and their state of preservation poor, I gave up the attempt either to copy or describe any of them. I must leave that to future students who can afford to spend at least a month in that interesting place. Elsewhere [2] I have given expression to my opinion that stucco images are

[1] In this "dragon frame" as well as in that of the stucco sGrol-gser in the northern temple we notice a curious development of a well-known decorative motive of Indian art. It is very common in the architecture of Java, where archæologists are in the habit of describing it as the *Kāla-makara* ornament. Some, however, prefer the designation *Garuḍa-nāga* ornament. In the present instances the central figure at the top is undoubtedly a Garuḍa, but the two dragons at the sides still bear the character of *makaras* (Ed.).

[2] *History of Western Tibet*, p. 51.

a. Crossing the Spiti River by a rope bridge.

b. Lotsabai Lha-khang Monastery, Nako.

PLATE XIII.

a. Figure of rNam-par-snang-mdzad or Vairochana in the Lotsabai Lha-khang Monastery, Nako.

b. Figure of sGrol-gser or the yellow Tara in the Lotsabai Lha-khang Monastery, Nako.

PLATE XIII.

a. Figure of rNam-par-snang-mdzad or Vairochana in the Lotsabai Lha-khang Monastery, Nako.

b. Figure of sGrol-gser or the yellow Tara in the Lotsabai Lha-khang Monastery, Nako.

of later date than the times of Rin-chen-bzang-po. Since I wrote this statement, I have had to change my opinion. Stucco images of very artistic design were fashioned in the eleventh century. And as regards Nako, all the monks were unanimous in asserting that the images of this monastery were of the great Lotsaba's time. In a godown here we found an ancient wooden mask such as are used by the lamas in their devil dances. We bought it for one rupee. The present day masks are made of stucco, and differ widely from this ancient specimen. I found only a single inscription in this hall, written on the wall with black ink. It reads *so-rdi,* a word which I cannot explain.

The southern temple is called *dKar-byung-lha-khang,* the 'White Temple.' We were not allowed to enter it, as a lama was occupying it for meditation.

The northern temple is called *Lha-khang-gong-ma,* 'Upper Temple.' It contains the stucco image of sGrol-gser, the yellow Tārā, in an elaborately carved wooden frame (Plate XIII, b). This is one of the rarer forms of this popular deity, the Tibetans being more interested in the white and green Tārās. Of the latter deity, there is a representation in stucco in the same hall. The yellow Tārā is surrounded by frescoes representing the eight medicine Buddhas (*sman-bla*).

The eastern temple is also called *Lha-khang-gong-ma,* 'Upper Temple'. It contains only frescoes. Opposite the door, there is a seated Buddha surrounded by his disciples. To the left of this picture is found a blue rDo-rje-chang (Vajra-dhara). On the wall to the right of the door is the picture of Thse-dpag-med (Amitāyus), probably in his capacity of medicine Buddha (*sman-bla*) surrounded by his eight followers. All these pictures were furnished with Tibetan inscriptions in white colour. Only the following three names were still legible: *Sha-kya-thub-pa*; *Myang-ngan-med-mchog-dpal*; *Rin-chen-zla-ba.* Above the door, among other tutelary deities, there is a large fresco of King Kesar riding on a white *r Kyang* (wild ass). At Nako he is called *gLing-sing-chen-rgyal-po,* 'Great Lion King of gLing.' This may point to a connection between the pre-Buddhist religion of the Tibetans and the Buddhism of the eleventh century. I copied six Tibetan inscriptions in this hall, which are merely of iconographical interest. Most of the others were illegible. Besides the Tibetan inscriptions we found here a short inscription in Śāradā characters which we tried to photograph, but did not succeed, as it was written with brown ink on an orange ground. Much was not lost, however, as it is probably not of very ancient date.

Another little temple to the south of the village of Nako is called *sLob-dpon-zhabs-rjes,* 'Footprint of the Teacher.' It is built over a natural rock showing a footprint of more than human size. Above the rock is placed a stucco figure of Padma-sambhava. The temple is furnished with frescoes of as ancient a type as those in the Lha-khang ched-po (*ched-po* is the same as Tibetan *chen-mo,* 'great'). They also have the same glassy polish which is found on the before-mentioned pictures. This little temple was probably erected in the eleventh century, together with the great monastery. Thus, we are led to surmise that already in the days of Rin-chen-bzang-po, this footprint on the rock was believed to be that of Padma-sambhava who lived two and a half centuries earlier.[1]

Opposite the present town, on the other shore of the little lake of Nako, there are the extensive ruins of the ancient town, with the Jo's (chief's) fort above it. This ancient town is said to have been destroyed by the Ladakhis, probably on one of their punitive expeditions against their vassal kings of Guge. Where the present village stands, there used to be only stables in earlier days, as was also the case in Li. The chiefs of Nako are still in existence, and a votive tablet by one of their ladies was found and copied in the temple of Lo-tsa-bai-lha-khang. All the *maṇi* walls round about Nako are of recent date, like those of Li, the most ancient name mentioned on them being that of Metar (Mahindar) Singh of Bashahr.

North-west of Nako, there are a number of deserted villages which show that in former days the cultivated area about Nako was larger than it is at present. I gathered the following names as those of the now deserted settlements: Khartag, Jadong, Gulbug, Bemgrol and Therang thangka. Most of them were deserted a long time back, but one of them only six years ago. Two or three people had lost their lives when the water course was mended, which was considered a sufficient reason for giving up the settlement altogether. Let me add that Nako was one of the places visited by Csoma de Körös.

We reached the village of Chang on the 24th July, after a march through a mountain desert without any special interest. The locally famous monastery of Tra-shi-tong-yang (*bKra-shis-mthong-dbyangs*) is situated on the opposite bank of the brook of Chang, on a rock, in the middle of a deserted village. We were not in a position to visit the temple, as its key had been taken to Tibet by the lama in charge. The monastery is asserted to have been founded by Padma-sambhava, and to contain his image. The lamas belong to the 'aBrugpa order.

Here again, in former days, all the peasants had to live on the rock around the monastery and castle, where there are many ruined houses. In the middle of the present village of Chang, there is a life-size stone statue of Avalōkitēśvara half buried in a *maṇi* wall. It is a very rude and ugly image. The small figure of Amitābha can be plainly seen in his headdress. The statue has only two arms and is painted white. The legend which is connected with this image, is of some interest, because it is a version of a tale connected with Langdarma's persecution of Buddhism.[2] The Chang legend runs as follows:—Many centuries ago, the image was carried down from some higher place by a flood. The Chang people found it, and tried to carry it up to the Tra-shi-tong-yang

---

[1] The earliest picture of Nako village and monastery is found on Plate XXII of *Reise des Prinzen Waldemar von Preussen*, 1845. Of particular interest are the slanting roofs of several houses shown in that picture. Dr. Hoffmeister, who was of the Prince's party, gives the following items with regard to the ancient images of the Nako temples. In one of the halls, the travellers were shown the following images: Dordschi Simba (*rDo-rje-sems-dpā*); Nanatheia (*sNang-ba-mthā-yas*); Vinschin-jungne (*Rin-chen-byung-ldan*); Thevadna (?); Nabarnangse (*rNam-par-snang-mdzad*), and a frame-work with a Tschakium (*Khyung*, Garuḍa). This was evidently the *Lha-khang-ched-po* temple. In another temple, they saw a Dulma (*sGrol-ma*) with a Tschakium (*Khyung*, Garuḍa) above her. This was evidently the *Lha-khang-gong-ma* temple.

[2] See *Ladrags rGyal-rabs* under Langdarma.

monastery, believing that this monastery would be the most suitable abode for the statue. However, a hundred men could not move it. Then a clever lama guessed that the image wished to be set up in its present place. And lo, when they tried to take it there, a single man could easily carry it.

On the evening of the 24th, I went to have a look at the castle of Kyahar which is only three miles distant from Chang. This castle is more imposing and of greater dimensions than I have yet seen in these mountains. It is supposed to have been built by the king of Rāmpur (in about 1650 A.D.) who probably wished to fortify the frontiers of his new territory. People told me that the castle was famous for its beautiful frescoes, and I was sorry not to be able to go and examine them. I asked, however, Mr. Cargill, of the Public Works Department, whom I met a few days after in Spiti, to go and inspect the pictures, if his journey should take him that way. He told me afterwards that he had actually been to Kyahar and made inquiries about the frescoes. People told him that there had been pictures, but that they had all disappeared. On the way to Kyahar, I noticed a short inscription in Ṭākarī on one of the boulders on the roadside. It is unintelligible, but interesting, as testifying to the use of that script in these parts.

I was told that there is a small, but ancient monastery at Kyahar, which local tradition also connects with the famous Rin-chen-bzang-po. It is called Lha-brang and belongs to the Gelugpa order. Although I was assured that it contained ancient pictures, I could not manage to visit it. Nor did I see the ancient stone sculpture at Kyahar which is said to be similar to the Avalōkitēśvara of Chang, mentioned above.

On a rock below the present village of Kyahar are extensive ruins of a deserted village. I am told that the people of Kyahar were invited to settle round the present stately castle, and therefore exchanged sites.

On the 26th we started on our march through a desert which separates Spiti from the Bashahr State. We had to spend three days in absolutely bare and uninhabited country, before the first village of the territory of Spiti was reached. The first march took us to the Zangzam bridge, which spans a tributary of the Spiti river. Here the road leads through Tibetan territory for several miles, and the camp on the bridge as well as our next camp at Horling was on Tibetan ground. There are several sulphur springs in the vicinity of the bridge, which contain rather hot water. The natives have hewn out little basins in which they bathe. Crystallized sulphur and some white salt (probably borax) are found near the wells. I collected some water plants which I found growing in the hot sulphurous water.

The 26th July was spent in the same desert on our march to Horling, a desert camping-place on the Spiti river. I had expected to have an archæological holiday in this uninhabitable region. But that was not so. Strange to say, we passed by *maṇi* walls, from time to time, and several of the stones placed on, or by the side of, the walls, were of unusual interest. I found here four or five stones which must have been carved in the 15th century. They contained the names of the great reformer Tsong-kha-pa and three of his contemporaries, mKhas-grub-pa (1384-1437), Lha-dbang-blo-gros (1388-1462), and dGe'adun-grub (1389-1473). What points in particular to their ancient origin is the fact, that in these inscriptions the *e*, *o* and *u* vowel signs are all directly joined to their consonant bases. These stones were, in all probability, put up on the roadside during the Lamaist reformation, and later on placed on or near *maṇi* walls. They testify to the enthusiasm with which Tsongkhapa's reformation was welcomed in these tracts.

A still more interesting inscription I found on a *maṇi* wall at the desert camping place of Horling. This *maṇi* wall was erected by a man of the Tibetan village of rGyu-mkhar, the *Shugar* of the map, during the reign of a king who resided at Tsaparang (spelt *rTsabarang*, on the stones). When I read this, I could not help thinking at once of the Jesuit priest, d'Andrada, who states that he had found a Tibetan king at Tsaparang favourably inclined towards Christianity. This statement of the Jesuit has been subjected to serious doubts by modern writers on Tibet. They could not believe that a 'king' should ever have resided at the now unimportant village of Tsaparang. But d'Andrada is vindicated as we know now that Tsaparang was the capital of a sovereign whose power was acknowledged even as far as Spiti. At the same time when the tablet was carved, Tsaparang was the capital of the kingdom of Guge, the largest vassal state of the Western Tibetan empire. As far as my knowledge goes, the kingdom of Guge has had three capitals : the first was mTho-lding (Tholing), the second, Tsaparang, the third Garthog. The genealogical tree of the kings of Guge has been preserved in Tibetan historical works. The original line of these kings came from Zangskar, as stated above. Their dynastical name was *Lde.* The Lde dynasty came to an end in the principal line, and was superseded by a *rMal* dynasty. When the rMal dynasty became extinct, a member of a side branch of the original Lde dynasty was invited from Purang and became king of Guge. Then the historical information ceases. The name of the king who is mentioned on the votive tablet, is Khri-bkra-shis-grags-pa-lde. This name is not found in the genealogical tree, and therefore he must be one of the later members of the second Lde dynasty from Purang. He cannot well have reigned before 1600 A.D., for *maṇi* walls were hardly ever constructed before that time ; nor can he have reigned much later than 1630 A.D., for about that time Indra Bodhirnam-rgyal, a younger brother of the king of Leh, was made vassal king of Guge, and in 1650 A.D., Guge was annexed by Lhasa and received a Tibetan governor. It is, therefore, very probable that Khri-bkra-shis-grags-pa-lde is the very king whose acquaintance was made by d'Andrada in 1623 A.D.

This supposition is strengthened by the discovery of a similar votive tablet which I made three days after at Tabo in Spiti. This contained the name of the same king and gave Tsaparang as his residence. But what is still more surprising, is the occurrence of the following short passage on the same tablet : "He who clears away all the apostacy and darkness at the great palace of *Tsabarang rtse.*" The man who carved this inscription was evidently displeased with the Tsaparang king's inclination towards Christianity. So was the king of Leh ; for it was probably on this account that he placed his younger brother on the throne of Guge. I think, we shall have to accept d'Andrada's account of his mission to Tsaparang without any severe criticism.

a Monastery of Tabo.

b. Row of one hundred and eight *stupas*, Tabo.

Not far from our camp at Horling, on the plain towards Lhari, I found a large stone containing an inscription of Tsongkhapa's time. It mentions, besides the names of the reformer and one or two of his contemporaries, those of an ancient lama-king of Guge, Byang-chub-'od, of the famous lama Rin-chen-bzang-po of the year 1000 A. D., and also that of the Tabo monastery. This shows that in the 15th century people believed in a connection between the Tabo monastery of Spiti, and the great priest-kings of Guge.

From Horling, the high and beautiful snow mountains near the village of Chang, which belong to the group of the Purgyul peaks and are over 22,000 feet high, can be seen. We had already admired them on our way to Shipke, when we were much closer to them (Plate X, a). At Namgya, I had heard the following ditty about them :—

Tise gangskyi rgyalpo yin
Purgyul rii rgyalpo yin
Maspang mthsoyi rgyalpo yin.
" Kailāsa is the king of glaciers,
Purgyul is the king of mountains,
Manasarowar is the king of lakes."

At Horling the coolies from Chang, pointing towards the Purgyul group of mountains which is here called Gung-ri (perhaps the *Kungrang* of the maps), said that on those mountains was the fabulous 'aBa-yul, the abode of spirits. Its inhabitants are believed to be numerous, but ordinary people can neither see nor hear them. It is only very good men or lamas who are capable of perceiving anything. When such a pious man approaches that region of eternal snow, he hears the voices of its invisible denizens or the barking of their ghostly dogs, but sees nothing. This tale reminds me strongly of a passage which I had repeatedly found in inscriptions with reference to the Kailāsa mountains :—*dgra bcom bzhugs gnas Tise,* ' Kailāsa, the abode of those who have conquered all enemies' (*arhats*). The ice mountains evidently are not only the abode of the gods, but also that of the dead who, according to the belief of the Tibetans, have acquired paradise.

We reached Lhari, the first village of Spiti, on the 28th July. Although this village is possibly connected with the history of gNya-khri-btsam-po, the first king of Tibet, it is nowadays a very poor place. It consists of only a few scattered houses. Above it, on the side next the brook, there are the extensive ruins of an ancient castle, called Serlang, the former abode of the Lhari people. Below the village there are very many ancient rock-carvings, among which we note, in particular, the ibex and the *svastika.* One of the carvings appears to represent the 'willow of the world' with its six branches and six roots, one of the symbols of the pre-Buddhist religion of the people. Another symbol appears to represent the sun and the moon. Dilapidated as Lhari is now-a-days, I cannot escape the impression that it is a very ancient settlement.

On the 29th July, we marched to the famous Gelugpa monastery of Tabo which is only three miles distant from Lhari (Plate XIV, a). When we were approaching it, I said to Pindi Lal : "You see, popular tradition connects this monastery with Rin-chen-bzang-po who lived 900 years ago, and an inscription at Horling showed us that such traditions were also current in the 15th century. But what is the use of all these traditions? We must have literary proof that a monastery actually goes back to those early days; if possible, we must have a document of those very times, on which it is plainly stated that the erection of the monastery actually took place at that time. I wonder if ever we shall be able to prove any such assumption!" As I said this, I little thought that a few hours after, I should have ample proof in hand.

In the vicinity of the Tabo monastery are many rows of 108 small *mchod-rten*, but one of them numbered at least 216 (Plate XIV,b). They were the forerunners of the *maṇi* walls in Western Tibet. Besides these rows, there are many ruined *mchod-rten* round about, and countless rock carvings. The latter represent mostly the ibex and the *svastika* and are possibly of pre-Buddhist origin. On the hill side, almost like cave dwellings, are the winter houses of the lamas.

The temple buildings are found on the plain above the river. They are surrounded by a high mud wall. I made a plan of the whole establishment and these are some of the measurements taken. Extreme length : 313 feet, 7 inches ; breadth 257 feet 3 inches. Within this enclosure exist seven temple-halls, and a great number of *mchod-rten.* The monks took me from one temple to another without showing me the principal hall. They said that only a Commissioner (the highest personage they have ever heard of) could be permitted to enter there. I tried in vain to convince them that, with regard to their treasures, I was in as high an office as a Commissioner, until I produced two rupees. Then the doors to their holy of holies were thrown open, and I presume that nothing of interest was purposely concealed from us.

The principal hall is called rNam-par-snang-mdzad. The length of this hall with additional apse is 63 feet, 14 inches and its breadth 34 feet, 10 inches. The principal image is a white stucco statuette of rNam-par-snang-mdzad (Vairôchana) consisting of four complete figures seated back to back (Plate XV, a). Along the walls, 6 or 7 feet above the ground, there are thirty-two raised medallions with exceedingly well executed stucco figures of life size (Plates XV, b ; XVI and XVII, b). Nobody in the monastery at present knows whom they represent. But I am inclined to believe that they represent the thirty-three Hindu gods.[1] The figure of Gaṇēśa, which would make up the full number, seems to have lost its original position above the door. It is now found on the altar, below rNam-par-snang-mdzad (Plate XVII, a). One of the figures by the side of the door was recently furnished with a new head like a modern Lamaist dancing mask, the old head having been lost (Plate XVII, b).

In the apse, behind rNam-par-snang-mdzad, there are four standing stucco figures and a seated figure of Buddha on a lion throne. Above it there are exceedingly well executed figures of flying spirits (Gandharvas?).

[1] This identification seems to me to be open to doubt as, according to the Brahmanical conception at least, "the thirty-three gods" include no goddesses. Neither is Gaṇēśa one of them. Their number is made up by 12 Ādityas, 8 Vasus, 11 Rudras, Indra and Prajāpati : *Śatapatha-brāhmaṇa* 11, 6,215. The Rāmāyaṇa (3, 20) substitutes the Aśvins for the two last mentioned deities. [Ed.]

PLATE XV.

a. Image of rNam-par-snang-mdzad or Vairochana in central hall of Monastery, Tabo.

b. Female figure on wall of central hall of Monastery, Tabo.

a. Two female figures on wall of central hall of Monastery, Tabo.

b. Two male figures on wall of central hall of Monastery, Tabo.

a. Ganesa and other images in front of main image in Monastery, Tabo.

b. Three figures on wall of central hall of Monastery, Tabo.

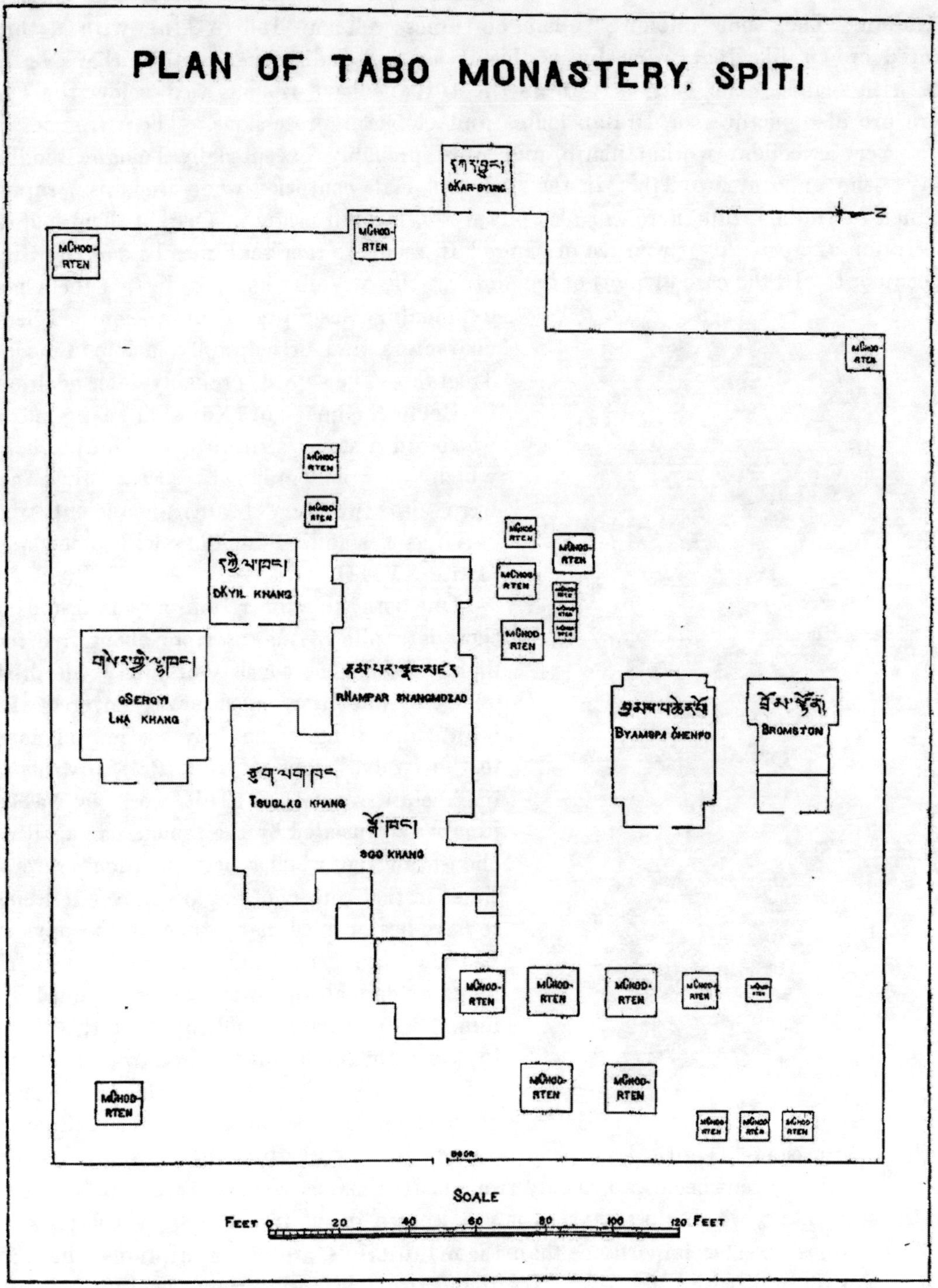
PLAN OF TABO MONASTERY, SPITI
N
dKAR-BYUNG
mCHOD-RTEN
dKYIL KHANG
gSERGYI LHA KHANG
RNAMPAR SNANGMDZAD
TSUGLAG KHANG
SGO KHANG
BYAMSPA CHENPO
BROMSTON
DOOR
SCALE
FEET 0 20 40 60 80 100 120 FEET

Fig. 2.

The walls are completely covered with paintings. Some of the pictures are distinctly Indian. They show ancient Indian costumes well: an Indian king with a three-pointed crown like that worn by Bōdhisattvas, and Indian men with turbans or felt hats with brims. The hats as well as the turbans have ribbons tied below the chin. There are also pictures of Indian ladies and elephant processions. These frescoes are all of very excellent workmanship, and were probably executed by Indian Buddhist monks who emigrated to Tibet in the 10th and 11th centuries, when Buddhism rapidly declined in India. But there are also picturesof Tibetan origin. One of them had the inscription *Gu-gei-sde*, 'province of Guge.' It seems to represent members of the Guge government. In the case of most of the pictures the meaning has been lost. Others have explanatory inscriptions in ancient Tibetan characters and orthography, a few in modern Tibetan. They are probably later additions.

Fig. 3.

Below the image of rNam-par-snang-mdzad, we found a stone sculpture of Mañju-ghōsha which we photographed. (Fig. 3). There were also two very beautiful ancient wood carvings of standing Buddhas with attendants. (Plate XVIII).

On both sides of rNam-par-snang-mdzad, there is a pile of manuscripts about five feet high. Each pile consists of many hundreds of loose and disarranged leaves covered with beautiful writing. The leaves seem to belong to the twelve books of the *Prajñā-pāramitā* in Tibetan translation. This work by Nāgārjuna was translated by the famous lama, Rin-chen-bzang-po, who has been mentioned several times in the course of my account. It seems to have been copied many times in the days of Rin-chen-bzang-po, and copies were distributed among all the monasteries founded by him. So far I have found copies of this work in the orthography of his own times in three different places, but nowhere have I seen so complete a copy as in Tabo. The value of such a manuscript for critical purposes is enormous. Works like the *Prajñā-pāramitā* have up to the present been known only from modern manuscripts or wood-prints. Here, on the other hand, we obtain a text, as it was known in the translator's own days.

Of almost greater importance than the manuscripts, are the inscriptions which are written on the wall with black ink. We found two long inscriptions behind the image

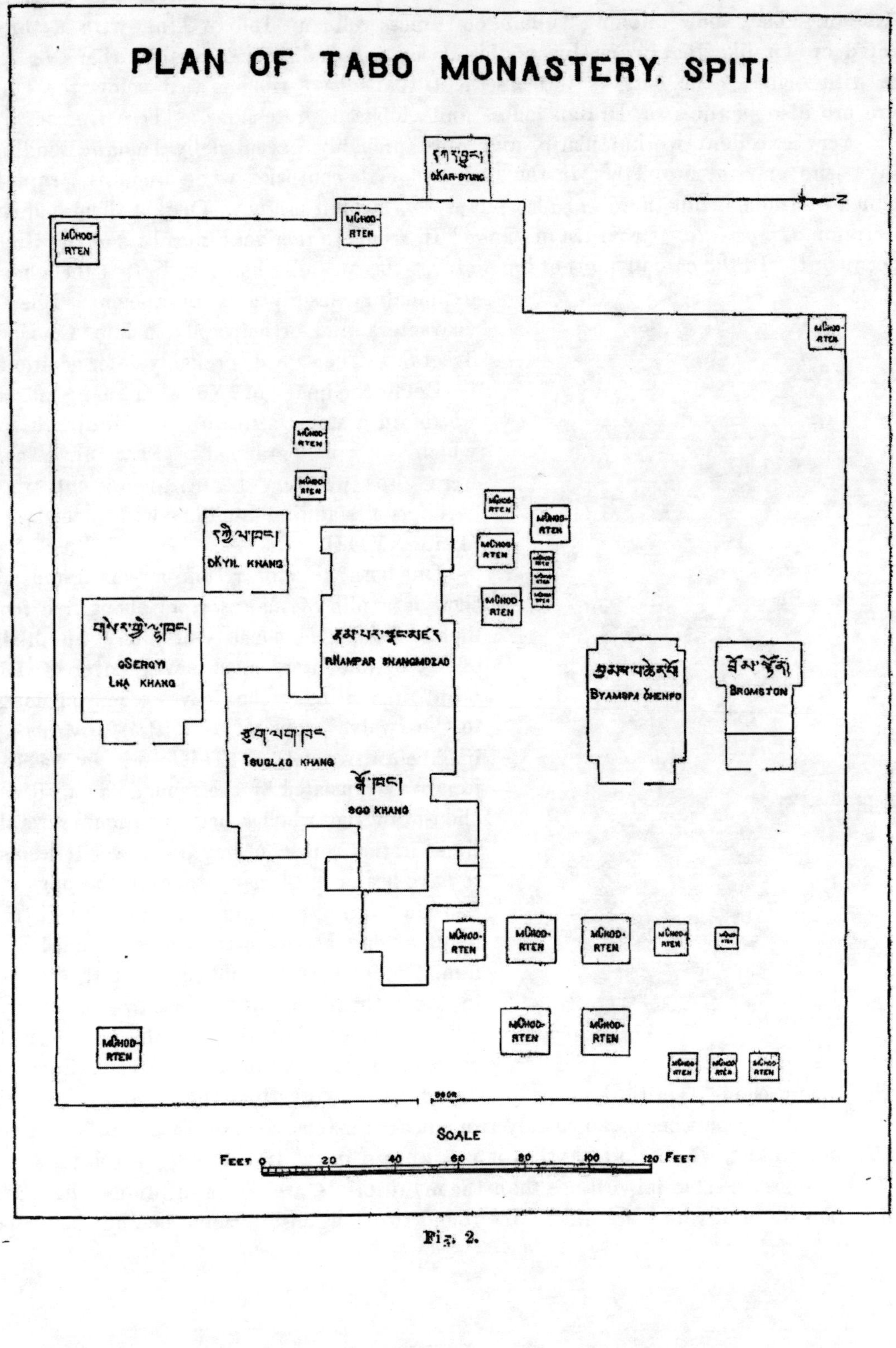
PLAN OF TABO MONASTERY, SPITI
N
dKAR-BYUNG
mCHOD-RTEN
dKYIL KHANG
gSERGYI LHA KHANG
RNAMPAR SNANGMDZAD
TSUGLAG KHANG
SGO KHANG
BYAMSPA CHENPO
BROMSTON
DOOR
SCALE
FEET 0 20 40 60 80 100 120 FEET

Fig. 2.

The walls are completely covered with paintings. Some of the pictures are distinctly Indian. They show ancient Indian costumes well: an Indian king with a three-pointed crown like that worn by Bōdhisattvas, and Indian men with turbans or felt hats with brims. The hats as well as the turbans have ribbons tied below the chin. There are also pictures of Indian ladies and elephant processions. These frescoes are all of very excellent workmanship, and were probably executed by Indian Buddhist monks who emigrated to Tibet in the 10th and 11th centuries, when Buddhism rapidly declined in India. But there are also picturesof Tibetan origin. One of them had the inscription *Gu-gei-sde*, 'province of Guge.' It seems to represent members of the Guge government. In the case of most of the pictures the meaning has been lost. Others have explanatory inscriptions in ancient Tibetan characters and orthography, a few in modern Tibetan. They are probably later additions.

Fig. 3.

Below the image of rNam-par-snang-mdzad, we found a stone sculpture of Mañju-ghōsha which we photographed. (Fig. 3). There were also two very beautiful ancient wood carvings of standing Buddhas with attendants. (Plate XVIII).

On both sides of rNam-par-snang-mdzad, there is a pile of manuscripts about five feet high. Each pile consists of many hundreds of loose and disarranged leaves covered with beautiful writing. The leaves seem to belong to the twelve books of the *Prajñā-pāramitā* in Tibetan translation. This work by Nāgārjuna was translated by the famous lama, Rin-chen-bzang-po, who has been mentioned several times in the course of my account. It seems to have been copied many times in the days of Rin-chen-bzang-po, and copies were distributed among all the monasteries founded by him. So far I have found copies of this work in the orthography of his own times in three different places, but nowhere have I seen so complete a copy as in Tabo. The value of such a manuscript for critical purposes is enormous. Works like the *Prajñā-pāramitā* have up to the present been known only from modern manuscripts or wood-prints. Here, on the other hand, we obtain a text, as it was known in the translator's own days.

Of almost greater importance than the manuscripts, are the inscriptions which are written on the wall with black ink. We found two long inscriptions behind the image

PLATE XVIII.

Ancient wood carvings in central hall of Monastery, Tabo.

of rNam-par-snang-mdzad, immediately above the ground. Their low position indicates that they were meant for people accustomed to sit on the floor cross-legged. The inscriptions are of varied character. One of them is historical; it speaks of the foundation of the Tabo monastery about nine hundred years ago, and of people who were connected with that event. The other inscription is admonitory; I feel inclined to call it "blessing and cursing," but there is more of cursing in it than of blessing. It speaks of the many punishments to be inflicted on such lamas as do not live up to the standard of the law. There is no end of chopping off members of their bodies. I wonder if these regulations were ever carried out. To return to the historical inscription; It tells of a renovation of the Tabo monastery by Byang-chub-'od, priest-king of Guge, forty-six years after the monastery had been founded by *Lhayi-bu Byang-chub-sems-dpa* (*'Byang-chub-sems-dpa*, the son of the gods'). The latter name is evidently that of the king of Ladakh, who is mentioned in the Ladakhi chronicles as one of the early rulers of that country. He is spoken of with much respect in this inscription. His advice was repeatedly asked by the king of Guge, and thus the inscription confirms the statement of history, that the kings of Ladakh were the recognised suzerains of the Guge princes. Besides these two royal names, the inscription contains also those of the two most important lamas of the period, *viz.*, Rin-chen-bzang-po, and Atīśa, the latter being called Phul-byung, which is his Tibetan name, as already stated by Jäschke. The inscription says that Rin-chen-bzang-po was made a 'light of wisdom' by the agency of Atīśa. This is apparently a reference to the controversy between the two lamas, which ended with Rin-chen-bzang-po's acknowledgment of Atīśa's superiority. Of this event we read in the historical book dPag-bsam-ljon-bzang. As this inscription was evidently written in the times of king Byang-chub-'od, c. 1050 A.D., it is of the utmost importance for Tibetan palæography. The type of its writing is different from that of earlier datable documents, as well as from later ones, say, of Tsong-kha-pa's time. It, therefore, enables us to distinguish manuscripts or inscriptions of the 11th century. Of this important question, I will treat later on, when we shall have examined several more records of the same times. Besides these two important inscriptions, there are many more of the same period on the walls around, and as there are also numerous objects of art and paintings in this large hall, it would require at least a full month to do it justice from an archæological point of view.

The gTsug-lag-khang is a smaller hall with frescoes, to the left of the principal hall. Most of the pictures refer to the story of Buddha's life, beginning with the descent of the white elephant from heaven. On both sides of the door were painted the four Lōkapālas, as we find them so often. On the right and left wall there was the medicine Buddha with his followers, Śakya thub-pa, Rin-chen-zla-ba; Myang-ngan-med-mchog-dpal; Chos-grags-rgya-mthsoi-dpal; gSer-bzang-dri-med; mNgon-mkhyen-rgyal-po and mThsan-legs. Most of the pictures in this hall were furnished with explanatory inscriptions in modern Tibetan. Like all the remaining halls, it had apparently been renovated in a sweeping way. All the ancient frescoes and inscriptions had been scratched off, and new pictures painted on the old walls.

When we were at Tabo, we met a native painter, who was prepared to renovate everything. The monks of the monastery had been told that Government would undertake to pay for necessary repairs in their temples and had asked the Assistant Commissioner to let them have the services of an artist. Accordingly, Mr. Howell, I.C.S., had ordered a painter to go to Tabo and apply his art to its ancient walls. Fortunately, he had not yet started work in the principal hall, but in all the other halls, there remained little which had not been destroyed either by him or by previous artists. I told the man that he was on no account to touch the walls of the central hall, and when I met Mr. Howell about a week later in Spiti, he promised to give strict orders that no further attempt should be made to "improve" this precious relic of the past.

The gSer-gyi-lha-khang is another picture hall to the left of the preceding one All the pictures in it are modern, and it has an inscription *Oṁ maṇi padmē hūṁ* in *Lañihsa* characters running round the four walls.

The dKyii-khang is a picture hall behind the preceding. As the roof is not watertight, the pictures have suffered much through leakage. The principal picture shows rNam-par-snang-mdzad, but I could discover no inscriptious in it.

In Lha-khang-dkar-byung, a picture hall behind the preceding, the central picture shows Buddha with two disciples ; to the left of this group we see Tsong-kha-pa. The other pictures in this hall can no more be explained. There were no inscriptions.

The picture hall Brom-ston was evidently named after the famous pupil of Atīśa, called by that name, the founder of the bKā-gdams-pa sect. It is situated on the right hand side of the Central Hall. It was probably erected in Brom-ston's time, but nothing remains of ancient relics, besides the interesting door of *thang-shing* (Deodar wood) which is decorated with well executed carvings of Buddhist saints. The style of carving is very different from the present Tibetan style, and is a distinguishing characteristic of the half Indian Buddhism of the 11th century. This hall is without inscriptions and the principal picture in it represents Buddha with his two disciples.

The seventh hall called Byams-pa-chen-moi-lha-khang contains a huge stucco statue of Maitrēya seated on a chair. The top of his head may be 18 to 20 feet above the ground. This hall contains pictures of Tibetan architecture, perhaps four to five centuries ago, such as the monastery of Tashilumpo (bKra-shis-lhun-po) and the Potala palace of Lhasa. But most of the other pictures in this hall are modern restorations or inventions. Here I noticed a Wartu inscription, probably an *Oṁ maṇi padme hūṁ* formula. This hall has also a door carved with Buddhist figures in Indian, not Tibetan style. The central figure on the lintel, however, is Gaṇēśa.

Besides these seven principal halls, I must also mention the entrance hall to the principal temple, Lha-khang-chen-moi-sgo-khang. It is furnished with paintings, for instance Tsong-kha-pa with two disciples, one of whom was called mKhas-grub.

The thick darkness of most of the Tibetan temples is a great hindrance to archæological research. My work had to be done in a different way from that done at Pompei or in the Turkestan deserts. At Pompei and in Turkestan every article which comes to light, is valuable and has to be taken up, labelled, and put aside. In an inhabited place

PLATE XIX.

a. Drangkhar, the capital of Spiti.

b. Rope bridge near Lithang.

like Tabo, I had, however, to select among hundreds of inscriptions and objects of art, those which were of real value for the study of Tibetan history and art, which meant a close examination of many objects and records in a badly lighted place. When, finally, the most interesting had been decided upon, the second part of our work, photography, and copying in writing as well as in colours, began. Considering the very great difficulties he had to encounter, I must say that Pindi Lal achieved wonders with his camera. But the little light that entered this hall through a minute hole in the ceiling was not sufficient for the lamas, whom I set to work on the paintings and wall inscriptions. Then we thought of our small supply of candles and by giving three of them to our helpmates, we made three Tibetan hearts happier than they had ever been. None of them had apparently ever possessed a candle, and now think of the grand sport they had, working in a dark corner of the temple with a real European candle by their side. No Maharaja could have taken greater pride in the electric light newly introduced into his capital.

Within the walled enclosure about the temples, there are many *mchod-rten*, and several of them have frescoes inside. There is also a botanical curiosity in this court; for here we find the only apricot trees existing in the barren and cold country of Spiti which is separated by a girdle of deserts from all the neighbouring territories of Tibet, Ladakh, Lahul, and Bashahr.

The next morning, when we had left Tabo, I found on our march to the village of Phog (map Pok), the beforementioned votive inscription of the times of the Tsaparang king on a *maṇi* wall outside the village. On the other bank of the Spiti river, we saw the large monastery of Nathang with many terraced fields round about it, some under cultivation, but most of them bare. The monastery is built in three stories, the one above always a little narrower than the one below it, like a pyramid of three steps, thus reminding me of the Alchi (and also of the mTho-lding) monastery. Nathang also is said to have been founded in the days, when the Tabo monastery was built. During summer, there is not a single lama residing in it.

In the village of Phog, I met with Mr. Cargill of the Public Works Department, who was on tour through these outlying districts examining the bridges. He invited me to dinner, and I spent a very pleasant evening with him.

On the 31st July, we arrived at Drangkhar called *Brang-mkhar* or *Grang-mkhar* in inscriptions (Plate XIX, a). The monastery of this town, the capital of Spiti, is called *Lha-'od-pai-dgon-pa*. *Lha-'od* seems to be the local pronunciation of *Zla-'od*, the name of a famous lama who was born in 1121, according to the Reu-mig. Zla-'od-pa would then mean "a follower of Zla-'od." He is apparently the founder or renovator of the monastery which now belongs to the Gelugpa order. The monks assert that it was not only of earlier origin than the Tabo monastery, but also earlier than the times of Srong-btsan-sgam-po. They have, however, nothing to show of really ancient relics. They explain this fact by stating that the monastery was plundered many times, lastly during the Ḍōgrā war, which is in agreement with my History of Western Tibet. Traces of the ravages of that war may be plainly seen in all the monasteries of Spiti which we visited on our journey, with the exception of Tabo. Why did Tabo alone escape destruction? I am inclined to believe that Tabo was under Bashahr in those times, and that the Ḍogrās did not wish to interfere with the government of that state. We found three, probably modern, stucco statues in the central hall. They represent Byams-pa (Maitrēya), seated crosslegged, with a kind of tea-pot in his hand; Buddha; and the lama Chos-drag, a contemporary of Srong-btsan-sgam-po. The statue of Chos-drag looks like the illustration of the same personage in Grünwedel's *Mythology*.

There are frescoes on the walls of this temple, but now only very little of them can be made out. The following figures could be distinguished: 'Od-dpag-med (Amitābha); Padma-sambhava; and dGe-bai-bshes-gnyen (Kalyāṇa-mitra).

Above one of the doors there is an inscription in modern characters and orthography which, I was told, contained the name of dGe-bai-bshes-gnyen. I found it impossible to read it in the dark.

Above the entrance to the monastery, there is suspended the stuffed skin of a goat. I was informed that this goat during her lifetime occasionally became possessed with a spirit which made her jump about in an extraordinary way. Therefore she was treated kindly and fed well by the monks, and after death she was stuffed, to serve as a lasting memorial of herself.

Drangkhar is one of the few towns of Western Tibet which still stand on their original site, *i.e.* on the top of a rocky spur, and thus it is in its entirety an interesting relic of the past. The most ancient picture of this fortress is a lithograph after a drawing by Trebeck who was here in 1820. From this we learn that since then the town has not altered much in general aspect. The uppermost place on the rock is occupied by the castle which is now in possession of the Nono (chief) of Spiti. It was built by the Ladakhis who used to have a garrison here. There are tales current about the last days of Ladakhi rule, when the place was captured by the Spiti people, and its inmates were thrown down from the rock.[1] Judging from the ruins in the vicinity, the castle was much larger in Ladakhi times, than it is now. The present building, therefore, gives no idea of what it was like formerly.

We spent Sunday, the 1st August, in this interesting place, and on Monday, the 2nd August, we marched to Kaze (map Kaja). On the road, near Lithang, we saw a rope bridge of the old style, plaited of willow branches, as they still are in Lahul and Zangskar. (Plate XIX, b). When we were approaching Kaze, we saw the stately palace of Kyu-ling (*Skyid-gling*), the Nono's residence, on the opposite bank of the stream.

In a side valley of Kaze, high up on the rocks, there is the bTang-rgyud or Sa-skya-gong-mig monastery which belongs to the Sa-skya-pa order of lamas. Although it has a certain fame on account of its antiquity, it is believed to be inferior to the Ki monastery. The Kaze monastery has always been favoured by the Nonos of Spiti, one of whose members takes orders as a Sa-skya-pa lama, just as the kings of Ladakh have bestowed special favour on the 'aBrug-pa order of Lamas. Gong-mig means 'the upper eye,' and at the place, where this monastery can be seen peeping out of a world of rocks, a *mchod-rten*

[1] See my publication *Die historischen und mythologischen Erinnerungen der Lahouler.* Tale No. 17.

a. Fording the Brom-ston-chu.

b. View of the Brom-ston-gyi-sna.

was built. I should have visited it, had we not been far too tired for such a climb in the evening after our arrival, as well as next morning.

On one of the *maṇi* walls of Kaze, I saw a fairly old votive tablet dating from the time of the Ladakhi *régime* in Spiti. It was written in bad orthography and was in a poor state of preservation. The "national anthem" was similar to that of the Guge stones, but in the place where the Guge version has the Satluj (*gLang-chen-kha-bab*), here we find the Indus (*Seng-ge*[1]*-kha-bab*). What interested me particularly, was the spelling of the name Leh, the Ladakhi capital. We find it often spelled *sLel* in native documents, but the spelling *sLe* is also not infrequent. According to the ideas of the natives of Ladakh, the correct spelling of the name is *sLes*. The word *sLes* (or *sLas* in Lower Ladakh) signifies a walled enclosure, such as is set up by nomads. Leh is supposed to have developed out of a Tibetan nomads' camp. The Kaze inscription confirms this derivation, for here we find the name of the capital spelt *sLes*. I may add, that this spelling is corroborated by the Tibetan geographical work 'aDzam-gling-ye-shes where the same spelling is found.[2] The name of the capital of Spiti is spelt here *Drag-mkhar-rtse* (against *Brang-mkhar* on other stones). A nobleman, Ga-ga Sod-nams, is mentioned as having held the office of Resident at the castle, but the name of the king of Leh is missing.

We reached the Ki (*dKyil*) monastery at noon on August the third. Here I met with a messenger from Mr. Howell, Assistant Commissioner of Kuḷū; he handed me a letter from that gentleman, asking me to make the monks of the Ki monastery acquainted with the discovery of Buddha's bones at Peshāwar, and to suggest to them that they should make an application to the Indian Government to let them have the relics. I gladly agreed to Mr. Howell's proposal, in particular, because it gave me an opportunity to point out to them the difference between Buddha and Christ, of whom no bones have ever been found. But also for another reason I was anxious to visit the Ki monastery. In 1863 Mr. P. Egerton, of the Civil Service, made a tour through Spiti, together with our missionary, Mr. A. W. Heyde. A beautiful book illustrated with capital photographs, was the outcome of this journey. In this book we find the statement that the Ki monastery of Spiti was probably founded by Brom-ston, the pupil of the famous teacher Atiśa, in the 11th century. The travellers apparently heard a rumour of a connection between this monastery and Brom-ston, and if they had simply stated this, they would not have been wrong. But they went further. They found a note in Körös' Tibetan Grammar, to the effect that Brom-ston had founded a monastery called Rareng (*Rva-sgrengs*); and as a village in the vicinity of Ki is called Rangrig, Mr. Egerton jumped to the conclusion that the Ki monastery of Spiti was identical with the famous Rareng monastery of the 11th century. But we know from the geographical work 'aDzam-gling-ye-shes, that the Rareng monastery is situated in the Rong district near Lhasa. It is not to be wondered at, however, that no clear traditions about the origin of the Spiti monastery exist. We read in Moorcroft and Trebeck's travels, 1820, that the Ki monastery was thoroughly ransacked

---

[1] *Seng-ge* from Sanskrit *Siṁha*. "a lion."

[2] See S. Ch. Das' translation in *J. A. S. B.*, 1887. *sLes* would correspond to classical *lHas*.

in the petty wars between Kuḷū and Ladakh which preceded the Ḍōgrā war. And during the Ḍōgrā war itself it suffered even more severely. It is evident that Brom-ston must have some connection with Spiti and this monastery, from the fact that his name is found in certain localities in the vicinity. Thus, as we have seen, one of the temples of the Tabo monastery is called after him. Moreover, on our way from Kaze to Ki, we had to ford a brook called *Brom-ston-chu*; then, a little farther on, we passed by a rock called *Brom-ston-gyi-sna*, "Brom-ston's nose" or "the shrubbery of Broms-ton" (Plate XX). From the historical work dPag-bsam-ljon-bzang we learn that Brom-ston erected four monasteries, one of them at Ke in Mangyul (*Mang-yul-gyi-Ke-ru*). Mangyul is a name often used to signify the Western Tibetan Empire. Ke is a misprint for *Ki*. Whoever knows how carelessly Western Tibetan names are treated by Lhasa writers, does not wonder at their spelling *Ke* instead of *Ki*.

But the Ki monastery has been restored since the turbulent times of the Ḍōgrā war. (Plate XXI). It is a typical example of ancient monasteries of a certain period. In this type we find the principal temple on the top of a little conical hill, and the cells of the monks round about and below it. The aspect of the whole establishment is unusually pleasing, especially as it is situated in a wilderness of bare and barren rocks. Monasteries of the same type are found in Khrig-rtse, Me-ru, Chem-re, Ling-shed, dKar-rgya of Zangs-dkar, and probably in several other places.

As all the old books and idols had been destroyed by G͟hulām K͟hān,[1] the outfit of the Ki monastery is rather modern. The door is carved in present day Tibetan style, and the library contains modern blockprints. In the central hall, I noticed two stucco idols; one was called Yum-chen-mo, "great mother," probably a form of Tārā, the other sPyan-ras-gzigs (Avalōkitēśvara). There are several more stucco statues in the library opposite the temple, the most remarkable being Thse-dpag-med (Amitāyus), Shākya thub-pa, bLo-bzang ye-shes, the Paṇ-chen, who resided at Trashilhumpo from 1663 to 1737; Padma-sambhava with two of his fairies, one being called Lha-sha-man-da-re-ba (Mandārava) the other mKha-'agro-ye-shes-gtso-rgyal.

On the 4th August, we made preparations for our journey through the desert across the Pharang Pass, and on the 5th, we moved our camp four miles in the direction of the pass, especially as I wished to be near to Mr. Howell, the Assistant Commissioner, who was encamped at Lhanartsa, Spiti, at an elevation of about 14,000 feet.

On the way, not far from Kyibar (map Kibber), I noticed an ancient ruin of a temple built of sun-dried bricks, its walls sloping inward, as is always the case in Rin-chen-bzang-po's temples. It is called Lha-bla-mai-dgon-pa, and thus by its name it directly points to the great priest-king of Guge, Lha-bla-ma-ye-shes-'od, whose name we had found in an inscription at Poo. Local tradition says that King Lha-bla-ma or, as another man understood it, the gods (*lha*) and the lamas (*blama*) built it in one night.

At Lhanartsa I spent two enjoyable and instructive days with the Assistant Commissioner. Here I had an attack of malarial fever, and Mr. Howell did everything in

---

[1] *History of Western Tibet*, p. 163.

a. View of Ki Monastery.

b. Congregation of Ki Monastery.

his power to cure me and make me fit for the road. Mr. Howell was just engaged in revising the Spiti portion of the Kangra Gazetteer, and as he had the Nono of Spiti as well as lamas of various denominations encamped in the vicinity, our time was spent in a very profitable way. Let me briefly review the principal points of our enquiries about Spiti.

There are now-a-days five principal monasteries in Spiti, which represent three sects of Lamaism. The Tabo, Drangkhar, and Ki monasteries belong now to the Ge-lug-pa sect. The Kaze monastery belongs to the Sa-skya-pa sect, and the Pyin monastery belongs to the rNying-ma-pa. Whilst the four first mentioned monasteries do not differ essentially from Central Tibetan establishments, with which they keep up intercourse, the Pyin monastery has no connection with Lhasa, and maintains those traditions which have been banded down from the times of the most primitive Lamaism. I have already mentioned the wild appearance of its monks, and as Mr. Lyall tells us in the Gazetteer these monks were blamed for their uncivilised condition by a Lhasa emissary who travelled through Spiti. Mr. Lyall who saw these people perform a play, the substance of which was similar to that represented in the tale of Eka-śriṅa, describes also the head-dress of the Bu-rzhan, when performing. He says that they then appear with a head-dress formed of a mass of streamers of bright coloured silk. This observation is of great interest for this kind of head-dress seems to have been handed down in Spiti from the earliest time of Tibetan Buddhism. We read in the Yarlung part of the rGyal-rabs that king Ral-pacan had silken streamers tied to his locks, and that he was connected by such streamers with the lamas who surrounded him. The close connection of the rNying-ma-pa form of Lamaism with the pre-Buddhist Bon religion has already been noticed, and the Pyin monastery of Spiti seems to be a particularly favourable place to study it. I still regret that our limited time did not allow us to visit it. One of those Bu-rzhan lamas was in Mr. Howell's camp, and gave us much information. Unfortunately, his dialect was so unusual, that I could not make out all he said. The Bu-rzhan lamas of Pyin travel also to Leh where they give grand conjuring performances, one of their most famous feats being the breaking of a huge boulder on the belly of a boy.

We also made enquiries into the Tibetan system of clans, as it is represented in Spiti. In my article, "Notes on a language map of Western Tibet,"[1] I drew attention to the importance of the study of the Tibetan "father-brotherships" (*pha-spun*) from a historical point of view. As the Indian officials who hold office among the natives of Indian Tibet apply Indian methods, instead of Tibetan ones, in their administration of the country, this important institution has not yet been discovered. I hope that in the next census, Tibetan methods will be used for Tibetans. When Indian officials try to fix the individuality of a certain Tibetan, they generally ask him to state his own name and that of his father. The first question is answered readily, but the second question puzzles a Tibetan to such an extent, that it takes him sometimes several days to clear up the mystery as to who is his sire. How could he tell at once, as he has at least two, and often three fathers, whilst many others are ignorant of their own parentage. The individuality of a Tibetan is fixed by three names: (1) by his personal name, (2) by his house

[1] *J. A. S. B.*, Vol. LXXIII, pp. 362. ff.

name, (3) by his clan name. The latter name is the name of the *pha-spun*-ship ("father brothership") to which he belongs. As stated by Lyall in the Gazetteer, and as was also asserted in our presence, the *pha-spun*-ship is an exogamic institution, *i.e.* a boy of a certain *pha-spun*-ship is not allowed to marry a girl of the same *pha-spun*-ship. This interesting custom was already noticed by the most ancient Chinese authors who describe the Tibetans. Every *pha-spun*-ship has to look after the cremation of their dead, and monuments in commemoration of the dead, *mchod-rten* or *maṇi* walls, are generally erected by the whole *pha-spun*-ship of a certain village, and the name of the particular *pha-spun*-ship is found on the votive tablets of such monuments. The historical interest of these clan names lies in the fact that they are often local names, *viz.*, they indicate the locality from which a certain clan has immigrated into Western Tibet. Thus, from the names of the *pha-spun*-ships of Khalatse it can be proved that the greater part of the population of this village emigrated from Gilgit, a fact which is supported also by other evidence, in particular by the preservation of a prayer in Dardi to certain house deities. As our inquiries in Spiti showed us, Mr. Lyall had almost discovered the whole institution. He uses the word clan for them and calls them *ruspa* or bones, a name which is actually used for *pha-spun*-ship in Spiti. He had collected the names of six *ruspa* from Drangkhar, but he is wrong when he believes that the same *ruspa* are to be found in all the villages of Spiti. Some of the names may be found also in the other villages of Spiti, but quite new names also will turn up. From the six names he gives, we see at once that they testify to the presence of Tibetans in Spiti in early times, while they also suggest the presence of settlers from Kuḷū. The following four names are decidedly Tibetan: (1) *rGya-zhing-pa,* large field owners, (2) *Khyung-po,* 'Garuḍa-men,' a name which was very common during the pre-Buddhist times of Tibet, (3) *bLon-chen-pa,* 'great ministers,' the men of this clan are doubtless the descendants of some early Tibetan official of Spiti, (4) *sNyegs-pa,* this is a word which is found in the names of the earliest Tibetan records. Two of the names, given in the Gazetteer, do not appear to be Tibetan: *Henir* and *Nandu*. *Henir* signifies probably the Hensi caste of Kuḷū; *Nandu* I cannot explain. I hope that on the occasion of the next census, every Buddhist Tibetan will be asked to give his three names, his personal name, his house name, and his clan name.

On the 6th August I had sufficiently recovered to be able to start on our journey to the Lake Thsomo Riri of Rubshu. As we were very badly equipped for so trying a journey, Mr. Howell kindly helped us with as many of his provisions as he could spare. On the same day we travelled to Jugda, a small level spot on a brook in the midst of a horribly uneven country. On the 7th, we crossed the Pharang Pass, 18,300 feet high. The climb was very steep and trying, and as I felt that I could not do it walking, I mounted one of the spare yaks of our caravan. Another of the spare animals was used by Pindi Lal, but as there were no more available, the Khansaman as well as the Khalasi, who were hill-men from Kōtgur and Rāmpur, had to walk. It was, however, too much for them, and the Khalasi was unwell for a number of days after it. These simple folks who had never seen anything but the Satluj valley and surroundings, had

PLATE XXII.

a. Lake Thsomo Riri from the north.

b. Barley fields on Lake Thsomo Riri at an altitude of 15,000 feet.

become more and more alarmed at the increasing bareness and cold of the country we were travelling through, and were now on the point of giving up all hope of ever seeing human habitations again. Pindi Lal had from time to time raised their spirits by prophesying that, in about ten days, we should reach a great town, Leh, where there would be abundance of delicacies, such as sugar, *dal*, rice, and butter, the existence of which we had almost forgotten. In one of the last villages of Spiti, we unfortunately met a traveller from Ladakh who knew Urdū. They asked him how many days it would take us to reach Leh, and when this man said that it could not be done under twenty days, they gave up all hope of ever reaching it. The only topic of conversation among them, now, was the malign conjunction of planets (as they thought), under which their birth had taken place. However, we reached the top of the pass after all, and had a grand view over a large glacier directly below us, over many more glaciers hanging down from black rugged peaks, and a labyrinth of icy mountain ranges. And the thought came to them that they had to travel over these wild mountains with nothing but a little coarse flour in their provision bags. When then the yaks absolutely refused to jump across cracks in the glacier, and we had to cross deep fissures in the ice by sliding down one side and climbing up the other, when the mountain sickness in its most acute form assailed the poor Khalasi, he lay down on a boulder on the edge of the glacier and gave himself up to die. I had not kept my eye on him, and thus we had descended a good way, before Pindi Lal drew my attention to him, saying: "One man is missing." It was very unpleasant in this pathless country to return over the same boulders, but I had to send Pindi Lal back again to fetch the Khalasi. He brought him to our camp at the only level spot in the vicinity, called Drathang, 17,000 feet high. His face had become sallow, and his eyes had lost their lustre. The night was sure to be cold and his insufficient clothing as well as the small tent could not afford him sufficient warmth and shelter. I, therefore, cut one of my blankets in two, and gave him one half, and Pindi Lal gave him some of his clothing. Soon after, he came to my tent with the blanket in his hand. He could not believe that a blanket of scarlet colour should be his property. But when he was assured of the fact, there was a ray of light in his eye again. I am convinced that the expectation of one time or other showing this treasure to his relations, was one of the most powerful factors in raising his spirits, and ultimately restoring him to health.

On the next morning, he was mounted on a yak and expected to ride the whole way. That was, however, easier said than done. For the most part, no road of any kind could be distinguished, and we had to make our passage along the steep bank of a deep and broad river. Whenever the progress on dry ground was absolutely impossible, the yaks jumped into the water to wade or swim in it, which latter performance made me feel rather uneasy with regard to the photographic plates in the boxes on their backs. Pindi Lal, who was riding on one of the two horses of our caravan, had a narrow escape, when the ground under his horse suddenly gave way, and the horse, performing a somersault, fell into the river, the rider holding on to the bank. Whilst we were thus ploughing on slowly, I noticed that the Khansaman was staying behind, and when I found him, I saw that his face had become black. He appeared hardly able to support himself any longer. I found it easy to guess at his thoughts which seemed to be as follows: "Well" thought he, "have I not a right to be ill too? Did I not walk up the high pass yesterday? I cooked some food and got no reward; the Khalasi did nothing and got a red blanket." But part with the other half of my blanket? No, that I could not. Fortunately, I found two rupees in my pocket which I handed over to him, and lo, within no time he recovered so much that he was seen among the foremost yaks of our caravan.

We reached the desert place Umna on that day, and on the 9th August we marched to Nemaringmo camp which was distinguished by the proximity of a very extensive swamp, overgrown with a luxurious vegetation of alpine flowers, edelweiss, and red and yellow pedicularis. Leaves of wild rhubarb were conspicuous on the margin of the swamp. At noon of that day we stopped at a place called Raco lhamo, the 'Horn goddess,' where we noticed again signs of the occasional presence of man in these wilds in the shape of an altar of rude white stones covered with horns of sheep and goats. When entering the large swampy plain to the south of Lake Thsomo Riri, we saw a tower-like building in ruins which was explained to us as marking the frontier between Spiti and Kashmir. As the road from this camp to the lake was easier than what we had experienced during the previous days, it gave me time to review in my mind the times of Atīśa, which it was the good fortune of our journey to throw light upon. It is due in particular to the labours of Sarat Chandra Das, that we now know something of this interesting period of Tibetan Buddhism, when Western Tibet, and in particular the vassal kings of Guge, held up the torch of guidance for the whole of Tibet.[1]

King Lha-bla-ma-Ye-shes-'od of Guge (1025 A.D.), who resided at mTho-lding (his inscription at Poo will be remembered), was not satisfied with the Tibetan form of Buddhism, as it prevailed in his dominions, and resolved to purify it by bringing it into contact with Indian Buddhism. He gave a careful education to twenty-one Tibetan boys, the name of one of whom was Rin-chen-bzang-po, and sent them to Kashmir and other parts of India to receive instruction in Sanskrit and philosophy. Although through their agency the king secured the services of thirteen Indian pandits, most of the boys died from the unhealthy climate, and only two, one of whom was Rin-chen-bzang-po (Ratna-bhadra), returned to Guge.

Then the king heard of the famous teacher Atīśa at the monastery of Vikramaśila in Magadha and sent an embassy to him with a large quantity of gold to invite him to come to Guge. Atīśa gave the following answer to the king's messengers: "Then it would appear that my going to Tibet were due to two causes: first, the desire of amassing gold, and second, the wish of attaining sainthood!" and so he remained in Vikramaśila.

King Ye-shes-'od interpreted Atīśa's words in a different way from what a European would have done. He understood that the great teacher had not yet been offered

[1] A detailed account of this period is found in Sarat Chandra Das' '*Indian Pandits in the land of snow,*' and the Tibetan text underlying this tale was published by the same author in the *dPag-bsam-ljon-bzang*.

a. dKor-dzod Monastery, Rubshu.

b. Residence of Nomad Chieftain, Rubshu.

gold enough, and began to work a gold mine which had just then been discovered by his minister. There, however, he came into conflict with a Muhammadan king of Garlog (Turkestan), who claimed the mine for himself. In the ensuing war, Ye-shes-'od became a prisoner of the king of Garlog, who said he would release him only on condition that a ransom, consisting of solid gold of the size and shape of the captive king's person, was paid. Gold was now collected all over Tibet, but when melted and cast to form a statue, the gold fell short of the quantity that would be required to make the king's head. The king of Garlog, who was not satisfied with the amount of gold offered, threw Yse-hes 'od into a gloomy dungeon to make him more miserable.

There he had an interview with the new king, Byang-chub-'od (the king of the Tabo inscription) who had continued collecting gold for his uncle's release. Ye-shes-'od advised his nephew not to use the gold for his own release, but for bringing an Indian pandit to Tibet. He said : " I am now grown old, and am on the verge of the grave. In none of my former births, I believe, did I die for the sake of Buddhism. This time let me, therefore, be a martyr in the cause of my religion." Thus they parted, and Lha-bla-ma-Ye-shes-'od died in prison.

Then we hear of another embassy of Tibetans to Vikramaśīla, who were almost robbed of their gold on the journey, and a religious assembly at this Indian monastery is described with its brilliant stars of wisdom and holiness who were all eclipsed by Atīśa. As the Indian monks would not have allowed their master to leave the country, Atīśa disguised his intention of going to Tibet by saying that he was going on a pilgrimage to the eight places of Buddhist sanctity,[1] which pilgrimage took him to Nepal. He was much honoured by the king of that country, called Ananta-kīrti, and performed various miracles and acts of piety on the journey. Thus he made all the robbers who wished to assassinate him, dumb and motionless like statues, until he had passed by, and at times, he lifted himself into the air a cubit above the saddle with a view to be distinguished from the others. A smile was ever on his face and Sanskrit *mantras* were ever on his lips. At a deserted camping ground, he saw three puppies left uncared for. He took them in the folds of his robes, saying " Ah, poor little ones, I pity you," and resumed his journey. The breed of these puppies, says the historian, is still to be seen at Rva-sgrengs in Tibet.

When the party entered Guge, they found one hundred horsemen all decorated with white ornamental equipments, sent by King Byang-chub-'od. The escort carried small flags and twenty white satin umbrellas. The band consisted of musical reeds, bag-pipes, guitars, and other instruments. With sonorous and grave music, and uttering the sacred mantra, *Ōṁ maṇi padmē hūṁ*, they approached the holy sage to offer him a respectful welcome in the name of the king of Guge.[2]

[1] The eight great places of pilgrimage (Sanskrit *mahāsthāna*) are 1st the Lumbinī Garden (modern Rummindei in the Nepal Tarai) where Buddha was born ; 2nd Bōdh Gayā where he attained enlightenment ; 3rd the Deerpark (modern Sārnāth) near Benares where he preached his first sermon ; 4th Kusinārā (modern Kasia ?) where he reached Nirvāṇa ; 5th th Jētavana near Śrāvastī (modern Sahēṭh-Mahēṭh), where the great miracle took place, 6th Vaiśāli (modern Basārh) where he was fed by a monkey ; 7th Saṁkāśya (modern Sankisa) where he descended from heaven, and 8th Rājagṛiha (modern Rājgir) where he subdued the wild elephant. [Ed.]

[2] This reception seems to be represented among frescoes in monasteries of those times.

Atiśa had never yet tasted tea, and the first cup on Tibetan soil was offered him with the following solemn words: "Venerable sage, permit me to make an offering of this celestial drink which contains the essence of the wishing tree!" Atiśa said: "This curious cup of precious material contains an elixir of the wishing tree. What is the name of this drink which you prize so much?" The Tibetans answered: "Venerable sir, it is called tea. We do not know that the tea plant is eaten, but the leaves are churned in warm water, and the soup is drunk. It has many properties!" Thereupon Atiśa, who could pay compliments like any French abbé, remarked: "So excellent a beverage as tea must have originated from the moral merits of the monks of Tibet!"

The Manasarowar Lake pleased Atiśa so much that he stayed there for seven days. Then he proceeded to mTho-lding, the capital of Guge, where he was received by the king with due honours. Although all the lamas and noblemen rose respectfully when Atiśa approached them, the old lama, Rin-chen-bzang-po, would not rise, partly from envy, partly from weakness. But then Atiśa displayed his intellectual armour in such a brilliant way before the old monk that even he was conquered and ready to sit at the feet of the newcomer.[1] After a residence in Guge of two years, Atiśa proceeded to Central Tibet. He died at Nyethang near Lhasa at the age of seventy-three in the year 1053 A.D. The founding of the so-called half-reformed sects of Lamaism was due to his exertions. The most important of them is the bKa-gdams-pa sect. It was in monasteries of this sect that Tsong-kha-pa studied, before he started the great reform movement which ended in the creation of the Ge-lug-pa sect. The object of all these reformations was not, as is often supposed, to go back to the early Buddhism as it was preached by Gautama, but to build up a church which represented the doctrines of the Mahāyāna school of Buddhism in a pure form. The doctrines of Nāgārjuna were propounded by all the great teachers of Tibet. But the Kāla-chakra philosophy with its monotheistic tendencies was also favoured by them.

On the 10th August, we travelled to the southern end of the lake, and then along its western shore, and at sunset we arrived at bKor-rdzod (map Karzok. Plate XXIII). The sudden appearance of the monastery in that barren desert was such a surprise that it was at first difficult to believe in its reality. On this march, the Tibetan fauna was much in evidence. There were large herds of *rkyang* (wild asses which look like mules), and one of the *rkyang* came quite close to us and watched our caravan passing by. There were very many hares and marmots which did not show any signs of fear, and also the beautiful tail-less rats of Tibet looked at us curiously from behind many a stone. Whilst animal life was thus well represented on dry land, I could not discover any living being in the water of the lake. But as aquatic plants were plentiful it attracted wild geese and ducks, of which we saw a good number. As Drew says, gulls have their breeding ground on an island in the lake. In spite of the desolation round about, the scenery is very fine. Snowclad peaks, bare hills of brownish colour, dark

[1] This incident is referred to in one of the Tabo inscriptions, as stated above. Cf. *dPag-bsam-ljon-bang*, Part II, p. XVII.

PLATE XXIV.

a. *Mani* walls and *mchod-rten* at dKor-dzod.

b. Milking goats at dKor-dzod.

blue-green water, and dunes of yellow sand combine to make a picture like those sublime quiet landscapes, which have become familiar through Sven Hedin's Tibetan sketches.

The first European who visited the lake was Trebeck in 1820. Cunningham gives the legend of the lake which explains its unusual name. We heard the same legend at bKor-rdzod. Although the tale is quite without a point, Cunningham says that it is as good as many a Greek tale. The word *Thsomo* means 'lake,' and *Riri* is an exclamation used by people when driving yaks. According to the tale, an old woman came riding on a yak and made the animal wade into the water. She was shouting *Riri* all the time, and was finally drowned together with her yak. It is strange that Trebeck does not make any mention of a monastery on the lake, although he travelled along its western shore. All the same, the convent must have been in existence in his time, for in an inscription which I found on one of the many *maṇi* walls which line the lake shore, the expression *dGon-snying*, ancient monastery, was used with reference to it. These *maṇi* walls extend to about two miles in both directions from the monastery (Plate XXIV, a). The votive tablets on these walls contained the names of several chiefs of the Rubshu nomads who have their residence close to the monastery. Of royal Ladakhi names, I found only two mentioned, those of the two last independent rulers of Ladakh. But another tablet near the monastery contained a very beautiful hymn on Tibet, especially its western parts. This hymn was more of a geographical than historical character. We took an impression of this inscription, and I had to make an eye-copy in addition.

I visited the monastery next morning and was disappointed to hear that it was a modern structure, between fifty and sixty years old.[1] The old monastery stood on the brook, below the present site; but not a trace of it now remains. The few ancient images and other articles of worship were taken up to the present building. Among the antiquities pointed out to us, were several miniature *mchod-rten* of the usual type. Of all the stucco figures, and of a fine wood-carving in sandal wood, which represented Padma-sambhava with two of his fairy friends, it was asserted that fifty or sixty years ago they had been brought up here from gSham, Lower Ladakh. I suspect that these Rubshu people bought up the entire contents of a ruined monastery in Lower Ladakh. The principal stucco figure represents Buddha with two disciples, and another Padma-sambhava. The names of the other images, I did not try to ascertain, because the history of their date and origin will always remain obscure. I may mention here, that outside, near the site of the ancient monastery, I found a relievo representing Padma-sambhava, carved on a beautiful slab of snow-white quartz. I was greatly tempted to carry it off, but it would have been too heavy. One of the clay pots in the bKor-rdzod monastery reminded me of the stone age of Europe. It had evidently been made by plastering the inside of a basket with clay and then burning the basket. All the books at this monastery were modern Tibetan prints.

The neck ornament of a man at bKor-rdzod who acted as Lambardār, attracted my attention, because it was of cruciform shape, and could at first sight be taken for a Christian ornament. He said, he had excavated it from a high hill in the neighbourhood.

[1] A picture of the old monastery is found in Schlagintweits' *Reisen in Indien und Hochasien* Jena 1872-18.

I bought it from him for two rupees. It was made of a mixture of metals, similar to the Indian *khānsī*. It was a plain cross with beams of equal length, and at the end of each beam was found a double spiral as an ornament. As I was told by another man from Rubshu, there are ruins of ancient settlements and watercourses all over the country. They are found on high hills in Rubshu, and are ascribed to a tribe of Mon, the pre-Tibetan inhabitants of the country. These Mon must have been marvels of endurance. How they could have cultivated fields at those altitudes, is a mystery. The barley fields of the bKor-rdzod monastery are in Mr. Drew's opinion the highest in the world (Plate XXII, b). But those of the Mon settlers must have been higher still. According to Survey maps,[1] the altitude of bKor-rdzod is 15,600 feet, but according to Drew it is only 15,000 feet high. Drew gives the following numbers with regard to this lake: length 15 miles, breadth 3 to 5 miles; depth 248 feet. It may sound incredible that there should have been fields still higher than the present fields of bKor-rdzod whose harvest sometimes fails. But I remember that also on one of my former journeys, in Zangskar, I came across the ruins of a Dard settlement at an altitude where it was icy cold even in summer.

Whilst we were encamped at bKor-rdzod, the chief of the Rubshu nomads visited me, and to entertain him, I showed him the pictures of my "History of Western Tibet." He enjoyed them thoroughly, but he was struck with emotion on seeing the portrait of the ex-king of Ladakh with his son and retinue. As the ex-king was married to his own sister, this picture represented some of his nearest relations, and he implored me not to go away without making him a present of it. There remained no alternative for me but to tear the picture out of the book, and hand it over to him. It was however, fortunate for us, to have placed under obligation such an important personage through this little present. For, if we had not been in his favour, it would probably have taken a long time before the nomads found yaks for us. As matters stood, the yaks turned up in good condition next morning. In the same way, it was also our good fortune to have met with the Assistant Commissioner in Spiti. Otherwise we should certainly have had difficulty in getting transport animals from Spiti to the lake. It must be remembered that animals as well as men are scarce in these frontier regions, that the roads are difficult, if not dangerous, and that these frontier people can hardly be reached by any authority. Last year, as Mr. Howell told me, transport was absolutely refused to a traveller in Spiti, who obtained it only by using desperate means.

As we have been travelling on yaks for some time, and as we have before us many more miles of yak riding, it seems the proper place to say a few words about these interesting Tibetan animals. The first yak ride we had on our way back from Shipke, and the second on the journey from Spiti to the lake. All those yaks had rings through their noses, and could in a way be controlled by them, for it requires great anger on the part of the yak to make him indifferent to the pain which would be caused by his tearing himself free and running away. But the yaks which we received for our journey

[1] Survey Map of 1874. Sheet 46 gives Karzok as 14,960 ft. [Ed.]

a. Nomads' camp on Lake Thsomo Riri.

b. Yaks on the shore of Lake Thsomo Riri.

from bKor-rdzod to Nyoma on the Indus, and from Nyoma to rGya in Ladakh, were without this last touch of culture, a nose-ring. They had neither saddles, nor bridles, nor even nose-rings, they were absolutely undefiled products of nature. When I asked the nomads why even this last remnant of civilisation was not found on them, they said that this particular breed of yaks did not possess any noses. I was pitying the poor creatures for whom the roses had no scent, when I noticed that two little holes could be distinguished above the mouth. That in these circumstances it was no easy matter to use the yaks for riding, can well be imagined. In fact, their management was so difficult, that I would have gladly renounced this doubtful pleasure altogether, if the rarified air of those altitudes had not compelled me to use these uninviting beasts. When I was tired, I would tell one of the nomads to get me a yak for riding. Then all the men would run in front of the herd of yaks they were driving, shouting at them and waving their arms in the air, to make them understand that they were wanted to stop. A single one could never be made either to stop or to start. Their *esprit de corps* was so strong that they insisted on doing everything together. Now, when the herd was stopped, one of the unladen yaks was singled out for my use and seized by the horns. Naturally he disliked this treatment, and whilst he was dancing round the man, I was supposed to fly through the air and drop on the yak's back. As soon as I had reached my seat and seized its mane, the nomad would let go the horns, and off went the yak galloping up and down the hillside, until he had found his natural equilibrium, when he joined the herd again. The nomads had the kindness to select for me the least savage of their yaks, but the Khalasi and Khansaman had to take what remained, and that led often to exciting performances. I still see the Khalasi seated on the tail and hindquarters (for he had failed to drop down in the middle part of the animal) of a furious yak, which charged up and down with him on very uneven ground on the Thaglang Pass. Then, when the yak had found his place in the caravan of snorting beasts, he would look out for another yak, his adversary, and poke him with his horns. The opponent, naturally offended by this act of special attention, would pay it back in the same coin. In these continual fights, the yaks knocked a lock off one of our boxes, made holes in several others, and smashed the tripod of our camera. That they did not smash our own legs, was due to the continual care with which we watched these fights. Whenever one's own yak was charged by his adversary, one had to lift high the threatened leg, and join in the struggle by using one's stick and umbrella. There was, however, one weapon which was respected by all the yaks. That was the stone whip of Rubshu. We were now in the centre of a large treeless country, and thus it is not to be wondered at, that even the whip should be a stone implement. It was an oblong stone, three to four pounds in weight, with which the yaks were hammered on their hind quarters, whenever they showed signs of laziness. Curiously, the animals seemed to fear the sight of this stone implement more than its weight. The one I was riding on was often energetically hammered by a nomad behind me, a treatment which he endured with the utmost indifference. But the moment he saw another nomad using his stone against a yak in front of him, he shuddered with terror. When the hammering failed to make an impression, the stones were thrown at the yaks.

Once, the Khalasi had such a stone flung at his leg, which caused him to complain bitterly, as he was an official personage, but the nomads explained that it was intended for the yak.

On the 12th August, we had our camp by another mountain lake, called mThso-kyag (Kyaghar). This lake is only 2½ miles long and one mile broad. Its depth is 67 feet according to Drew. Its water is brackish, like that of the Thsomo Riri. There is no permanent habitation on its shore, but many stone walls have been erected by the nomads who often have their encampment on this lake. The scenery round about is very grand and of the same character as on the Thsomo Riri.

On the 13th August, we had our camp near Raldrong, where the Phuga brook enters the Indus. Opposite the confluence are the ruins of a Mon village. This is probably the deserted village mentioned by the late Dr. Shawe in his letter of the 19th July 1906, in which he advised me to visit Nyoma and surroundings. Dr. Shawe wrote as follows: "Some miles west of Nyoma are said to be the remains of an old Mon village, where I was told boxes, household utensils, and coins have been found (apparently in graves). Unfortunately I did not hear of this till I had left and was across the Indus, or I would have made enquiries. Coins should prove interesting and instructive." From the left bank of the Indus we could see deserted fields in terraces, a group of houses, and walls. As, however, the distance from Nyoma was fully ten miles, and we were perfectly exhausted from our long desert journey, I could not manage to visit the site. In Nyoma I tried to obtain some of the articles found by the people at this deserted village, but they pretended not to possess any such things.

On the 14th August, we marched to Nyoma, where we had our camp on the left bank of the Indus. Pindi Lal and myself crossed the Indus on a little raft of inflated skins. The river journey on this raft, where four men had to sit motionless on a single square yard, occupied fully half an hour. Pindi Lal got a slight touch of the sun, and a severe headache prevented him from enjoying the shade of the first willows after Kaze in Spiti, to which he had been looking forward. He was, however, brave enough to take some photos of objects of interest.

The elevation of Nyoma (Nimu, Nima, etc., on maps) is given as about 14,000 feet by Drew. This is certainly exaggerated. It could hardly be more than 13,000. Drew mentions the few large willow trees of great age at the village. They would not be found, we may be sure, at an elevation of 14,000. Besides, we saw very many young and thriving ones. Before speaking of our own experiences, let me quote Dr. Shawe's observations according to his letter of the 19th July 1906. He says: "Here (at Nyoma) are very fine remains of a castle and old town on the top of a rock (Plate XXVI, a). The buildings all more or less destroyed except the temple which is said to be of the same date as the rest, and contains a fine lot of small brass idols and other temple utensils. The town is said to have been built by bDe-skyong-rnam-rgyal (c. 1730 A.D.) whose name I also found on a *maṇi* wall. The only other king's name was Don-grub-rnam-rgyal (1790—1841), but there are many old *maṇi* walls, both of the ordinary and of the shelf type. On the plain behind the rock are extensive remains of a village which the people said was of the same date as the castle, but which appeared to me much older from the style of building, also two or three "step *mchod-rten*," but no ladder in the middle of sides (like those of the *Alchi-mkhar-gog* carvings). One old *mchod-rten* of the ordinary type, now fast falling to pieces, had a small door at either end, some three feet high, and the interior was very finely decorated with paintings of Buddha's temptation, his subduing demons, etc. The decorations of the ceiling were in relievo. It is by far the finest piece of *mchod-rten* decoration I have seen yet. The only rock carving I could find was a *migmang* (kind of chessboard) on a boulder, but no inscriptions on rocks at all."

As we see, Dr. Shawe himself did not feel satisfied with the people's statement that the town of Nyoma was built by bDe-skyong-rnam-rgyal. He found distinct signs of an earlier origin. The old types of *mchod-rten* especially, and the fact that one of them was beautifully decorated inside, point to an age of at least 900 to 1,000 years. I went to examine the temple which occupies the highest position in the now deserted town on the rock and belongs to the 'aBrug-pa order of monks. Since Dr. Shawe had been told that the temple was built in the 18th century, the monks had altered their opinion, and I was told that it dated from the days of King Seng-ge-rnam-rgyal (c. 1600). I was, however, not satisfied with an assertion which possibly had no real foundation and asked the monks to show me proof of this assertion. Then they brought me a book which had been dedicated to the monastery by Seng-ge-rnam-rgyal and actually contained a dedication sheet on which the names of the king and his illustrious queen bSkal-bzang could be distinctly read. Of course, a document like that goes to prove only that Senga ge-rnam-rgyal took a certain interest in the settlement, and possibly renovated the temple. It is difficult to believe that there was nothing before Seng-ge-rnam-rgyal's days in a pleasant valley like Nyoma, and ancient *mchod-rten* distinctly point to a time, earlier than this king. One of the many painted flags (*thang-ka*) in this temple, particularly interested me, for it not only contained an idealised portrait of Seng-ge-rnam-rgyal's friend, the great lama sTag-thsang-ras-pa, but also scenes of the royal household 300 years ago. I wanted by all means to have it photographed, and as Pindi Lal was not well enough to climb up to this temple above the present town, I asked permission to take the picture down to the bungalow. This request was not granted, until I had interviewed a high lama of Hemis who was touring in the district.

On this picture we see a number of whitewashed houses, one or two stories high. They look exactly like the present Ladakhi houses and also have a red or black band round the roof, just as the present monasteries have. Then we see the inside of the royal kitchen with five or six people busy at work, and the male and female members of the royal family in separate rooms. Below the houses are painted two processions which approach the buildings from right and left. The men on the right hand side are riding on mules or *rkyangs*, and those on the left are walking, carrying presents, perhaps tribute. The chief value of the picture lies in the fact that the costumes of those times are painted so well. Seng-ge-rnam-rgyal is the king who is credited by popular tradition with the introduction of the Ladakhi type of dress, as it remained unchanged down to the time of the Ḍōgrā war. In a collection of Tibetan proverbs which I acquired from a man from rGya some years ago, and which is among the manuscripts brought to Simla, there is a proverb which refers to the change of dress under this king. There it is stated that the king, whose name *Seng-ge* means "lion," said that he was willing to honour his subjects by giving them one of his ears; thus the men received the high black cap, called *seng-ge rna-mchog*, "lion's ear" which I find pictured by Drew.[1] The same proverb informs us that the great tiger lama (*sTag* means a tiger) favoured the women by giving them his spotted skin. Thus the dark blue dress of the Ladakhi women with its red and yellow spots was introduced. The picture in the Nyoma monastery does not, however, show the new fashion, having possibly been painted before its introduction. All the male persons wear turbans, as was the fashion in Western Tibet from c. 1000 A.D. downwards. The royal ladies are distinguished by their rich *berags*, fillets of leather which are covered with precious stones. Although I have not yet been able to trace them on pictures earlier than c. 1530 A.D., I am convinced that this fashion goes back to examples of old Indian art, where the Nāgas and Nāgis were represented by a human figure with a snake growing out of the back and over-topping their heads. The *berag* of the Ladakhi women which begins in the middle of the back and becomes broader over the head, looks like the representation of a snake. Perhaps the Ladakhi women wished to look like Nāgis, because these water fairies were famous for their beauty.

We spent Sunday, the 15th August, on the left bank of the Indus river, opposite Nyoma, and resumed our journey on Monday the 16th. Our next aim was Leh, and as the road along the Indus river was impracticable at that time of the year, I had to decide which of the two other roads we were to take, the road by Drangtse (map Tankse), or that by Phuga. As regards the Drangtse road, it attracted me much on account of a description Dr. Shawe had given me of it. The Phuga road, on the other hand, would take us to rGya, the antiquities of which I had previously examined. I decided for the latter route, but I will quote Dr. Shawe's letter on the Drangtse road to show the reader what we missed. He says in his letter of the 19th July 1906 :—

"I was told yesterday by one of the men that at Sakti you only visited the newest of the three old castles—the oldest being a mile or two up the valley. I am sorry I did not know when there. I saw few, if any, rock carvings in Sakti, except a *migmang* (see p. 57) on a boulder. At Drangtse is an old castle and village on top of a rock, destroyed by the Dogras. It is in very fair preservation, some of the streets being quite recognisable. Around Drangtse are numbers—thousands—of rock carvings of the usual ibex and yak type, but no Indian bulls, as far as I saw. At first I thought there were no inscriptions. and nobody could or would tell of any; but later, on top of a large rock or boulder, I found a number of carvings of some of which I enclose original copies. One, a *chorten*, had a long inscription beneath in letters which appear to be mostly, but not entirely, Tibetan, and on another boulder a line in Persian characters. Two or three carvings of crosses

[1] *Jummoo and Kashmir*, p. 240.

were rather interesting; I give copies. Another carving about a mile out, on the road to Pangkong (lake) of a stag hunt, thus [drawing]. A large and rough outline of Buddha on a rock seems to be fairly new—newer than some *chortens* on the same rock. I found no kings' names or votive inscriptions on *maṇis* at Drangtse, and the clay tablets were all of the *chorten* type, without letters, as far as I could see. Chushol yielded nothing of antiquarian interest, and I found nothing more till I got to Nyoma on the Indus."

Let me now add a few notes on Dr. Shawe's most valuable observations. I may remark that he was the first traveller who ever passed through this district with his eyes open to objects of archæological value. In 1906, I had travelled with Dr. Shawe as far as Chemre (*lCe-bde*) where we had investigated the monastery built by Seng-ge-rnam-rgyal. We became thoroughly convinced that there had existed a monastery previously on the same site. I went up the valley from Chemre to Sakti on a hurried visit, and as Dr. Shawe points out, in his letter, visited only the latest of three ancient castles. The first European traveller who visited the Chemre-Sakti valley, was Moorcroft in 1820. He also noticed the "fort" of Sakti which was already in ruins in his time. What he saw was also "the newest of the three old castles." Thus, the two older ones still remain to be investigated. Moorcroft[1] says: "On the face of the mountain, forming part of the eastern limit of the valley, stood the fort of Sakti, a pile of buildings surrounded by a wall and towers, the whole built of granite blocks cemented with clay; the houses were unroofed, but the walls were mostly standing. This fortress was evidently intended to command the northern entrance of the valley, but it was taken and dismantled by the Kalmaks nearly two centuries ago and has never been repaired."

The Kalmaks who dismantled this fortress, were evidently the Mongols and Lhasa Tibetans under Thse-dbang of Galdan, who after having beaten the Ladakhis in the battle of Zhamarting, besieged them in the fortress of Basgo. On their way to Basgo, 1646, they probably destroyed all the fortresses of eastern Ladakh. As we learn from Moorcroft, the Chemre-Sakti valley was under the command of the famous Ladakhi minister Bang-kha who ruled over seventy villages. The family of these Bang-khas evidently had the hereditary office of 'defender of the eastern gates of Ladakh. Their principal castle was the gSer-khri-mkhar of Igu, in the neighbouring valley, where there are many ancient ruins, among them walls with frescoes in front of huge carvings of Bōdhisattvas. One of the great generals of bDe-ldanr nam-rgyal (c.1630 A.D.) was a Bang-kha-pa from Igu. We also find a Bang-kha-pa in a high position of command during the first part of the Ḍōgrā war, when he did not quite justify the confidence placed in him.

As regards the other places of archæological interest mentioned by Dr. Shawe, they were not noticed by Trebeck on his way to the Pangkong lake. But Trebeck gives an interesting description of a festival he witnessed at Drangtse. As regards the inscription "mostly, but not entirely Tibetan," Dr. Shawe's copy of it was sent to Dr. Vogel, who said that it probably dated from c. 700—900 A.D., judging by the form of the characters used. It contained the Buddhist formula *Yē dharmā*, etc., which,

[1] *Travels*, Vol. 1, p 426.

according to my observations, played the part of the *Ōṁ maṇi padmē hūṁ* among the Ladakhi Buddhists of those times. The Indian characters, used by them, bear a remarkable resemblance to the Tibetan characters, for which reason I have come to the conclusion that the Tibetan script was developed in the western parts of Tibet, probably under the influence of Kashmir and Turkestan Buddhism.[1] This inscription may possibly give a clue to the date of the Maltese crosses found by Dr. Shawe in the vicinity.[2] Christianity in its Nestorian form was somewhat powerful in Turkestan about 900 A.D. and, although I do not venture to assert that there was a Christian community at Drangtse in those days, I think it not improbable that the ancient inhabitants of Drangtse had become acquainted with Christian forms of crosses. It is very probable that trade connections between Ladakh and Turkestan existed as early as 700 – 900 A.D. The Ladakhis were probably ready to try the efficacy of the Christian crosses for the sake of experiment, just as they swallow pages of Christian books nowadays, if swallowed pages of Buddhist writings have not the desired effect.

I was told that there was another deserted Mon settlement above Nyoma on the left bank of the Indus. When our caravan started for Phuga on Monday the 16th August, I made a special trip to this old site which is called Staglung. On my way thither I passed by the village of Ngod (*Mud*, or *Mad* of the maps) on the right bank of the Indus, which is known for its monastery. I was told that the Ngod monastery was of more recent date than the Nyoma one, and that it was erected by Ngag-dbang-rnam-rgyal, the step-brother of Seng-ge-rnam-rgyal who had been obliged to take religious orders. Staglung is about seven miles distant from Nyoma (or better Nidar) and is situated in a very dry side valley near the Indus. There I found a rocky hill covered with ruins of houses, the single rooms of which were very small. As there are no traces of ancient fields round about, it is probable that Staglung was not a village, but a monastery. Below the rock is a number of ancient *mchod-rten* (about 15 to 20) and several rows of 108 small *mchod-rten*, all of which are built of sun-dried bricks. In two of the larger *mchod-rten* we found cremation tablets of clay, painted red. Two of them contained an inscription of the *Yē ḍharmā* formula in an ancient type of Tibetan character. This would point to Tibetan influence before the abandonment of the establishment.

As the word *'aBrog-pa* (Dard) is never used here at Nyoma, nor in Rubshu, to signify the pre-Tibetan inhabitants of the country, I believe that the word *Mon*, which is here always used for them, refers to the Dard settlers of Rubshu and Nyoma district. At any rate, the Dards of Da state expressly in one of their songs that they once colonised Rong-chu-rgyud, which is the site of the present village of Nyoma and

[1] See my article: *The Kingdom of gNya khri btsanpo*, in *J. A. S. B.*, Vol. VI. p. 93.

[2] These crosses were again examined by Rev. S. Schmitt of Leh in 1911. Mr. Schmitt found inscriptions in an unknown script, running from top to bottom, in the vicinity of the crosses. Professor A. Grünwedel of Berlin points to the similarity between the Drangtse inscriptions and the Nestorian tomb-inscriptions treated by Chvolson of St. Petersburg. Dr. A. von, Le Coq pronounces the language of the inscriptions to be Soghdian. The word *S[a]mark[a]nda* may be read without difficulty. According to Professor F. W. K. Müller, the Drangtse inscriptions were carved by pilgrims and dated.

PLATE XXVI.

a. Ruins of Nyoma.

b. Mon *mchod-rten* at Rumrtse.

surroundings[1]. But the Dard civilisation apparently went beyond the present Tibetan boundary, for on Sven Hedin's new map I find a district near Ruthog called Monyul, a name which evidently refers to a former colonization by Mons or Dards.

On the 17th August, we passed by the borax and sulphur mines of Phuga, 14,300 feet high, and saw some of the hot springs in the valley. The houses near the mines were uninhabited, but did not appear to be very old. It was apparently here that the Ladakhi kings obtained the sulphur which they sent to Kuḷū between 1650 and 1836 A.D. In Kuḷū, this sulphur was exchanged for iron according to the trade contract between Ladakh and Kuḷū.[2] In one of the old *mchod-rten* at the upper end of the Phuga valley, we found a terra-cotta inscribed with Indian characters. This makes it probable that the mines were worked already by the ancient Mons (or Dards). As there are so many hot sulphurous springs in the valley, some even in the middle of the river bed, the air is in many places full of sulphurous gases.

We crossed the Phologongkha Pass (16,500 feet) on the same day, and had our camp on the shore of another large lake called mThso-d kar (White Lake) by the Tibetans, and "Salt Lake" by the cartographers. The elevation of this lake is 14,900 feet according to Drew. The first European to visit this lake was Trebeck, who passed by it in 1820, on his journey to Spiti. He calls it Thog ji chenmo, which is evidently the name of the monastery Thugs-rje-chen-po on the shore of the lake. This justifies our conclusion that this little monastery was already in existence in 1820. I was told that the present buildings were erected only a few years ago, instead of an older establishment which consisted mainly of cave dwellings. The present monastery contains only a few modern Tibetan books and a stucco statue of Avalōkitēśvara, after whom it is called, *Thugs-rje-chen-po*.

In the vicinity I noticed a cave, the entrance to which was closed by a stone wall, and this stone wall again had several clay seals impressed on it. Both kinds of seals showed complicated designs of the *svastika*. It is probable that some evil spirit was believed thus to be shut up in the cave. From one of the little houses near the monastery was suspended a piece of wood shaped like the male organ, painted red. As we read in the chronicles of Ladakh, "King Lha-chen-rgyal-po (c. 1050—1080 A.D.), provided with untiring zeal the recluses that lived in the neighbourhood of the Kailāsa and the three lakes with the necessaries of life." This passage undoubtedly refers to the Manasarowar lake in the first place, but it may also refer to the lakes of Rubshu, for I am fully convinced that, although no ancient remains have been discovered in them, yet the monasteries on the Thsomo Riri as well as on the Salt Lake are of great age. On the Pangkong Lake no monastery exists.

As the Salt Lake is surrounded by marshes, it does not make such a pretty picture as the Thsomo Riri, and the Khyagar Lake. The best view is probably obtained from the site of the little monastery. The following notes are taken from Drew who gives a very interesting geological account of this lake. The former level of the lake, as shown

[1] See my translation of the eighteen songs of the Bonona festival, *Ind. Ant.*, Vol. XXXIV, p. 93.

[2] See the account of the trade in my pamphlet '*Die religiösen und historischen Erinnerungen der Lahouler.*'

by distinct marks on the hillside, was 320 feet above the present level, and at that time the lake covered between 60 and 70 square miles as against its present eight square miles, the small fresh-water sheet included. This change of level is explained by him as being due not only to the erosion of dams, but also to the diminution of the humidity of the air. The salt lake produces various kinds of salt. On the northern shore of the lake, common salt is deposited. This is collected by the nomads who trade with it. It is consumed all over Ladakh, and even in Kashmir. Over part of the plain round about the lake, a carbonate of soda, called *patsa* (Bathsa) by the Tibetans, is found. This is the salt of the poor, and of animals. Another mineral found in the vicinity is called *gurm.* It is a mixture of sulphate of magnesia with a compound of soda. The depth of the lake is only 30 feet at the eastern end, its deepest part.

We had our next camp at Debring, on the southern side of the Thag-lang Pass, and exchanged our yaks from Nyoma for others from Rubshu. Debring is a nomads' camping ground which is furnished with several *maṇi* walls and *mchod-rten*, although there are no houses.

CHAPTER III.

The Indus Valley.

a. LADAKH.

We crossed the Thag-lang Pass (17,500 feet high) on the 19th August, and marched to the village of rGya (13,500 feet high), the first village of Ladakh, on the road from Rubshu. Before entering rGya, we passed by the ancient remains of the village of Rum-rtse (map Ramcha) which is asserted to have been a Mon settlement. When Moorcroft halted here in 1820, the whole population of this little village, who had never seen a European before, fled in terror, leaving their houses empty.

What may be called the necropolis of the ancient Mons of Rum-rtse, is situated on a plain above the trade road, about two miles above rGya. It consists of a number of large single *mchod-rten*, and many well-preserved rows of 108 little *stūpas.* The present inhabitants of Rum-rtse said that all those *mchod-rten*, having been the work of Mons, were not reverenced by them. The Mons and the Tibetans had nothing in common, they said. Although we examined some of the ruined *mchod-rten* at the site, we did not find any inscribed tablets in them. We took a photo of a rather well-preserved specimen of these *mchod-rten* which was of the so-called ladder type, as we find it represented among the ancient rock carvings near the Alchi bridge. The lower part showed remains of stucco frames which, I suppose, originally enclosed stucco figures of Buddha. This kind of ornamentation is not found on Tibetan *mchod-rten.* If a Tibetan *mchod-rten* has stucco relievos, they represent lions, Garuḍas and other animals. These are not found round the base, but round the middle portion of the *mchod-rten.* Another of our photos shows some of the well-preserved rows of little *stūpas* (Plate **XXVI, b**).

Opposite, and a little below the necropolis, on the other bank of the rGya brook are the ruins of the ancient castle and town of the Mons, called Rum-rtse-mkhar, with cave dwellings close by. The most conspicuous building in the old town was a round tower of great dimensions. Unfortunately, our limited time did not allow us to visit the site. The rGya district altogether is so full of ancient remains that an archæologist could profitably spend a couple of weeks here.

There is another ruined castle (called *mKhar-gog*), on a spur in a side valley to the left, between Rum-rtse and rGya. Although I could not trace any traditions regarding it, it is apparently of Mon, *i.e.*, pre-Tibetan, origin. Besides, there are many ancient Mon *stūpas* in various places between Rum-rtse and rGya. The two large *mchod-rten* seen by Moorcroft on the road before entering rGya, are apparently still in existence. They are of Tibetan origin, and probably not more than two centuries old.

The site of the old settlement of the Tibetans at rGya is called *rGya-mkhar*. It is situated on a spur of the right bank of the rGya brook. From Moorcroft's account it appears that in 1820 A.D., the site was no longer inhabited and that Moorcroft's town of rGya was identical with the present, which is situated on the left bank of the brook. He says[1] : " Opposite to the town, on a lofty ridge of rocks, was a large pile of houses, formerly inhabited by the raja; and lower down, one belonging to the lama." The ruins of this ancient Tibetan town are still very picturesque. Higher up on the same hill are several ancient watch-towers. When Moorcroft was in rGya, he found one of the ancient chiefs of the district still in authority. He had friendly intercourse with this man whom he calls a raja. He says : " The raja whose name was Tsimma Panchik, was a short stout man about fifty." Of course, there were no kings of rGya, not even a vassal king. The title of raja (*rgyal-po*) may have been given to the chiefs, because they were related to the Ladakhi kings. Now the line is extinct, and all records being lost, I found it impossible to establish the identity of Moorcroft's Tsimma Panchik. It is even difficult to make out what Tibetan name may underlie Moorcroft's spelling of it. I suppose that the man was called Thse-dbang Phun-thsogs, pronounced Tsewang Puntsog. I asked several people at rGya if they could remember the names of the last members of their line of chiefs, and they gave me the following three names ; (1) bKā-blon-Thse-bstan ; (2) Nono bSod-nams jo-rgyas ; (3) bKra-shis (or Thse-ring) bZang-grub. More they could not remember. It is, however, possible that on a votive tablet on one of the *maṇi* walls at rGya the name of Moorcroft's friend may yet be discovered. Thus an inscription on a *maṇi* wall below rGya, of the time of bDe-ldan rnam-rgyal (c. 1630 A.D.) contains the name of one (or two ?) probable ancestors of Moorcroft's Tsimma Panchik, *viz.*, Nono bSod-nams-lhun-grub, 'father and son.' In this inscription the castle of rGya is called rGya-mkhar-rmug-po, ' the dark red castle of rGya.' On another *maṇi* wall in the vicinity of the preceding I found a tablet which is of interest on account of its reference to the state of Ladakh during the times following the battle of Basgo, 1647 A.D.

---

[1] *Travels*, Vol. I, p. 234.

It gives the name of the Lhasa commissioner who for a time was regent of Ladakh and who, as the chronicles prove, intended to make himself the independent ruler of the country. His name is given here as rGyal-bai rgyal-thsab rJe-btsun Mi-pham-mgon. But unfortunately, there was no time for copying these inscriptions in full, nor for making impressions of them.

Behind the present village of rGya, on the left bank of the brook, there is a plateau studded with a number of ancient, mostly ruined *mchod-rten*. They are still held in veneration by the present inhabitants of rGya (Plate XXXI, a). This is remarkable, because many of these *mchod-rten* which are called *Lha-bab-mchod-rten*, undoubtedly go back to Mon times. And had not the people of the neighbouring village told us plainly that they were indifferent to everything connected with the Mons? The difference may be this, that whilst the Mons of Rum-rtse did not succumb to Tibetan influences, the Mons of rGya did. We found several types of cremation tablets with Indian inscriptions, containing the *Yē dharmā* formula. The characters employed are of c. 700—900 A.D. according to Dr. Vogel's estimate. But there were also several tablets which showed the same formula in Tibetan characters. The difference between the Tibetan and Indian characters rests mainly in this, that in the Tibetan version the aspirated mediæ are indicated by an ordinary media furnished with a subjoined *h*, whilst in the Indian version *gh*, *dh*, and *bh* are expressed in simple characters. Besides, the Tibetan version has the tripartite *y*, whilst the Indian version has a later form of the *y*. In two cases, there were two tablets showing almost exactly the same design, but the characters used for the inscription were Tibetan on one of them, and Indian on the other. Among the *Lhā-bab-mchod-rten*, there were also the ruins of an ancient monastery of unknown origin, built of sun-dried bricks. I am almost convinced that the town of rGya is mentioned in the time of King Sadna legs, c. 850, in the chronicles of Ladakh. There it is stated that King Sadna legs built the temple of sKar-chung-rdo-dbyings in the province of rGya (*rGya-sde*). This could, of course, also be translated by "Indian Province" or "Chinese Province." But it is very unlikely that a Tibetan king should have built a monastery in a district, the hold on which was always uncertain. It is a pity that the name of the ruined temple in the middle of the *Lha-bab-mchod-rten* has become entirely lost.

On the 20th August, we left rGya for Mar-rtse-lang (map Marsahing), the Marsilla of Moorcroft. Below rGya, we passed by a high *lhatho*, an altar of the pre-Buddhist religion, with a few houses and fields in the vicinity. It is the *Latu* of Moorcroft, and soon we reached the houses and fields of a small settlement, called Rong.[1]

We made a short halt at this place, because I wished to examine the site of some ancient graves, called *Mon-gyi-rom-khang*, "graves of the Mons." The first who told me of the existence of these graves, was our evangelist dGā-Phun-thsogs of Kyelang, who is a native of rGya. He had told me that he had been inside them when a shepherd

[1] On the map this village is indicated by the name of *Latho*.

PLATE XXVII.

a. Site of Mon castle at Rumrtse.

b. Ruined monastery at Miru.

boy. He said that then the graves were quite accessible ; that he went down a staircase and came to rooms furnished with boards of pinewood, on which were placed numbers of skulls. A native of Rong whom we met, also asserted that the graves were very deep and furnished with masonry walls. As regards pinewood, I must say that it is a very rare article at rGya, which place is nowadays 150 miles away from the nearest pine tree. When we looked at the graves, we saw only pits in the ground for the superstitious people of Rong had closed them up with earth. As my observations later on in Leh showed me, it is very probable that these ancient graves of Rong belong to the same period as those of Leh, which I have much reason to attribute to the period of the " Empire of the Eastern Women." This State bordered on Ladakh, if it did not include parts of Eastern Ladakh. The Leh graves as well as those of Rong are furnished with masonry walls. Both contained numbers of skulls, a circumstance which points to the custom prevalent in that empire of burying all the higher officials along with the chief. The fact that the skulls were placed on boards in Rong, seems to show that the corpses were cut to pieces. Also at Leh the skulls as well as the vases containing the bones were originally placed on boards which became rotten when irrigation water entered the graves. Most of the larger pots at Leh had holes in the bottom, which shows that they probably had fallen down from a higher position. As excavations in Rong would have been possible only at a considerable sacrifice of time and money, I abandoned the idea for the present.

The next village on the road along the narrow valley from rGya to the Indus is Meru, pronounced Miru. It has a monastery in ruins which was famous in olden days (Plate XXVII, b). It is situated on a hill above the trade road. Its temple occupies the uppermost position on the top of a little conical hill, and the now ruined cells of the monks surround it below. It used to be one of the important monasteries of Ladakh, but its founder is not known. It lost much of its glory, when King Seng-ge-rnam-rgyal made it the " mother " of the Hemis monastery which he built in the Shang valley. On that occasion, not only the " spirit " of the Meru monastery was carried off in a bundle of twigs, but also most of the images were transferred to Hemis. But Meru had to suffer a still greater injury during the Ḍōgrā wars, when it was plundered, and the monks expelled. At present, there is not much remaining in the temple hall ; one of the frescoes is, however, of unusual interest as it represents Gog-bzang-lha-mo, the mother of Kesar and one of the great pre-Buddhist deities of the Ladakhis. This picture is probably of ancient origin, although it had apparently been renovated from time to time. It was painted at a time when Bon-po art was largely influenced by Buddhist art. The complexion of the goddess is a beautiful white, whilst her hair is black. The hair is raised over the forehead and furnished with a ribbon and a diadem of pearls. Her ear ornaments (probably shells) are white and spiral-shaped, and her dress is white with blue and red seams. In her hand she carries a white cup.

Opposite the monastery, there is a hill with cave dwellings, probably the most ancient inhabited locality at Meru. It is called *Baho* (' Caves').

The place where the inhabitants of Meru had to live before they built their present houses in the bottom of the valley, is a hill spur on the right bank of the rGya river where there are extensive ruins of houses. As has been stated above, during the ascendency of the Ladakhi kings people were not allowed to live among the fields, probably to prevent their trespassing too much on valuable ground. But, as we learnt from Moorcroft's account of rGya, the lofty sites on the top of rocks were already partly abandoned during the times of the last king, Thse-dpal-don-grub-rdo-rje-rnam-rgyal (1820 A.D). From his account it appears that at Meru also people lived in their present houses in 1820.

Several miles below Meru, the rGya brook discharges into the Indus, and at this place is situated the village of Ubshi (Moorcroft's *Ukshi*). In this village we noticed several *mchod-rten* of great age which were known to the inhabitants as *mchod-rten* of the Mons. We examined the interior of one of them and found the walls inside covered with ancient frescoes which were apparently painted with two colours only, indigo blue and brownish red. There were any number of rows of figures of blue complexion seated cross-legged. Their garments were white with red seams. The larger pictures in the centre of the four walls were too far gone to allow of any identification. The headdress of these blue figures was somewhat unusual; it looked as if the ends of a long hair-pin projected on each side. Later on, when I had examined several more similar frescoes at other ancient sites, I came to the conclusion that the Ubshi pictures represent Nāgas (*Klu*), and that these ancient *mchod-rten* may be Bon-po, and not Buddhist, structures.

We spent the night of the 20th and the 21st August at Martselang. Here I had a pleasant surprise in meeting one of the Leh mission ladies, Miss Schurter, who had travelled through the desert wilds of Rubshu from Kyelang to Leh, accompanied only by two Christian Tibetans from the former place. I might have caught her up much earlier, if she had not been alarmed by rumours of the approach of a very untrustworthy sportsman (myself !) which caused her to make double marches to escape him.

Martselang is situated at the lower end of the Shang valley (the *Changa* of Moorcroft), which contains the Hemis monastery. This monastery which was built by king Seng-ge-rnam-rgyal only about 300 years ago, has acquired quite unusual fame among European visitors to Ladakh on account of its devil-dances. These are performed here in June (originally probably on the occasion of the summer solstice), a convenient time for Europeans to attend them, whilst most of the other monasteries have the same performance in winter. The monastery was also frequently referred to fifteen or eighteen years ago, when the Russian traveller Notovitch surprised the world by stating that he had found in it a copy of a new Christian gospel written in Pāli. A great deal of learned correspondence then took place which proved that Notovitch's extraordinary find was a forgery. The interesting Tibetan account of the foundation of this monastery was brought to Europe by the Schlagintweits, and the Tibetan text with an attempt at a partial translation was published by Emil von

Schlagintweit.[1] I hope to find time to prepare a reliable version of this interesting document. Although the Hemis monastery is not very ancient, yet it contains images of a type which is found only in monasteries of the 10th or 11th century. When the monks are asked to state the place of origin of such statues, they say that they were brought here from Lhasa. I wonder if that can be true. It seems to me that a more likely explanation is that these images were brought here from Meru, which is, as already stated, the "mother" monastery of Hemis.

At Martselang we saw again many ancient *mchod-rten* of the Mon type, and all along the road, from this place to Chushod, these *mchod-rten* were much in evidence. I may add that it is very much the same on the other bank of the Indus, *e.g.*, at Khrigtse, Raṇbīrpur, and Sheh, where they are numerous. At Raṇbīrpur, I remember having seen even several specimens of the ladder type in fair preservation. The conviction that we are travelling here on ancient Buddhist ground, grew very strong on me. It is not impossible that the present village and monastery of Khrigtse are identical with the castle of Khri-btsegs-'abum-gdugs mentioned before Srong-btsan-sgam-po, who was the first Buddhist king of Tibet, and with the monastery of Khri-rtse mentioned under King Mes-ag thsoms (705—755 A.D). Local names in Sanskrit which are found here and there in Ladakh, date from the times of this more Indian than Tibetan form of Buddhism. The names of Meru, and Sakti (Skr. *Śakti*) have already been mentioned. I may add the names of Muni and Kanika (= Kanishka ?) in Zaṅgskar, and Tar (Skr. *Tārā*, on account of the Svayambhu Tārās at that place), Hari rtse (Summit of Hari). The greater part of the Ladakhi local names are certainly Tibetan, but not a few are of Dard origin. In connection with the latter statement let me point to the many names which have the Dard word *hem* (Skr. *hima*) or *hen* "snow," as one of their component parts, *viz.*, Hembabs (Dras), Henasku, Hema la, Hemis. Of other plainly Dard names like Hanu, Hunupatta, Garkunu, Chanegund, Hibti, Esu, etc., I cannot yet explain the etymology. The name *Raṇbīrpur* is a modern Ḍōgrā name.[2] A few ancient Indian personal names also have been preserved in folklore and inscriptions. Thus, the ruined castle opposite Stag-sna is called the castle of king Surgamati (Skr. *Sūry-amati*, "Sun-mind") and among the old royal names on inscriptions at Khalatse we find Shirima (Skr. *Srīmān*) and (probably) Satyamati ("Truth-mind"), besides several others.

When riding along the left bank of the Indus river, we could see the villages, castles and monasteries on the right bank, a visit to many of which would amply reward archæological research. The conical hill of the Khrigtse monastery always looks picturesque, and so it is with the Stag-sna monastery which is built on a rock between two arms of the Indus. The buildings of this monastery look almost like a royal castle. It was built with the greater care, because it was the residence of several members of the royal family who had taken orders in the 'aBrug-pa sect. The erection of this monastery in its present shape is attributed to Ngag-dbang-rnam-rgyal, the step-

[1] "*Buddhism of Tibet.*"

[2] The place is named after Raṇbīr Singh, the son and successor of Gulāb Siṅgh and the second Ḍōgrā ruler of Kaśmīr.

brother of Seng-ge-rnam-rgyal. The village of Sheh (*Shel*) on the right bank has also many attractions. It was apparently the capital of Ladakh, before the old kings of Leh, the professed descendants of the mythological king Kesar, were expelled. Here are the most ancient royal rock inscriptions, but the best preserved of them will probably remain inaccessible for some time for the natives of Sheh, being afraid of a devil who has his abode exactly in front of the best of them, have erected a wall which conceals the entire inscription.

We crossed the Indus at Choglamsa. The water was so high, that it flowed over part of the bridge, and we had to ride through deep water for several hundreds of yards on the bridge as well as on the left bank. At Choglamsa we met two ladies of the Mission who had come to the bridge to welcome Miss Schurter, and on the road through the sandy desert below Leh we were welcomed by several more members of the Moravian Mission. We rode along the long royal *maṇi* walls south of Leh which had astonished Moorcroft ninety years ago, and entered Leh with thankful hearts, for we were all much in need of a good rest. Here in Leh we again received letters, the first since leaving Poo four weeks before, and also a remittance. But a more powerful inducement to continue our work was the approval of our past doings, which found expression in Dr. Marshall's letters.

b. LEH.

The name of *La-dvags* is not mentioned in the Tibetan chronicles before the reign of king Nyi-ma-mgon, c. 900 A.D., when it is stated that it was in the hands of Gesar's descendants. The kings Lha-chen-she-srab and Khri-btsug-lde (c. 1350 – 1400 A.D.) seem to have resided chiefly at Sabu; and only the kings from 'aBum-lde onward, (after 1400 A.D.) resided permanently at Leh. As has already been mentioned, the original name of the town is not *sLel*, as it is now-a-days spelt, but *sLes*, which signifies an encampment of nomads. These nomads were probably in the habit of visiting the Leh valley at a time when it had begun to be irrigated by Dard colonizers. Thus, the most ancient part of the ruins on the top of the rNam-rgyal-rtse-mo hill at Leh are called 'aBrog-pai-mkhar (Dard castle), and of the supposed Dard graves at Leh, we shall have occasion to speak again.

The first European to visit Leh was apparently the Jesuit Desideri who visited Ladakh in 1715 during the reign of King Nyi-ma-rnam-rgyal whom he calls Nima namgial. The Jesuit was kindly received by the king, but as the Muhammadan traders plotted against him and undermined the king's confidence, he soon left the town and travelled to Lhasa. I regret to say that I have not yet seen a satisfactory account of this interesting and important journey.[1] A relic of Desideri's mission was discovered by the next European visitor to Ladakh, Moorcroft. He found at Pashkyum an old Bible on which he makes the following remarks :[2] " A Sayid, who seemed to act as his [the Pushkyum Raja *i.e.* vassal chief's] ghostly adviser, produced a book which had descended

[1] The best seems to be : Carlo Puini, *Il Tibet, secondo la relazione del viaggio del P. Ippolito Desideri.*

[2] *Travels*, Vol. II, pp. 22 ff.

from his grandfather to the Raja, and which proved to be an edition of the Old and New Testament from the Papal press, dated in the year 1598. It was bound in Morocco, with the initials I. H. S. surmounted by a cross, stamped on each side of the cover. How it had come there no person could inform me, but it might possibly have been given to the former Raja by Desideri, who visited Ladakh, although it is very doubtful if he reached Lé. The Khalun and Khaga Tan. zin made, at my request, very particular inquiry regarding any evidence of a European having been at Lé before us, and no proof nor tradition of such an occurrence could be traced." I feel confident that a critical edition of Desideri's diary will establish beyond doubt the fact that Desideri actually visited Leh.

But although Moorcroft was the second instead of the first visitor to Leh, his description of his visit is of the greatest importance in historical as well as geographical respects. Moorcroft visited Ladakh fourteen years before the kingdom lost its independence. He spent two years at Leh, and as he was a very keen and intelligent observer, his description of the kingdom is of unique interest. Trebeck, Moorcroft's travelling companion, who was a clever draftsman, made a pencil sketch of Leh, which was reproduced in the account of their travels, and this picture of Leh, the oldest known to exist, no archæologist would willingly lose. The reason why Moorcroft spent such a long time at Leh was his attempt to arrange for the king of Ladakh's tendering his allegiance to the East India Company. It took him a long time to win the confidence of the Ladakhi king, Tuntuk namgial (*Dong-rub-rnam-rgyal*) and his Prime. Minister, Tsiva Tandu (*Thse-dbang-dong-rub*). But when they were ready to tender their allegiance, their offer was declined by the East India Company. How different the fate of Ladakh would have been, had it been accepted. Moorcroft had no doubts then, that Ladakh would soon be swallowed up by Russia, for the Prime Minister showed him a letter from the Emperor of Russia to the king of Ladakh which had been brought there by a Jew, six years before. Moorcroft and Trebeck became eye-witnesses of some little warfare between the Ladakhis and Baltis, and between the Ladakhis and the Kuḷū State; they also saw the seditious placard at Leh, in which the unsatisfactory rule of the king was contrasted with the excellent rule of his predecessor, his brother, who had died young. There is simply no end of most interesting information in Moorcroft's account, and I hope to be spared to edit the Ladakhi portion of his journal with notes from the Tibetan point of view.

Let me now quote Moorcroft's description of Leh, in 1820, and contrast it with the Leh of the present day. He writes: [1] "Lé, the capital of Ladakh, is situated in a narrow valley, formed by the course of the Sinh-kha- bab[*Sengge kha-bab, i e.*, the Indus], and bounded on the northern and southern sides by a double chain of mountains running east and west, the highest of which are from eighteen hundred to two thousand feet above the plain. It is built at the foot and on the slope of some low hills, forming the northern boundary of the valley, and separated by a sandy plain about two miles broad from the river

[1] *Travels*, Vol. I, pp. 315 ff.

It is enclosed by a wall, furnished at intervals with conical and square towers, and extending on either side to the summit of the hills. It is approached by a double line of the sacred structures or manis, frequently noticed in the journal, and houses are scattered over the plain without the walls, on either hand. The streets are disposed without any order, and form a most intricate labyrinth, and the houses are built contiguously, and run into each other so strangely, that from without it is difficult to determine the extent of each mansion. The number, it is said, is about a thousand ; but I should think they scarcely exceeded five hundred. They vary from one to two or three stories in height, and some are loftier. The walls are in a few instances wholly, or in part of stone, but in general they are built with large unburnt bricks : they are whitened outside with lime, but remain of their original colour inside. They are usually furnished with light wooden balconies ; the roofs are flat, and are formed of small trunks of poplar trees, above which a layer of willow shoots is laid, which is covered by a coating of straw, and that again by a bed of earth."

From this description we learn that in 1820, although the general character of the houses was the same as it is nowadays, yet the ground plan of the old town must have been very different from that of the present town. It is true that even then some houses existed outside the walls, but the town proper was enclosed by a fortified wall. The two large bazaars which form such a conspicuous feature of the present town of Leh were not yet in existence. As popular tradition asserts, the large bazaar of Leh was laid out by the Ḍōgrās after the war of 1834-1842, and the new bazaar was made in 1897 by Captain Trench, British Joint Commissioner. I have been told, the Schlagintweits give a very minute description of Leh as it was in 1856, when the large bazaar was already in existence. Where this description is to be found, I have not been able to trace. A few remains of the walls of Leh are found right in the middle of the present town, where there is also one of the ancient crooked gates. This gate, which is a little north-east of the great mosque at the end of the bazaar, marks the extent of the former town towards the south. All those houses which are found between the rNam-rgyal rtse-mo Hill and this gate, belong to the old town of Leh, of Moorcroft's time. He makes special mention only of three conspicuous buildings, *viz.*, the royal palace, the Chamba (Byams-pa, *i.e.*, Maitrēya) and the Chenresi (sPyan-ras-gzigs, *i.e.*, Avalōkitēśvara) Monasteries. These three buildings are still in existence, and will be referred to in due course. The following conspicuous buildings of the old town must also have been in existence in Moorcroft's time, although he does not make any reference to them. The house *Blon-po* ("Minister") is situated directly below the castle, on the south-west corner ; the *dGon-pa-so-ma,* (New Monastery) is situated on the south-eastern corner of the same castle. It is the scene of the devil-dances which were witnessed by Moorcroft. Both these buildings can be distinguished on Trebeck's picture of Leh. Below the dGon-pa-so-ma and the Byams-pa monasteries, is situated the *mKhar-chung* ("the little Palace"), and exactly below the latter the ruined site of the house *bKā-blon* ("Prime Minister"), possibly the very same house in which Moorcroft was received in audience by the then Prime Minister. West of the house *bKạ̄-blon* we see the house *Tạ-go-che.* The

PLATE XXVIII.

a. Clay pots from Dard graves, Leh.

b. Skulls from Dard graves, Leh.

To-go-che used to be an official who ranked between a minister and a *Grong-dpon*, or mayor. The present representative of the To-go-che is Munshi dPal-rgyas, the chronicler of Ladakh. To the west of his house we find the house *Grong-dpon* or "Mayor," and below it the old Byams-pa (Maitrēya) monastery. But on Trebeck's sketch of Leh we see two high palace-like buildings behind the Maitrēya and Avalōkitēśvara Monasteries, of which no trace remains. What were the names of these two buildings? From the chronicles of Ladakh we learn that a "new palace" was built above the sPyan-ras-gzigs Monastery during the reign of King Thse-dpal-rnam-rgyal. That would account for one of those buildings. During the reign of the same king mention is also made of a "*Theg-chen-gong-ma* Hall." As, however, nothing definite is said with regard to its situation, we do not know whether it is a room in the old castle or the building shown on Trebeck's sketch between the large royal palace and the "New Palace," behind the Avalōkitēśvara Monastery.

We could not possibly examine all the antiquities of Leh within four weeks, but we did some work, and I now wish to describe what we found.

We were just entering Leh, when I heard that somebody had again opened the ancient Dard graves near the *Teu-gser-po*, about two miles above the Commissioner's compound in the Leh valley. This is the same site on which Dr. Shawe and myself had done some excavation work in 1903. As I did not wish anybody else to take away the more important objects of interest, I asked Mr. Schmitt of the Moravian Mission to go with me to the graves on the 23rd August. This we did, and the two Christian boys who accompanied us proved very useful in opening the graves, which involved very hard work. The roof of the grave is more than a yard below the present level of the ground. It consists of large unhewn stones of rectangular shape, each about 1½ yards long, and a foot or so broad. The walls of the grave consist of masonry of unhewn stones. It is about two yards long, 1½ yards broad, and at least six feet deep. We had not yet reached the bottom, when we stopped our excavations. Originally the roof of the grave was probably above the ground. Later on, the deposits accumulated and buried it. But destruction did not set in, as I believe, until a field was made above it. Then, the continual flood of the irrigation water destroyed all the woodwork and many of the bronze implements began to oxydize. I suppose that the Leh graves originally contained wooden boards just like those at rGya.

The grave contained clay pots of various sizes, a few entire, but most of them in fragments (Plate XXVIII, a). The largest pot, of which only fragments came to light, may have had a height of three feet, and its diameter was probably not much less. The smaller pots, which were rarer than the large ones, had a height of 10 to 15 cm. There were also small, saucer-like vessels of clay, probably lamps. The natives who were with us at once asserted, that the pottery of the grave was distinctly different from present day Tibetan pottery. The pottery of the grave is not wheel-made but hand-made and characterised by very small handles. When Dr. Shawe and myself visited this grave (or another in the neighbourhood) in 1903, we found two elegant pots of medium size which were ornamented with designs in dark red colour. These pots were kept by

Dr. Shawe in his house, and photographed by Miss Duncan.[1] This time we could not find a single pot with painted designs in the grave. But there were linear ornaments impressed on several of them. The only places in Ladakh, besides the graves, where similar hand-made pottery with dark red ornaments has been found, are the ancient ruined castles of sBalu mkhar and Alchi mkhar gog. A plate showing such pottery is reproduced in my article "Archæological Notes on *sBalu mkhar*."[2] Another collection of such ornamental sherds was made at *Alchi mkhar gog* on our expedition and brought to Simla. These ornaments are all of a very primitive type. They consist of spirals, ladders, and a zigzag band; and occasionally there are bunches of lines which may represent grass or reeds.

As most of the pots had holes in their bottoms, I was led to believe that they had fallen down from some higher position, probably from wooden boards (as are said to exist in the rGya graves). When the irrigation water entered, the boards decayed and gave way. As I had previously observed, when examining the graves with Dr. Shawe, most of the pots were filled with human bones. This circumstance seems to indicate that the ancient inhabitants of the Leh valley indulged in the gruesome practice of cutting the corpses to pieces and filling clay pots with the fragments. This custom, which is also found in other parts of the globe, is asserted by the Chinese to have been in vogue in the "Empire of the Eastern Women." Some of the pots had old cracks and carefully bored holes on both sides of them. Thus the art of mending broken pottery with strings must have been known to the race which built these graves.

There were, it appears, between fifteen and twenty skulls in one single grave (Plate XXVIII, b). How many, exactly, it is difficult to state now, as we were not the first to examine the grave. When we opened a grave in 1903, Dr. Shawe carried home three of the skulls. He took measurements of them and writes with regard to them in his letter of the 14th November 1905, as follows: "All the skulls I got are very decidedly egg-shaped. The measurements taken with an ordinary pair of compasses (we have no proper 'callipers' here) along the antero-posterior and longest transverse diameter of the roof of the skull are (approximately) $6\frac{3}{4} \times 5$ inches, $6\frac{3}{4} \times 5\frac{1}{4}$ inches, and $6\frac{3}{4} \times 5\frac{1}{4}$ inches. Against these, the similar measurements of a skull which I got in Baltistan from a Musulman grave, presumably that of a Balti, are $6\frac{5}{8} \times 5\frac{5}{8}$ inches." If we convert these measurements into the ordinary centigrade formulas of cephalic indexes, we obtain the following numbers: three skulls from the Leh grave: 74,70; 77,77; and 77,77. Balti skull 82,82. Unfortunately, on our visit to Leh last year, even a pair of compasses could not be obtained, and I therefore cannot give any numbers. But as I have acquired an experienced eye for forms of skulls, I venture to state that all the skulls we found in the grave last year, were most distinctly dolichocephalic, and the formulas 74 to 77 would probably suit them all. We had also an opportunity to compare them with two skulls taken by Mr. Schmitt from the graves below Leh which date

[1] This photograph was reproduced in Miss Duncan's "*A Summer Ride through Western Tibet,*" p. 148, where the painted ornament appears quite distinctly.

[2] *Ind. Ant.*, Vol. XXXIV, pp. 203 ff.

Plate XXIX.

a. Bronze objects from Dard graves, Leh.

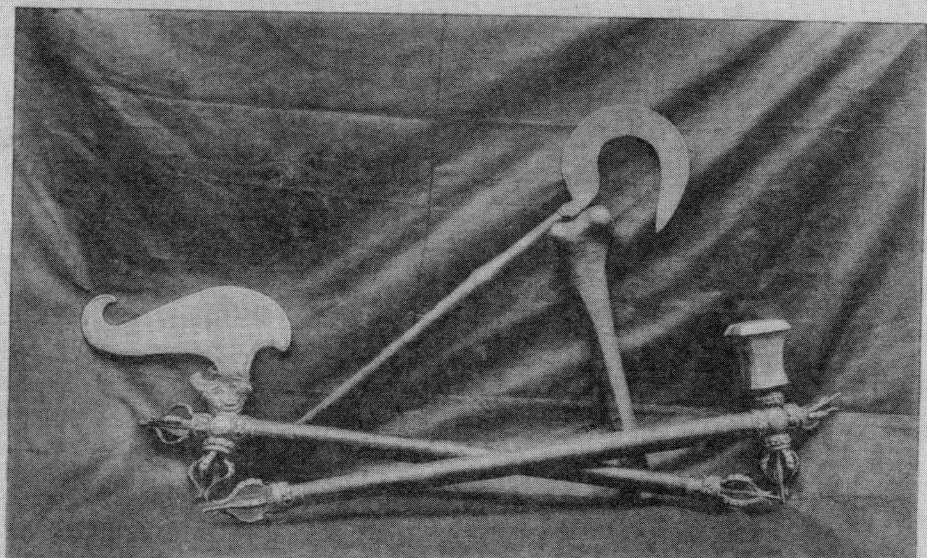

b. Implements used in devil dances, Leh.

from the last epidemic of small-pox in Leh, about a hundred years ago. These skulls from the small-pox graves appeared to be decidedly brachycephalic, when compared with those from the ancient grave. As dolichocephalic heads are a characteristic mark of the Dards of Hanu, Da, and other Dard places of Ladakh, we are led to believe that the people who built the ancient graves were probably of Dard stock ; at any rate they were not of Tibetan, but of North Indian origin.

Besides human skulls, a head of a sheep, and a horn of an ox were also found in the grave. These are apparently remains of a sacrifice, or gifts to the dead.

The grave contained also a number of bronze implements, some in fairly good preservation (Plate XXIX, a). Most of them were, however, much corroded, and covered with a thick layer of verdigris. First of all, I may mention small square leaflets of thin bronze furnished with an embossed ring, of which we found hundreds. Whether they were used for ornamental purposes, or as coins, I find it impossible to decide. Then there were numerous bronze beads, of round as well as of oblong shape, small and large, the largest thicker than a finger. Later on we discovered little pendants of bronze, of bell-like form, with triangular holes and a ring at the top. They were probably inserted between the bronze beads of the necklace. When we took photos of the bronze implements and other articles, we found a glass bead among the bronze beads. It was of mother-o-pearl colour, and looked like Roman or Greek glass. Dr. Marshall informs me, however, that this kind of glass is found all over Asia.

Once, when I had made arrangements to go to the grave and continue my exploration, I was prevented from doing so by an attack of malarial fever. Then Mr. and Mrs. Reichel of the Moravian Mission offered to go in my place, and they brought home several more very interesting finds. In particular, there were a number of bronze buttons of various sizes with a loop on the reverse. Some of them were of ordinary size, about half an inch in diameter, but others were much larger, nearly two inches in diameter. The largest had a scalloped edge, like an Indian one-anna piece. None of them contained an inscription. The smallest were quite plain, the largest had an elaborate spiral ornament, and those of medium size, a star ornament. I suppose that these buttons were worn by ancient officials as a distinguishing mark of rank, just as is the case in China nowadays.

Some other round pieces of bronze may have served as mirrors, such as are still found in Ladakh. Some fragments were probably the remains of bronze pots.

On the 28th August, three of our Christians went again to the graves of their own accord. They found many more bronze implements, several of them in fairly good preservation ; for instance, a can with a spout of excellent workmanship, though quite plain and without any ornament ; a seal with a cross-pattern engraved on it; an entire bracelet with a pattern of little circles. Although we could trace decorative designs on several fragments, there was no vestige of any script.

In addition let me say that fragments of iron implements came to light also, and that Mr. and Mrs. Reichel discovered the only gold article that was in the grave. It is of a shape similar to the mouthpiece of a trumpet, but its purpose is not known. Its ornamentation is a curved form of the Greek key.

After this description of the grave and our finds in it, let me enter into the question of its date and the nationality of the people who built it. As I have pointed out already, in connection with the rGya graves, the condition of these graves calls to mind at once the description of the form of burial practised in the "Empire of the Eastern Women," of the Chinese historians. There we read: "When a person of rank dies, they strip off the skin, and put the flesh and bones mixed with gold powder into a vase, and then bury it.........At the burial of the sovereign, several tens of the great ministers and relatives are buried at the same time!" The latter statement about this gruesome custom may account for the great number of skulls, sometimes as many as twenty, which are found in a single grave. As the grave contained large bronze buttons, obviously a mark of high rank, it is very probable that the Leh grave actually contained the remains of several "great ministers." This "Empire of the Eastern Women" has been described in the *Sui shu*, a book which was compiled in c. 586 A.D. Here it is called Nü-Kuo. Hiuen Tsiang also heard of this empire, and a little after his time, we read that the last queen died and was replaced by a king. The frontiers of this curious empire are given by the *Sui shu* as well as by Hiuen Tsiang. They are: Khotan, Sampaha (Ladakh), Brahmapura (Chamba State), and Tibet. From these definitions we may conclude that the empire comprised the Tibetan provinces of Guge and Ruthog, and possibly Eastern Ladakh. The empire was a Tibetan one, according to our Chinese authorities, and it therefore appears strange that the skulls of the Leh grave are not those of Tibetans, but of Aryans. My explanation would be that it is very probable that portions of Ladakh were for a time at least included in this empire. The value of our grave finds lies in this that they afford us a glimpse of the general state of civilisation which prevailed in this empire. As regards its date, the presence of iron besides bronze precludes the fixing of any very early date, say before the Christian era. The absence of any form of writing in the grave would perhaps point to a time earlier than 586 A.D., at which time, according to the Chinese, the Indian characters were used in the empire. In my opinion the grave dates from between 1 and 500 A.D.

Fortunately for me, I had finished my investigations, when Mr. Chatterji, Director of Archæology in the Kashmīr State, arrived in Leh with the message that it was the wish of the Maharaja that no further excavations of any kind should be undertaken in Kashmīr State territory.

The village of Skara (*sGa-ra* in native documents) is situated south of Leh and forms a kind of suburb of that town. On the 3rd September, I visited the ruins of the sGar-rtse Monastery at Skara. According to K. Marx this is the monastery "for four lamas only," founded by King 'aBum-lde, about 500 years ago. It was built on a crag resembling an elephant. This little monastery was destroyed by the Ḍogrās, at least so I was told. There was also another small temple erected below the ruin, occupied by one lama who belongs to the 'aBrug-pa order. No tradition regarding King 'aBum-lde has been preserved in the locality.

The village of Skara was formerly situated on a rocky spur to the right of the Leh valley, where there are still many ruined houses. The chief reason for evacuating the former site was said to be an epidemic. There are still many graves in a side-valley near it.

Probably the most ancient monastery at Skara is the one which is situated in a little ravine, between the rGar-rtse Monastery and the ruined village. Four walls are still standing, and there are traces of red colour (frescoes) on the walls. Close by is an underground room, in which we found a human skeleton of recent date.

Below this ruined monastery, there is a *mchod-rten* shaped like a "Mon *mchod-rten.*" It consists of a lower square room, on the top of which is placed a round pyramid. Locally this *mchod-rten* is known as the grave of a king. It actually contained human bones, notably fragments of a skull.

Not far from it, on the plain, there is a group of three ancient-looking *mchod-rten* of the usual shape. A man from Skara had extracted from them several ancient household utensils filled with grain. Out of these, he sold me a sieve cup made of very thin copper leaf.

At Skara my attention was drawn to a rather modern-looking round *mchod-rten* which was hollow and furnished with a door. Inside of it we found several cremation tablets of ancient style, some with Indian inscriptions. I was told that a few years ago an ancient *mchod-rten* was destroyed by a Muhammadan who built a house for himself at Skara. He carried all the tablets found in the old *mchod-rten* to the new one and hid them there. In the desert below Skara, there are the low mounds of several ancient *mchod-rten.* We found in them cremation tablets with Indian legends, very much like those at rGya.

In the desert between Skara and Spithug (*dPe-thub*) on the Indus, on a plateau below the western mountain range, there are the ruins of a large building called *Chad-pai-lha-khang*, "Temple of Punishment." The outer wall towards the east has a length of more than 100 feet. There is no wall on the west side. Perhaps it was left incomplete. I made a plan of it. I was told that in the days of the Ladakhi kings (no personal name could be remembered) two men were ordered to erect this temple as a punishment for some crime. No woodwork remains, and there are no traces of images or frescoes on the site.

In the desert east of Leh, there is a large *mchod-rten* of yellow colour, which is called *Ma-ṇi-gser-mo.* Popular tradition asserts that it is one of the most ancient here. On the western side of the dome there is a niche with a complete figure of a seated Buddha. It must formerly have had such niches on all four sides. Attached to it are two or three *mchod-rten* of more recent date. One of them was open, and contained all sorts of old rubbish, *viz.*, fragments of idols, pages of books, charms, and cremation tablets. We took away some of the better preserved tablets. In 1906 we obtained from the same *mchod-rten* a few sheets of manuscript in a modern Indian dialect which were sent to Dr. Vogel, for examination. As King *Seng-ge-rnam-rgyal* (c. 1600 A.D.) exhibited strong sympathies with the religions of India, the manuscripts may date from his time. Of more recent date are the pages of a Sanskrit book in Dēvanāgarī character. This book was used by the Ḍōgrās after the wars, 1834—1842 A.D., when they established a

Sanskrit school at Leh; but the school soon came to an end, and the book was then placed in this *mchod-rten.* *mChod-rtens* of this kind, which serve chiefly as receptacles for old and useless manuscripts, remind me strongly of the Jewish Genizas.

The hill behind the town of Leh is called rNam-rgyal-rtsē-mo. On the top there are the ruins of the royal palace which was built by bKra-shis-rnam-rgyal (c. 1520 A.D.) As I had often visited this site during my former stay at Leh, I had not intended to visit it again on this occasion. Owing, however, to the return of the Italian, Dr. Filipo de Filipi, of the Duke of Abruzzi's mountaineering expedition, with his wife and brother, it was decided to show them some of the sights of Leh. One forenoon was accordingly set apart for a trip to the top of rNam-rgyal-rtsē-mo, Mr. Reichel of the Moravian Mission accompanying us. I had no reason to regret having been of the party, for on this occasion I noticed a few things which I had overlooked before.

The Maitrēya temple on the rNam-rgyal-rtse-mo is apparently the oldest, and is in all probability identical with the "Red College" built by King 'aBum-lde, 500 years ago. It contains an inscription in praise of the reformer bTsong-kha-pa; and, among many other frescoes, a picture of the bKra-shis-lhun-po Monastery in Tibet. This picture shows the group of buildings which make up the large monastery, and there is a long inscription attached to it which is distributed all over the picture. Although this inscription, as well as the other one, is in very bad preservation, several sentences can be made out. As masons or architects are therein mentioned, it probably refers to a restoration of the temple. The name of a great minister, Phyag-rdor, is given in one of the inscriptions. He is possibly the same minister Phyag-rdor who is mentioned in the Daru rock inscription. I am inclined to think, for reasons which I will state later on, that Phyag-rdor served under Lha-chen Bha-gan, c. 1470—1500 A.D. In that case the inscriptions in this temple may date from the latter half of the 15th century. I ordered both of them to be copied. On the right and left hand side of the huge Maitrēya statue, there are fragmentary traces of two other statues which once stood there. This is in agreement with a statement in the *rGyal-rabs.*

There is another temple, of red colour, on the top of the same hill, namely, the temple of "the four Lords" (*mGon-khang*). This is the very one which was erected by king bKra-shis-rnam-rgyal c. 400 years ago, as stated in the chronicles. K. Marx was assured of its existence by bKra-shis-btsan-phel, his lama friend, but he was unable to visit it. It contains very artistically executed figures of "the four Lords" which are about from three to eight feet high. The principal figure represents rNam-thos-sras (Vaiśravaṇa). All four figures were covered with blankets; but these were removed with the exception of the one which covered Vaiśravaṇa. With regard to the latter image we were told that it is exhibited only once a year. The lama showed us, however, a fresco of Vaiśravaṇa on the wall, where he is represented in sexual union with his Śakti. As these images belong to the few in Ladakh which can be dated, they are of the greatest importance for the history of Tibetan art. Among the frescoes on the walls, I found one on the right hand side of the door which represented gorgeously dressed men with Yarkandi turbans on their heads. I could not understand the presence of these Muhammadan portraits in a Buddhist temple, until the lama in charge explained that they were Ladakhi kings. By the side of the picture, there is a long inscription in gold on indigo tinted paper, which mentions King bKra-shis-rnam-rgyal, the builder of the temple. From this inscription it appears that the picture represents this king who testified to his close attachment to the Turkomans by dressing exactly like them. As regards the Turkoman invasion under Sultan Ḥaidar during his time, it is very difficult to reconcile the Tibetan with the Turkish account. The latter is found in the Tārīkh-i-Rashīdī. Not only according to the Tibetan chronicles, but also according to inscriptions from Ladakh, he gained a signal victory over the Turkomans. According to the Tārīkh-i-Rashīdī, on the other hand, he was a servant of the Turkomans who held him in little honour.[1] I have come to the conviction that he was a very clever politician. bKra-shis-rnam-rgyal knew very well that he could not resist the first violent attack of the Turkomans with an armed force. He, therefore, concluded a treaty with them, and apparently took their side. He then very cleverly enlisted the energy of the Turkomans on his side, for co-ercing his disobedient vassal princes and unpleasant neighbours. Some of them were Muhammadans; for instance, the chiefs of Suru, Sod, Baltistan, and one in Nubra. It is rather remarkable, therefore, that the Turkomans actually went against and fought them. Whether the Lhasa expedition came to an end a few marches beyond the Manasarowar Lake, or eight marches from Lhasa, as stated in the Tārīkh, does not matter much. In the eyes of the Ladakhi kings, the chiefs of Guge as well as the Central Tibetans required suppressing. After the Turks had spent all their strength on the enemies of the Ladakhis, the latter rose against them themselves, and turned them out of the country. As the Ladakhi chronicles tell us, the corpses of the slain Turks were placed before the idols of the temple of the four Lords (*mGon-khang*). This is the reason why the male members of the royal family of Ladakh are shown wearing the Turkestan dress in the frescoes, whilst the female members are dressed in true Ladakhi fashion, wearing on their heads the *berag*, a leather strap covered with turquoises.

Above the temple of the four Lords (*mGon-khang*) are the ruins of bKra-shis-rnam-rgyal's palace. They include a little Lamaist monastery which is of no particular interest. Ruins of other parts of the ancient palace, for instance watch-towers, are found all along the ridge of the rNam-rgyal-rtse-mo hill. Some of the ruins are of a decidedly earlier date than the reign of bKra-shis-rnam-rgyal. For instance, I am told that the foundations of a certain round tower are commonly known by the name of *'aBrog-pai-mkhar*, "Dard castle." It may, therefore, be attributed to a building which was erected before the Tibetan conquest of Ladakh, in c. 900 A.D. A man from Leh brought me a fragment of a copper pot, which he said he had found on the top of rNam-rgyal-rtse-mo. It contained an inscription in ancient characters, giving the name of a prince: *rGyal sras dBang-(nya ?)-gsing dbang-po*, "Prince dBang-(nya ?) gsing dbang-po." As the word *rnam-rgyal* does not occur in the name, it may be the name of a younger son of a king of the first dynasty of Ladakhi kings. In the

[1] *Tārīkh-i-Rashīdī*, pp. 418 ff., 423 and 460.

Ladakh chronicles we read that one of their early kings had placed the bones of Buddha in his elephant incarnation on the top of the same hill. I made inquiries as to their whereabouts and was told that they had been deposited in a *mchod-rten* which was utterly destroyed by the Baltis about 1580 A.D. No trace of the relics remains.

On our way down from the top of the hill, we passed by the Great Palace of Leh which was erected by king Seng-ge-rnam-rgyal in c. 1620 A.D. As I knew from former visits, it is practically empty. We did not enter it, but photographed the carved wooden gate, the famous "Lion Gate" of Ladakh (Plate XXX, b). One of the rooms of the palace contains heaps of old manuscripts. All the paper is indigo-tinted, and the writing is in gold, silver and copper. As this collection probably represents the old royal library, or part of it, I asked Mr. Chatterji of the Kashmir State, to make arrangements to put the manuscripts into order again.

I heard rumours of the existence of ancient Indian Buddhist manuscripts at Leh and in other parts of Ladakh, Munshi dPal-rgyas, the representative of the To-go-che family being reported to be in possession of one. Fortunately for me, Munshi dPal-rgyas himself arrived in Leh soon after I had heard this, and readily showed me his old book. It was, however, not of Indian, but of Tibetan origin, being the eighth volume of the Tibetan translation of the Prajñā-pāramitā, and written throughout in 11th century orthography, gold on indigo-tinted paper. The wooden cover (Plate XXXVII, b) was ornamented with very beautiful ancient carvings, for which reason a photo was taken of the same. Munshi dPal-rgyas emphatically denied the existence of Indian manuscripts at the Hemis monastery, in spite of a rumour to that effect which had been brought to us. But he said that he had heard of the existence of a book, written in Lañthsā characters at the Sanid (or Muni) monastery in Zaṅgskar. This book may be identical with the old 'palm leaf' shown to the Rev. Mr. Bateson on the occasion of his journey through Zaṅgskar in 1908.

Mr. Meebold[1] also makes the statement that he was shown 'palm leaf' books at the Rangdum monastery of Zaṅgskar. These statements await verification. It is strange that Munshi dPal-rgyas should have bought his ancient book at Lhasa, as he says. The Prajñā-pāramitā, as already stated, was translated into Tibetan by Lama Rin-chen-bzang-po, who was a West Tibetan, and most of the copies of his book were distributed among the West Tibetan monasteries of his time. Sending them to Lhasa would have been of no use, as Buddhism had practically disappeared from Central Tibet in the 11th century, being introduced into the country again from West Tibet and Khams. But at a much later time, possibly only a century or so ago, a number of important books were carried off to Lhasa. So I was told at the Alchi monastery where no ancient manuscripts now remain. The history of Munshi dPal-rgyas' book may therefore be as follows: It was originally written for one of the Western monasteries. Then it was carried off to Lhasa; and was there again sold to a pilgrim for a high price.

---

[1] *Indien*, p. 264.

a. View of Leh.

b. Lion Gate of King's Palace, Leh.

Here I may add that I made another find of manuscripts of a very different character at Leh. In the Mission library at Leh, I found a good number of my old hand-written books which I had collected in former years and quite forgotten. As they contain many hundreds of pages of hitherto unpublished folklore, I carried them off with me and sold them to Government for the benefit of the Mission, together with another collection of unpublished folklore which I had still in my possession. Among these latter manuscripts was a sheet which contained a kind of introduction to the cryptic alphabet used in Tibetan seals. The inscription on the Dalai Lama's seal, among many others, is written in this alphabet. How gratifying it was to find that my sheet from Leh proved to be the correct key to the reading of the Dalai Lama's seal.[1] Among my treasures are several hymnals relating to the pre-Buddhist religion of Ladakh which, I hope, it will be possible to translate in course of time.

At Changspa, a village half a mile from Leh, there is the large residence of a family of ministers (*bka-blon*) of the former Ladakhi kingdom. In a garden-house (*rab-gsal*) belonging to the minister's estate are the remains of frescoes illustrating the Kesar-Saga. Several years ago, I ordered one of them to be copied by a local painter. This time, I had photos taken of three of them, in addition to a copy in colours executed by a local artist. The frescoes in the garden house will soon be gone altogether, and as pictures relating to the Kesar-Saga are very rare, I was resolved to save for science what could be saved. All the frescoes in this hall refer to a chapter of the Kesar-Saga, entitled *Ljang-dmag*, "the war against the country of Ljang," as we find it in the literary version of the Kesar-Saga. Let me remark that the famous epic of Tibet, the Kesar or Gesar Saga, is preserved in two versions which are very different from one another. One of them, the oral version, exists only in the mouths of the people, whilst the literary version is found in several manuscripts in Ladakh, and possibly even in woodprints. All my publications with regard to the Kesar-Saga deal only with its oral version. A manuscript of the literary version of the Saga is in the hands of the present ex-minister of Changspa. From an article by Schiefner[2] it is evident that it was the Changspa minister's Gesar manuscript, which was copied for the Imperial collection of manuscripts in St. Petersburg. Up to the present, nobody seems to have been able to read and translate it. This is very natural, considering the extreme difficulties of its language. K. Marx says that it is written in the *Khams* dialect. As there are people here at Changspa who can read and understand the Saga, their knowledge ought to be utilised for the benefit of science. I copied all the wall-inscriptions relative to the frescoes which it was still possible to decipher. The following notes on the dress of the pre-Buddhist divinities represented in the frescoes, may be of iconographical interest: dBang-po-rgyab-zhin has a red coat, and white cloak with blue seam; Gog-bzang-lha-mo is dressed in white, but her trousers are red, and she has a green shawl; one of her sons (Don-yod?) has a red jacket with green seams; another of her sons (Don-ldan?)

---

[1] Cf. *J. R. A. S.* 1910, p. 1205.

[2] Publications of the Imperial Academy of Science at St. Petersburg, entitled "*Des Missionar Jäschke's Bemühungen um eine Handschrift des Gesar.*"

has a white and green jacket and red trousers; Kesar has a red coat, and a white cloak with green seams; he sits on a red carpet, and the background behind him is blue.

There is a large pyramidal *mchod-rten* at Changspa which is called "the Kings' *mchod-rten*" by Europeans, and bKra-shis-sgo-mang by the natives (Plate XXXI, b). The present inhabitants of Changspa say that it was not erected by their ancestors, but by Turks or Mongols on one of their expeditions to Ladakh. The latter assumption is, however, difficult to believe. This old *mchod-rten* may go back to the times of the Mons or Dards. It is surrounded by rows of one hundred-and-eight *mchod-rten*. And this goes to prove that it cannot be of much later date than the 15th century, and may very well be of much earlier date. The *mchod-rten* has received its name *sgo-mang* "many doors" on account of the many little niches with which it is furnished. In all probability these niches once contained Buddhist images, but none now remain. On the whole, however, this old *mchod-rten* has been wonderfully well preserved and is still regularly whitewashed.

Not far from it are several stone sculptures in relievo which probably also go back to Mon or Dard times (c. 700—900 A.D.). The best of them shows a standing Buddha with Bōdhisattvas on his right and left (Plate XXXII, a). The one on his right who carries a vase is Maitrēya. The one on his left, and higher up, with a flower in his hand, is Avalōkitēśvara[1]. Above him, in the air, we see two flying figures (Gandharvas ?) On the reverse of the same stone is a four-armed figure, perhaps a Maitrēya, and a *mchod-rten* is carved on one of the narrow sides (Plate XXXII, b). I will not now describe all the stone sculptures of Leh and surroundings, because it would take too long, for there are many of them. A number have been mentioned or described in my article, "Archæology in West Tibet."[2] But I will mention another sculpture at Changspa near a group of houses, lower down, not far from the brook. It is enclosed by a masonry wall. This figure is furnished with an unusual headdress and seems to represent a Buddhist priest of the Mon or Dard times.

On a rocky hill to the west of Changspa, there are several crematories and some ancient *mchod-rten*. Higher up, on the same hill, are the ruins of the Ribug (Ri-phug) monastery. As the monastery was reported to be of ancient date, I visited it but could not, however, discover any inscriptions or documents referring to it. One of the *mchod-rten* close by is of an ancient type, but the cremation tablets contained in it are unfortunately without inscriptions. The temple hall being roofless, nothing remains of former frescoes except a few traces of colour on the plaster.

The ruined *mchod-rten* called Tsu-bkra-shis-'od-mtho is the largest in Ladakh. It is situated about 1½ mile from the Commissioner's compound, a little higher up in the Leh valley. We measured the circumference of its base at about 10 feet above the ground, a height at which the masonry rose clear above the surrounding rubbish, and found it to be 550 feet. It was erected by king 'aBum-lde, in order to cover up a crag which was believed to be harmful to the country, and is now in a very dilapidated condition.

---

[1] The kneeling figure on the proper left looks more like a human devotee. [Ed.]

[2] *Ind. Ant.*, Vol. XXXV, p 237, and XXXVI, pp. 85 and 148 ff.

PLATE XXXI.

a. Mon *mchod-rten* at rGya.

b. bKra-shis-sgo-mang, ancient *mchod-rten* at Changspa, Leh.

PLATE XXXII.

a. Rock-cut sculpture of Buddha with attendants, Changspa, Leh.

b. Rock-cut sculpture of Maitreya (?), Changspa, Leh.

On the 9th September, I went to the Teu-gser-po or Tiserru (as ordinary people call this ruined *mchod-rten*), accompanied by Mr. Schmitt of the Moravian Mission, Lobzang, a Christian and Meteorological Observer at Leh, Pindi Lal, and the Khalasi. Our object was to study the inside of the structure. When we had climbed up to half its height, we found a hole in the surface, the opening of a narrow shaft. Lobzang went down first of all. He came to a narrow room of triangular shape, which was perfectly empty. We then tried to dig a new hole in a different place, when suddenly a number of men, who had been working in the fields, rushed towards us terrified. They implored us not to open the Tiserru, as such a procedure would bring incalculable misfortune to the country. From their remonstrances we learned something about the history of the old monument. The story reminds us of European fairy tales, such as that of the devil being caught in a bottle. In King 'aBum-lde's times, there used to live a demon in a cavity of the rock Teu-gser-po. This devil, who had fire proceeding from his mouth, roamed about the country and destroyed the king's palace and portions of the town of Leh. To exorcise him, the huge *stūpa* was built above his abode. If we opened the *stūpa*, the people feared that the evil spirit which had been kept under custody for 500 years, might once more attain liberty. We pointed to the old holes in the building, and observed that he might have escaped long ago. But that was of no avail. At the same time, we were told that the old *stūpa* was not only a repository for devils, but for heavy gales also. When in the days of King 'aBum-lde, the country suffered severely from storms, several large clay pots were held against the wind with their mouths open. As soon as the wind subsided, their mouths were closed, and they were stored up in the *stūpa* with the storms contained in them. People were afraid we might find and open this ancient pottery, and that the country would be plagued with heavy gales again.

From the opposition which we met in this case from the peasants of Leh, it was plain to me that it is difficult to do archæological work in an inhabited country. The chronicles of Ladakh have only a very short note on this *mchod-rten*. They simply state that it was built, because "some fatality" had occurred at Leh. I am still of opinion that the idea of a devil living in this place has something to do with the ancient graves described above. These graves are situated in proximity to, and some of them possibly below the *mchod-rten*.

On the same day, I went higher up the Leh valley, following the desert road to the west of the cultivated area, accompanied by Pindi Lal and the Khalasi. Close to the village of dGonpa, we passed by the ruined site of an old town with *mchod-rten* of ancient type near it. There we found also a stone sculpture of some Bōdhisattva, enshrined in a masonry wall, with a *lhatho* (altar of the pre-Buddhist religion), in front of it (Plate XXXIV, a). As usual, the altar was furnished with many ibex horns. This ruined town may be the original site of the present village of dGonpa.

Marching upwards in the side-valley to the left of the village of dGonpa, we came to the ruins of an ancient temple, which is generally known by the name of Gya-mthsa. I had visited it occasionally, ten or twelve years ago, when I was stationed at Leh as a missionary. But the late Dr. Shawe of Leh was the first to draw attention to the fact that there are traces of circular medallions on two of its walls. In that respect rGya-mthsa reminds us of the ruined monasteries of Basgo[1] and Chigtan. Inside and below the medallions, Dr. Shawe noticed holes in the wall, as if sticks had once been stuck into it. He even found fragments of wood in two of the holes (according to his letter of the 27th October 1905). He supposed that these sticks had once served to support images. Our observations at the Tabo monastery of Spiti fully confirm Dr. Shawe's supposition. As will be remembered, in the Tabo monastery we found thirty-two raised medallions on the walls of the temple hall, and an image placed in front of each of them. After digging only a little way into the mass of débris below one of the medallions at rGyamthsa, we came across several pieces of plaster composed of clay, straw, and linen. This is exactly the material these images are made of. From our observations it follows that rGya-mthsa is probably of the same time as the Chigtan, Basgo and Tabo monasteries, *i.e.*, of the times of Rin-chen-bzang-po (c. 1000 A.D.). But let me add that my assumption is not supported by popular tradition. The present inhabitants of the valley do not even believe that the ruin is that of a temple, but assert that it once served as a summer house for a minister (*bkā-blon-gyi-dbyar-sa*).

On the other side of some adjoining fields, there are several ancient ruined *mchod-rten.* In one of them I found cremation tablets of the "miniature *stūpa*" type. When I threw one of them to the ground, it broke to pieces, and out of it came a very neat little tablet with an inscription in an ancient form of Śāradā. The inscription again contains the *Yē dharmā* formula, and its characters belong to the 11th century. Owing to its extraordinary receptacle, the characters of the inscription were as distinct as any I had seen up to this. I made an accurate copy of the inscription on the same day, and I am glad I did so. For, when my collection of clay tablets arrived at Simla several months later, the distinctness of most of the inscriptions had suffered much, in spite of very careful packing. Although I opened several more "miniature *stūpas*" in search of inscribed tablets, I did not find any other specimens.

On the 17th September, I visited Munshi dPal-rgyas in his own house, called *To-go-che*, at Leh. Mention has already been made of his old Tibetan book. This time he showed us some of the contents of his private temple, several printed flags of no particular importance, a few idols of the ordinary type, and a mask of an *Agu* (hero) of the Kesar-Saga (Plate XXXIII, a). This *Agu*, dGra-lha, who is worshipped in the Munshi's house, is also represented among the frescoes of Changspa. As I am told, several more masks representing Agus of the Kesar-Saga can be found also at the Lamayuru monastery. According to popular tradition, Lamayuru used to be the centre of the Bon religion of Ladakh. Munshi dPal-rgyas told me plainly that he was fully convinced that the religion of the Kesar-Saga and the Bon religion were absolutely the same. As will be remembered, the study of the Songs of the *Shar-rgan* festival at Poo leads to the same conclusion.[2] Then Munshi dPal-rgyas showed us the head of an

---

[1] See also beneath pp. 86, 100.

[2] *Cf.* above p. 21.

PLATE XXXIII.

a. Mask of Agu dGra-lha of the Kesar Saga, in possession of Munshi dPal-rgyas, Leh.

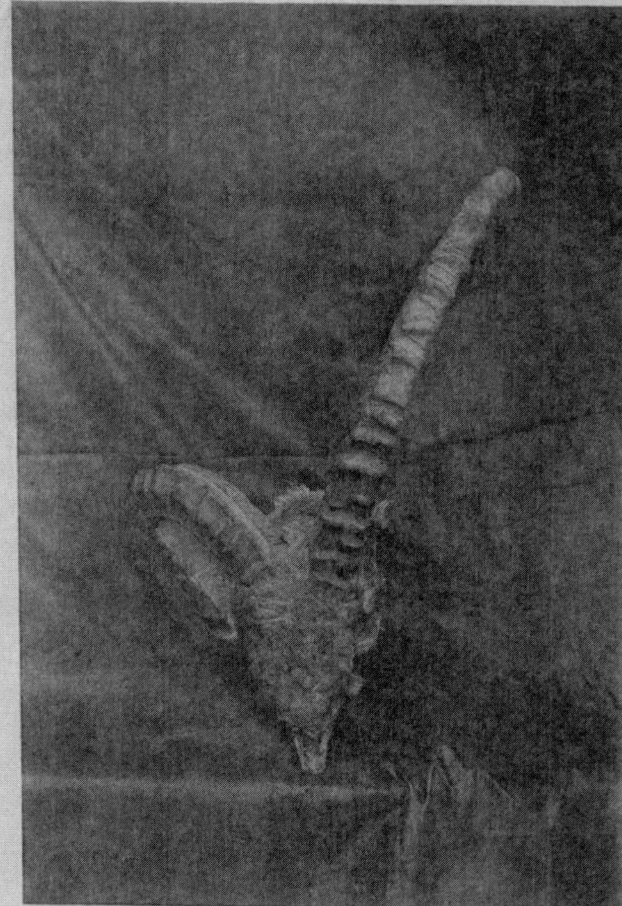

b. Head of ibex, believed to be that of Buddha in his deer incarnation, in possession of Munshi dPal-rgyas, Leh.

PLATE XXXIV.

a. Sculpture in ruined town at dGon-pa near Leh.

b. Rock-cut image of Maitreya on the Yarkandi road, Leh.

ibex in his possession, with the right horn crooked like an ammonite (Plate XXXIII, b). This head was found in Ladakh, and the famous lama bKra-shis-bstan-'aphel, who died in 1890, pronounced it to be the head of Buddha in his antelope incarnation. It is, of course, treated with proper respect by its owner, who will not part with it for anything. This is the second "bone of Buddha," which we have come across in Leh. The first is contained in a gaily coloured clay tablet which was brought to us for sale. It was said to have come from Lhasa, and the official seal stamped on its reverse indicates that a homœopathic measure of a Buddha relic was mixed up with the clay composing it. Mention has been made of another Buddha bone, that of Buddha in his elephant incarnation. With regard to the latter, Munshi dPal-rgyas said that it was a tooth of the Buddha elephant on which the mystic syllable *Oṁ* could be plainly read.

As I had suspected, Munshi dPal-rgyas turned out to be the writer of Dr. Marx's Manuscript C. Through Mr. Reichel's exertions I have come into possession of copies of the last two chapters of his *rGyalrabs*, and a comparison with Dr. Marx's translation shows that Munshi dPal-rgyas' text coincides with such passages of this version as are marked C-MS. As regards the "History of the Ḍōgrā war," Munshi dPal-rgyas has written no less than three different versions of it. He would perhaps never have thought of writing one, if Dr. Marx had not asked him to do so. The first account he wrote probably soon after the latter's arrival at Leh in 1886. This account was lithographed at Leh, and used as a school book. The Munshi seems to have soon found out that this account contained several mistakes, and therefore he wrote another version which he presented to Dr. Marx apparently in 1890; but the latter did not live to translate and publish the whole of this.[1] As Dr. Karl Marx's text was believed to be entirely lost, the text and a translation of Munshi dPal-rgyas' first version of his account of the Ḍōgrā war was published.[2] Mr. Reichel's manuscript contains the third version of Munshi dPal-rgyas' account. It is by far the best, and much fuller than his two preceding versions. I hope soon to be able to publish a translation of it. From what has been said, it follows that Munshi dPal-rgyas is quite an unusual man. Who else among the natives would have kept a certain subject of scientific interest in his mind for about twenty-five years, without being paid for it? Who would have continued his inquiries with so much patience and, discarding all his previous work, have started afresh, when more recent research showed him the truth in a new light? What a gain it would be to science if all historians were so conscientious!

Besides those already mentioned, it is necessary to refer to a few more buildings of importance at Leh. The mosque at the upper end of the Bazar is not the first of its kind at Leh.[3] The first mosque is a very small building; but the time of its erection has not yet been fixed. The Christian church is situated to the west of the "Great Palace" of Leh, behind the Bazar. North-west of the New Bazar is a small temple,

[1] One page of his translation is to be found in *J. A. S. B.*, Vol. LXIII, pp. 106 ff.

[2] *J. A. S. B.*, Vol. LXXI, pp. 21 ff.

[3] According to an inscription on a wooden board, preserved in the principal mosque, it was erected by a certain Shaikh Muhi-ud-Din in 1077 A. H., *i.e.*, apparently after the battle of Basgo.

belonging to the Hemis monastery. It is said to have been erected at the same time as this convent.

The old kings had two pleasure gardens near Leh. One of them was the *bKar-bzo* garden. It is the present Joint Commissioner's compound. The other one is the *Mu-rtse* garden. It is situated south of Leh, near a ridge of rocky hills running across the desert The latter garden contains the royal Polo ground (*Shagaran*). It is believed to have been planted by king Seng-ge-rnam-rgyal, c. 1600 A. D., who brought the game of Polo from Baltistan.

Below Leh, at the Tewar gorge, is the longest *maṇi* wall in the country. It was built by king bDel-dan-rnam-rgyal, and has the following measurements: Length: 1,931 feet 8 inches. Height: varying between 6 feet, 7 feet, 7·4 feet, 7·8 feet. Breadth: 39·6 feet. The *mchod-rten* at both ends are built on square ground plans, each side of the square being 49 feet long.

In conclusion, let me say that the Wazir of Leh, Chaudhari Khuṣhi Muhammad, a very well educated gentleman, and the Tahsildar, did their utmost to make me comfortable during my stay.

CHAPTER IV.

From the Indus to the Jehlam.

On Tuesday, the 21st September, we left Leh and marched to the village of sNyemo, 18 miles distant. Five miles below Leh, at Spithug (dPe-thub; map Pittuk), the road passes by the rock, on which King 'aBum-lde built his famous monastery 500 years ago. This monastery can be entered only with special permission of the *sKu-shog* [1] and as such a *sKu-shog* was not present at Leh, we had to give up the idea of visiting it. On the top of the same rock can be seen also the ruins of some older building, probably a castle. On the plain below, we found a ruined *mchod-rten* of ancient type, which contained cremation tablets of the shape of miniature *stūpas*. These tablets had an inscription in Indian characters impressed on them. Pandit Mukund Ram of Kashmir, to whom we showed such a tablet, was fortunately able to read the inscription. It again contains the *Yē dharmā* formula, which in this case is written in an early type of Dēvanāgarī characters, say, of the 11th or 12th century A.D. On the western prominence of the rock we noticed several very flat relievos, representing bTsong-kha-pa and his disciples. It will be remembered that the Spithug monastery was erected in honour of that reformer. This type of relievo which probably dates from the 15th or 16th century, is very different from the old type as it is represented at Leh and Changspa. The new type reminds us of the flat, carved figures often found on slabs placed on *maṇi* walls.

The trade road passes through the lowest extremity of the village of Phyang. This is a pity, for the village is well worth a visit. I should have visited it, in spite of everything, if at the time of our expedition, the thought had dawned upon me, that Phyang

---

[1] *sKu-shog*, the incarnation of its first abbot.

(spelt *Phyi-dbang*; map Phayang) is probably the most ancient town of Western Tibet. Unfortunately, I had not then yet started my studies of the geographical names contained in the account of gNya-khri-btsan-po's empire. Subsequent studies have shown me that practically all the places mentioned in the Ladakhi account of gNya-khribtsan-po's kingdom exist in Ladakh, and that the village of Phyi-dbang is in all probability identical with Phyi-dbang-stag-rtse, the earliest capital of Tibet.[1]

The Phyang (Phyi-dbang) monastery is a stately building of much later date. It was erected by King bKra-shis-rnam-rgyal (c. 1500—1532 A.D.) and belongs to the 'aBri-khung-pa sect of lamas. This monastery comes into view when the plain on the right bank of the Phyang brook is reached. At this place King bKra-shis-rnam-rgyal raised a long flagstaff on an elaborate pedestal. As we know from the chronicles, this flagstaff was intended to serve as a place of refuge for all those who were guilty of a *crimen læsæ majestatis*. It is quite possible that King bKra-shis thought of the crime committed by himself, when he erected the flagstaff. Had he not plucked out his elder brother's eyes and deprived him of his royal power? No doubt, bKra-shis himself had good reason to embrace the flagstaff most cordially. The pedestal still remains and is generally known by the name of *Thar-chen*, "great flag." From a note in Dr. Marx's "Three Documents" we learn that the Phyi-dbang monastery contains a beautiful collection of ancient armour.

A plain called La-dvags-gong-khai-thang stretches from the village of Phyi-dbang to the village of Umla (Umbla ?) in the west. Halfway between the two is situated the little village of Daru. The *maṇi* walls of Daru contain votive stones mentioning King bDe-ldan-rnam-rgyal, c. 1630 A.D., and a minister Thse-dbang-don-grub (c. 1822 A.D.). These walls have little ruined houses built on one end which are known by the name of *Man Khang* (*Maṇi Khang*). These huts were built by the people who erected the *maṇi* walls, to serve as hospital stables for horses which had become exhausted on the long march across the great plain.

We examined and photographed the rock with sculptures at Daru. Thanks to the historical information contained in the Leh inscriptions of the rNam-rgyal-rtse-mo hill, the sculptures and inscriptions on the Daru rock can nowadays be dated with more certainty than it was possible a few years ago. I made a first attempt at dating them in my article, "Archæology in West Tibet,"[2] when I tried to identify King Lha-chen-kun-dgā-rnam-rgyal, whose name appears on the Daru rock, with Lha-rgyal (c. 1250 A.D.) of the chronicles. But even then I had to assume that part of the inscription was probably of later date, judging by the name of a lama which occurred in it. Now, the rNam-rgyal-rtse-mo inscriptions give the name of a great minister, Phyag-rdor-jo, who is also mentioned on the Daru rock. Phyag-rdor-jo of the rNam-rgyal-rtse-mo inscriptions is plainly stated to have been a contemporary of King

[1] This question has been fully treated in my article, "The Kingdom of *gNya-khri-btsan-po*," *J. A. S. B.* 1910, p. 92. Here we must distinguish between the chronicles of Ladakh and the chronicles of Central Tibet. Whilst the places mentioned in the former book are found in Ladakh, the places mentioned in the latter book are found in the vicinity of Lhasa. See "Yarlung" in the geographical work *'aDzam-gling-ye-shes* translated by S. Ch. Das.

[2] Cf. *Ind. Ant.*, Vol. XXXVI, pp. 89 ff.

bKra-shis-rnam-rgyal. Here at Daru his name is found connected with a king Kun-dgā-rnam-rgyal. The question, therefore, naturally arises: Are bKra-shis-rnam-rgyal and Kun-dgā-rnam-rgyal the names of one and the same king or not? Was *bKra-shis kun-dgā-rnam-rgyal* the full name of this king? Up to the present, only two inscriptions of bKra-shis-rnam-rgyal have been found, one on the rNam-rgyal-rtse-mo, the other one at Alchi. Neither of them contains the name *bKra-shis-kun-dgā-rnam-rgyal* as the name of a king; both give *bKra-shis-rnam-rgyal.* It is, therefore, possible that king Lha-chen-Bha-gan, the founder of the *rNam-rgyal* dynasty of Western Tibet, did not only give names ending in *rNam-rgyal* to his sons, but took a new name ending in *rnam-rgyal* for himself, that name being Kun-dgā-rnam-rgyal. The minister Phyag-rdor-jo would then appear to have served two kings, father and son, which is not at all uncommon. Similar cases are found in the history of the Tibetans as well as in that of other nations. If we say, therefore, that the Daru sculptures and inscriptions date roughly from the year 1500 A.D., we shall not be far wrong.

On the western end of the plain, called La-dvags-gong-khai-thang, there is a rock called bLa-ma-guru. It has an eroded hollow on one side which looks as if a man had left the mark of his head and shoulders in mud. This hollow is believed to have been formed through Padma-sambhava's sleeping on the rock on one of his journeys through Indian Tibet. The rock is worshipped by the people, who smear oil or butter on it. The *Oṁ maṇi padme hūṁ* formula has been carved twice upon it.

At sNyemo we photographed the ancient castle on the river, called Chung-mkhar (Plate XXXV, a); and also the stone sculpture of Jo-mo-rdo-rje, the ancient abbess of the nunnery at sNyemo. These antiquities were discovered by me in 1906.[1]

On the 22nd September, we marched to Saspola, by way of Basgo and Likir. Before reaching Basgo, a little north of the road from sNyemo, the ruins of an ancient temple can be seen (Plate XXXV, b). It is built of sun-dried bricks and is of the type of Rin-chen-bzang-po's temples. It particularly reminded me of the Tabo temple. The number of raised medallions on its walls is thirty-two as in Tabo; and there was probably another medallion above the door.[2] I made a plan of this temple which, according to the best traditions, dates from the days of the great lama Rin-chen-bzang-po. Popular tradition connects it, without any reason, with an invasion by Turks or Mongols.

Not far from the ruined temple are two ancient *stūpas* of the "ladder" type, and also the remains of a third *stūpa* of the same kind. In the latter we found cremation tablets with inscriptions containing the *Yē dharmā* formula, in exactly the same type of ancient Śāradā as had come to light at rGyamthsa near Leh. The Basgo and the rGyamthsa monasteries are evidently of the same period.

The temple of Byams-pa (Maitrēya) at Basgo is apparently the only well preserved building in the place. In my article, "Archæology in Western Tibet," I wrongly attributed it to King Seng-ge-rnam-rgyal. As it contains the inscribed portrait of Thse-dbang-rnam-rgyal I and those of his two brothers, it was evidently erected by him,

---

[1] *Cf.* my article "*Archæology in Western Tibet,*" *Ind. Ant.*, Vol. XXXVI, pp. 88 ff.

[2] The arrangement of the medallions is shown on Plate No. IV of my article *Archæology in Western Tibet.*

PLATE XXXV.

a. Ruined castle Chung-mkhar at sNyemo.

b. Ruined temple near Basgo.

was to make another search. The monastery is very picturesquely situated on a little hill inside the valley. This time the lamas showed me a long inscription written with black ink on one of the walls, which contained the history of the monastery, as they asserted. Although it dates only to the times of Thse-dbang-rnam-rgyal II, who repaired the building after a conflagration, I ordered it to be copied. After a long introductory hymn the inscription gives the names of several ancient kings of Tibet, gNya-khri-btsan-po, Tho-tho-ri-snyan, Srong-btsan-sgam-po, Khri-srong-lde-btsan, sKyid-lde-nyi-ma-mgon, and of some famous Buddhist teachers. Then follows a Buddhist account of cosmology which concludes with a list of the most famous palaces of the Ladakhi kings, the seats of king Thse-dbang-rnam-rgyal. Finally, a few dates are given, connected with the history of the monastery. It is stated to have been founded by Lama Lha-dbang-chos-rje and King Lha-chen-rgyal-po. We must not, however, believe that these two persons were contemporaries. King Lha-chen-rgyal-po lived in the eleventh century, and the lama is most probably identical with the famous pupil of bTsong-kha-pa, Lha-dbang-blo-gros-chos-rje, who lived in the 15th century. The passage should be understood in this sense:—King Lha-chen-rgyal-po founded the monastery in the 11th century. In the 15th century, Lama Lha-dbang-chos-rje converted the lamas to the reformed doctrines of the Ge-lug-pa order, and thus founded the monastery afresh as a Ge-lug-pa establishment. Then it is stated that seven generations after Lha-chen-rgyal-po, King Lha-chen-dngos-grub arose, and that he introduced the custom of sending all the novices to Lhasa. This statement is given in exactly the same words as we find it in the rGyal-rabs. Then we read: "Eighteen generations after him," but the name of the king who reigned then has been scratched out, as well as any notes referring to him. Now, if we search in the chronicles for the name of the king who reigned eighteen generations after Lha-chen-dngos-grub, we find the name of bDe-legs-rnam-rgyal, the unhappy prince who after the battle of Basgo was compelled to embrace Islām. I have already drawn attention to the fact that votive tablets with the name of this king have not yet been found in Ladakh. They were apparently all destroyed. The Likir inscription is an instance of a similar kind. The lamas could not suffer the name of the apostate king to figure in the inscription, and therefore it was obliterated.

Below the monastery of Likir (Klu-dkyil), there is a large *mchod-rten* which contains frescoes inside. They represent bTsong-kha-pa and other lamas of his times. Painted above the door, a very strange figure is found which looks very much like one of the ordinary representations of Srong-btsan-sgam-po. I was told by the lamas that it represents a lama of Srong-btsan-sgam-po's times. The figure wears a three-pointed hat of white colour and carries two leopard skins under his arms. The lower part of this *mchod-rten* is a room, square in ground plan, which the lama said was the earliest temple at Likir, and was already in existence when Lha-chen-rgyal-po built the monastery.

On the 23rd September, we went to Alchi on the left bank of the river. On the way thither, at Saspola, we photographed the two ancient ruined *mchod-rten* which are attributed to Rin-chen-bzang-po's time (Plate XXXVI, b). On the remains of the larger one has been erected a modern monastery, called Byams-pa-dgon-pa.

PLATE XXXVI.

a. *mChod-rten* of Rin-chen-bzang-po at Basgo.

b. *mChod-rten* of Rin-chen-bzang-po at Saspola.

a. Wood-carving in gSum-thsag Temple, Alchi.

b. Ancient book cover from Lhasa.

The famous monastery of Alchi is situated to the east of the village. It is called rNam-par-snang-mdzad, and according to popular tradition is of Rin-chen-bzang-po's times. We could distinguish the following six different temples :—

(1) Lha-khang-so-ma.—It is an insignificant square hall with a small *mchod-rten* in the middle, but several of the frescoes appear to be of ancient date. Some of them refer to the Buddha legend, whilst others seem to represent persons of the times when the pictures were painted. The head-dress of these people is quite unusual, and at first I took it for a kind of white top hat. A closer examination showed, however, that it represented a certain type of turban. What looks like the top of the hat, is in reality the turned-up end of the linen of the turban. I noticed two inscriptions in this hall. They were written in a kind of Ṭākarī character; but I have not yet met any one who was able to read them.

(2) gSum-thsag, meaning " Three Stories."—This temple has three stories, each narrower than the one below, and the general appearance of the temple is that of a stepped pyramid. The ancient temple of mTho-lding in Guge was probably of the same type. gSum-thsag is the only temple at Alchi on which the old wooden gallery and the trefoiled wooden arches have been preserved (Plate XXXVII, a). It gives us an idea of the appearance of the ancient Buddhist temples of Kashmīr. All the woodwork, especially the many columns, were covered with mythological carvings, and all the columns had on the inner side of their richly decorated capitals figures of jumping animals, apparently lions, stretched forth towards each other. But what reminded me of Kashmīr most of all, were three trefoiled arches under high pointed gables, exactly like those of the ancient stone temples of that country. On closer inspection it became evident that only the middle arch was of perfect shape, and that the two on the right and left were rude imitations of it. The middle one contains a wooden image of a Buddha seated in the earth-touching attitude, the one to the right (of the spectator), the green Tārā (sGrol-ma), and the one to the left, Vajra-sattva (rDo-rje-sems-dpa). I am of opinion that these two statues were inserted later on in place of two more ancient ones. All the woodwork is painted red, except the arch of the green Tārā, which is blue. Inside the temple are three stucco images, larger than life size, of the following Bōdhisattvas: Vajra-pāṇi (Phyag-rdor) which is painted yellow; Mañjuśrī (*'aJam-dbyangs*), the tallest, which is painted red; and Avalōkitēśvara (*sPyan-ras-gzigs*) painted white. At the feet of Avalōkitēśvara we found an inscription recording the restoration of this temple under King bKra-shis-rnam-rgyal in the 16th century. It is interesting that in this inscription, the amount of red, blue, and gold colour which was contributed by various peasants of the neighbourhood, is mentioned. King bKra-shis-rnam-rgyal's court painter was apparently an Indian who knew the Mughal art of painting. When he restored the temple, this artist preserved the old outlines of the 11th century as far as possible; but in the choice of colours, he was more original than the old masters had been. For a large part, the walls had been covered with endless repetitions of the Buddha figure in the same colours. He brought variety into their dress, haloes and backgrounds. Whenever a picture had disappeared altogether, he invented new

and in the Byams-pa temple of Basgo, we find the portraits of the royal founders by the side of the door. Whilst at Basgo the name of the king is found written below the picture, at Leh the inscription containing the name of the king is found on the other side of the door, as is the case here. The king wears a diadem, and his yellow mantle shows large round spots of blue or purple colour with the figure of a lion or tiger in each of them. His girdle shows a chequered pattern of white and red. In his hand he bears an axe of fanciful shape, and he is shaded by an umbrella. His son (probably Lha-chen-rgyal-po) is dressed in a similar manner, and the queen has her hair plaited in many little pigtails. The principal image in this shrine is of course Vairōchana (rNam-par-snang-mdzad). The temple door is most elaborately carved in Indian style (Plate XXXIX, a), and on both sides there are two narrow chapels which contain huge stucco figures.

(4) Lo-tsa-bai-lha-khang.—This temple is in a line with the first and second temples described above, but farther north. It contains a statue of a seated Buddha and a portrait painting of Rin-chen-bzang-po, the founder of the monastery. There is also an image of this lama in the same hall, but the monks say that it was modelled after the fresco. The hall is also furnished with an ancient, well carved door, and there are a few fragments of carved wooden pillars.

(5) 'aJam-dbyangs-khang.—This temple contains a large stucco image of the Dhyānibuddhas of the four regions, the one towards the east being painted yellow, that towards the south white, that towards the north red, and that towards the west blue. Below them, there are more images and the sixteen emblems of happiness, *i.e.*, the eight ordinary emblems of happiness with additions. Among them we could distinguish the pair of fishes, the wheel, the parasol, and even a cross, which is evidently intended to symbolise the four quarters of the globe. This hall is also furnished with beautifully carved door-beams and pillars. But the best wood-carving is that of a standing Buddha which is found above the door outside. It is already very brittle and will probably not last much longer.

(6) Lha-khang.—This temple is situated a little way to the south of the preceding ones. It contains only pictures and has suffered much by the rough treatment of the children of the village. A figure of Gaṇēśa is painted above the door. On one side of it are painted historical scenes; for instance a group of West Tibetan noblemen on horseback, hawking. On the other side are pictures of Buddhist saints and lamas, all furnished with inscriptions. I ordered Puntsog to copy all the decipherable inscriptions; but the copying of the many interesting frescoes I had to leave to some future explorer. The inscriptions contain mostly names, belonging to well known lamas. The following is a list of such lamas as are known to me: Klu-grub (Nāgārjuna); Arya-rdeba (Ārya-dêva); Natropa (or Naropa); Tilipa (or Telipa); Loipa (or Luipa); Kumara and Dharma-ki(r)ti of Srong-btsan-sgam-po's time; Kamala(śila), Ananta, Shantipa (Śāntirakshita) of Khri-srong-lde-btsan's time; E(n)-tra-bhodhe (Śrīlendra bodhi) of Ralpacan's time. The latest seem to be Zla-ba-grags-pa and Kun-dgā-snying-po of the 11th century. A further reason for attributing the frescoes and inscriptions of this temple to the 11th or 12th century, is that the orthography employed in the inscriptions shows signs of considerable age (*myi* and *mye* instead of *mi* and *me*).

Besides the temples mentioned above, there is at Alchi a great number of ancient *mchod-rten* and *mchod-rten* gates with four doors. Several of them contain pictures similar to those noticed at Basgo and Ubshi, *i.e.*, Buddha-like figures of blue complexion. They probably represent Nāgas, and these gates and *mchod-rten* may be of Bonpo origin. But there were so many that it was found impossible to register them all.

Let me add a few words with regard to Tibetan palæography, based on a comparison of the Alchi and Tabo inscriptions of the 11th century. Besides the Alchi and Tabo inscriptions of the 11th century, the following datable inscriptions of ancient Tibet are known: (1) The Endere manuscripts, excavated by Sir M. A. Stein in Turkestan. The latest date which can be attributed to them is the year 788 A.D., but several appear to be earlier. (2) The inscription of Khri-srong-lde-btsan in Lhasa of c. 780 A.D. discovered and edited by Dr. Waddell.[1] (3) The inscription of king Ral-pa-can in Lhasa, of c. 810–820 A.D.[2]

The most archaic of the Endere relics have the following peculiarities:—

(1) The *i* vowel sign is often inverted.

(2) In several cases, the final consonant of a syllable is written below the first.

(3) The article is in many cases *pha* and *pho,* instead of the ordinary *pa* and *po.*

(4) Ordinary *c* and *ts* are in many cases replaced by *ch* and *ths*; and *ch* and *ths* both have *g, b,* and *d* prefixes attached to them.

(5) When *m* precedes *i* or *e, y* intervenes.

(6) Words ending in *r, l,* or *n*, are furnished with a *d* suffix, called *drag.*

If we examine the Tabo, Poo and Alchi inscriptions of the 11th century, with regard to the peculiarities of the Endere manuscripts enumerated above, we find that they exhibit only the two last mentioned peculiarities, *viz.*, *y* intervenes between *m* and *i* or *m* and *e*; and *r, l,* and *n* are often furnished with a *d* suffix. Thus we see that during the period from the 8th to the 11th century, the Tibetan orthography has come much nearer to its present state. The *i* vowel sign, for instance, is no more found inverted, but always in its present position. At Alchi we found the *i* vowel sign only once inverted and that was probably due to want of space. From this observation we may conclude that all those inscriptions which contain inverted *i* vowel signs, may be older than the 11th century. As regards the position of the *e* and *o* vowel signs on the right or left upper end, or above the consonant base, it varies with the age of inscriptions. I am of opinion that the compilation of the *bKa-'agyur* and *bStan-'agyur*, in c. 1300 A.D., marks an epoch in Tibetan palæography. It probably put an end to the intervening *y* between *m* and *i* or *e*, and to the suffixed *d.* From the year 1300 A.D. onwards Tibetan orthography presumably remained stationary, and the age of an inscription after 1300 A.D. can be estimated only by the form of its compound letters, and the position of vowel signs on or above their consonant bases.

---

[1] *Ancient historical edicts at Lhasa* in *J. R. A. S.* 1909, pp. 923 ff.

[2] See my reading and translation *Ep. Ind.*, Vol. X, pp. 89 ff.

a. Carved door in rNam-par-snang-mdzad Temple, Alchi.

b. Fresco in gSum-thsag Temple, Alchi.

On our way back, from Alchi to Saspola, I visited the site of a ruined castle called Alchi-mkhar-gog, which once guarded the Alchi bridge. I found a number of sherds of pottery with dark red designs. The pottery was not wheel-made, but rudely shaped with the hand. As will be remembered, entire specimens of pottery with dark red designs were found in the ancient graves at Leh. On the boulders round about the ruined castle are found many inscriptions of officers who once resided here. As I have shown in my article " Archæology in Western Tibet, " most of these epigraphs may be attributed to the times of King Nyi-ma-mgon, in the 10th century, and his immediate successors. We took a photo of one of them.

On the 24th September, the principal caravan under Pindi Lal, marched to sNyurla, by the ordinary road. I myself went to sGyera on the left bank of the Indus, accompanied by Puntsog, my assistant, and Labpa, the Khansaman. From sGyera, I went up the valley, to visit the famous monastery of Mang-rgyu. Just below it, we passed a very rudely-executed rock sculpture which represents Mañjuśrī. The inscription below it mentions King Phun-thsogs-rnam-rgyal of the 18th century. It is the latest rock sculpture in West Tibet which I have seen.

The Mang-rgyu monastery consists of four temples standing in a row, with their doors towards the East like so many others of the same period.

(1) Byams-chen (or Lōkēśvara).—This temple contains a huge stucco image ; but the present lamas are uncertain whether it represents Maitrēya or Avalōkitēśvara. I should think that it represents the former. The door is furnished with ancient wood carvings of Indian type.

(2) 'aDu-khang (or Thugs-rje-chen-po).—The door of this temple is ornamented with ancient wood carvings of artistic workmanship, which represent the five Dhyāni-buddhas with Vairōchana (rNam-par-snang-mdzad) in the centre. We found an ancient and much effaced inscription in this hall near the door. I ordered it to be copied. Neither a personal nor a local name has been preserved in it, and it contains hardly a single coherent sentence. But the preserved fragments afford several instances of intervening *y* between *m* and *i*, and for this reason I feel inclined to attribute it to the 11th or 12th century. Local tradition connects the Mang-rgyu monastery with Lama Rin-chen-bzang-po. In another part of the same hall, we found a short fragmentary inscription giving the name of a forgotten prince, possibly a younger son of one of the kings of the first dynasty of Ladakh. It reads *Jo-no-chung-Khri-stod-'adi,* " the younger prince Khri-stod."

(3) rNam-par-snang-mdzad.—This temple contains a number of stucco images, some of which reminded me of the thirty-two at Tabo. On the wall outside, there is a long inscription recording the renovation of the monastery under King Thse-dbang-rnam-rgyal II (?) If the present ugly pictures in this and most of the other temples are the result of that renewal, it was absolute barbarism. The principal hall has lost its ancient door.

(4) 'aJams-chung (or Mañjuśrī).—This temple also contains a huge stucco statue, concerning the identity of which the present lamas do not seem to be agreed. They do not know whether it represents Mañjuśrī or Maitrēya. The frescoes of the hall have

escaped renovation and reminded me of similar pictures I had seen at Alchi. Here also were pictures of monks with patchwork gowns of many colours.

(5) Tretapuri (Tīrthapuri).—This is a large *stūpa* which is enshrined in a ruined house. The name of the building would point to its former occupation by a community of heretics (Skr. *tīrthika*), as they were found in Tibet by Atiśa on the occasion of his advent into the country. Judging by the images contained in it at the present time, however, it is now as Lamaist as any other temple at Mang-rgyu. There were four stucco images of the following Lamaist deities : 'aJam-dbyangs, (Mañju-ghōsha) painted yellow, in the eastern corner ; sPyan-ras-gzigs (Avalōkitēśvara) painted white, in the southern corner ; and Phyag-rdor (Vajra-pāṇi) painted blue, in the western corner ; and further the reformer bTsong-kha-pa (Sumati-kīrti), resplendent with red, orange, and yellow, in the northern corner.

At the time of its foundation, the Mang-rgyu monastery may have equalled the Alchi monastery in splendour. Now-a-days it is far inferior to it.

On the 25th September, we marched to Khalatse, on the right bank of the Indus. Half way we passed by a gorge which forms the entrance to the valley of the village of Tar. I should not have visited the latter, if rumours had not been current that a very ancient rock inscription had been discovered there by Mr. Chatterji and others. Just below the village of Tar, there is a rock, on which people believe they can see twenty-one figures of the goddess Tārā (sGrol-ma) which have come into existence of themselves. There used to be a high flagstaff in front of this rock. These *svayambhū* figures of Tārā may account for the name of the village. It was probably called Tārā originally, the name having become abridged to Tar. Lower down the valley, we found very well moulded clay representations of Tārā in a *mchod-rten*. In the village we examined the "famous" inscription mentioned above. It contains only the name of King Tlhse-dpal-rnam-rgyal, the last independent ruler of Ladakh, and is very fragmentary.

We arrived at Khalatse just in time to prevent the boulders containing the oldest inscriptions of Ladakh from being broken. There are several rocks near Khalatse bridge, bearing ancient Kharōshṭhī inscriptions, and one with an ancient Brāhmī inscription. As a new bridge was under construction, many boulders, some with interesting rock carvings and inscriptions had been blasted ; and the boulder with the Brāhmī inscription had already been marked for blasting. I spoke to the Public Works overseer in charge, as well as to the authorities at Khalatse, and entreated them to preserve these invaluable stones. I hope that this may not have been in vain. We took photos of the Brāhmī, the longer Kharōshṭhī,[1] and the old Gupta inscriptions. The latter is found in the close vicinity of the mGo-chen *mchod-rten*. Some of the ancient rock carvings were also photographed, and impressions taken of the royal Tibetan and the Kharōshṭhī inscriptions. The mGo-chen *mchod-rten* belong to the

[1] Our photograph of the longer Kharōshṭhī inscription was sent to Professor Rapson of Cambridge. He writes in his letter of the 23rd September 1910, as follows : "The title *Maharajasa* is quite clear. After this comes the name beginning with *A* and ending with the genitive termination *sa*. Four or five syllables intervene, but I am not quite certain about any of them. Above the king's name is a date which I read—with some doubt as to whether three strokes at the end are part of the date or not—as 100+20+20+20+20+4 [+3]; that is to say 184 or 187."

site of a ruined Dard castle at Khalatse. They were photographed and a plan was made of the whole ancient site.

As regards the antiquities of Khalatse, they have been described by me elsewhere[1]. I do not wish to repeat here all I have said in my previous articles, and, therefore, I will simply give a list of the more important of those antiquities :—(1) certain places of the cult of the pre-Buddhist religion in the neighbourhood, (2) Indian inscriptions extending over a period of more than one thousand years, several of which have already been mentioned. (3) A number of royal Tibetan inscriptions near the bridge. (4) Besides the ancient custom house (*sBalu-mkhar*) which is only three miles from Khalatse, there are three more ruined castles at this place, one being of Tibetan, and the others of Dard origin.

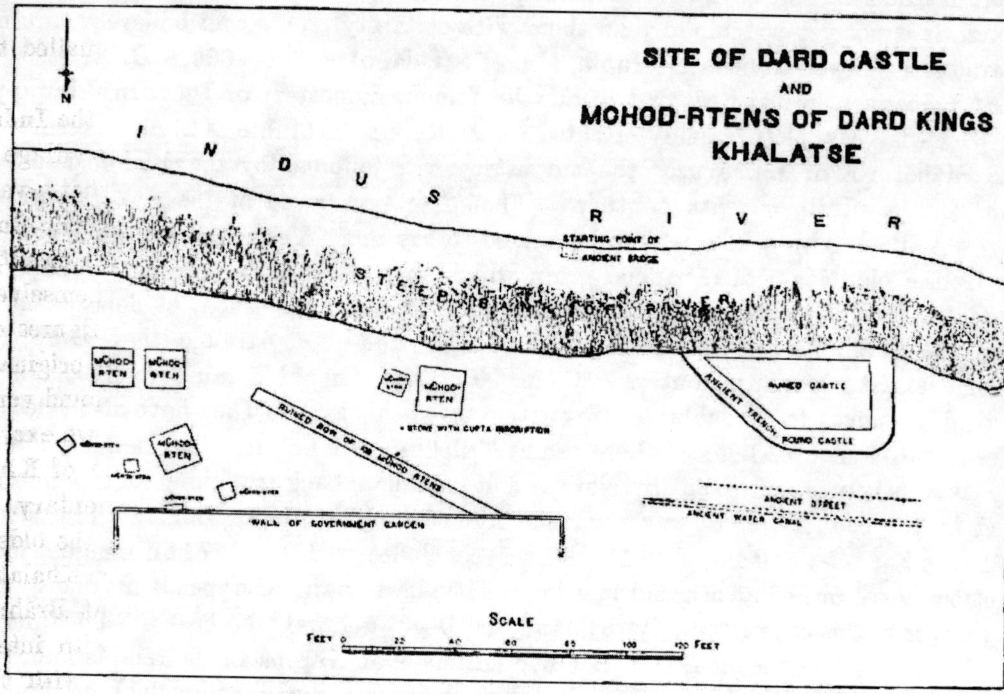

Fig. 4.

Whilst we were at Khalatse, the people of the village sold me a good many antiquities which they had found either in their houses or at ancient sites in the neighbourhood, *viz.*, sBa-lu-mkhar, Brag-nag-mkhar, or Brog-pai-mkhar. Among them was a stone knife, a stone axe, to be used without a handle, several stone lamps, beads of bone, stone charms, ancient female head-dresses, a bone knife, a stone inkpot, a pair of goggles made of turnips, etc.

Our Christian evangelist at Khalatse had become a father a few weeks before, and the people of the village had made presents of "flour-ibex" to him and his wife. He

[1] "*Historische Dokumente von Khalatse,*" in *Z. D. M. G.*, Vol. LXI, pp. 583 ff, and "*The Dards at Khalatse,*" *M. A. S. B.*, Vol. I, No. 19.

gave me one of those figures, which are made of flour and butter, and told me that it was a custom in Tibet and Ladakh, to make presents of "flour-ibex" on the occasion of the birth of a child. This is quite interesting information. I had often wondered why there were so many rock carvings of ibex at places connected with the pre-Buddhist religion of Ladakh. Now it appears probable that they are thank offerings, after the birth of children. As I have tried to show in my previous article,[1] people used to go to the pre-Buddhist places of worship, in particular, to pray to be blessed with children.

On the 30th September, we left Khalatse and travelled to Lamayuru. When we arrived on the left bank of the Indus, after crossing the Khalatse bridge, I examined again the three stones with inscriptions, which I had discovered there several years ago, and again made careful copies of the inscriptions, which later on I sent to Dr. Vogel. Although it is not yet possible to read them with certainty, Dr. Vogel believes the kind of character employed to be later Gupta, almost Śāradā, of c. 600—800 A.D.

At Lamayuru, we visited, first of all, the famous monastery of the 'aBri-khung-pa order which is very picturesquely situated on a steep rock (Plate XL, a). According to the Māhātmya of Lamayuru, the monastery was founded by the Buddhist priest Naropa in the ninth or tenth century. When Naropa arrived at the site, the whole valley was filled with a lake which he caused to dry up.[2] The monastery received its name from a plantation of sacrificial grain which mysteriously grew into the shape of the *svastika* (*gYung-drung*). It is interesting that there are traces of deposits of a former lake all around the mountains of Lamayuru, and it is strange that Drew in his book does not make any mention of them. But the Ladakhis must really have a geological instinct, to be able to invent stories of this kind. They have also tales of the former existence of lakes at Leh and at Trilōknāth in Lahul. The name *gYung-drung* was of course not given by Naropa, but must date back to a time long before he arrived in the country, as it was then the foremost place of the Bon religion which is called *gYung-drung-bon*. The Māhātmya concludes with a tale of an image which cannot be moved out of its original position. The 'barbarian' who spends his energy on it in vain, is in this case Dīwān Hari Chand, the Ḍōgrā general who beat the Tibetans in 1842 A.D. I asked the monks, if they had an image of Naropa in the temple hall, to which they replied in the affirmative. We were shown a rather modern looking stucco statue of Naropa in the library which also contained images of several more lamas connected with him, for instance, Tilopa, Marpa, Milaraspa. They seem to belong to a complete set of figures of the bKā-brgyud lamas. These bKā-brgyud lamas who are something like church-fathers of the 'aBrug-pa order of lamas, are enumerated in inscription No. 128 from Kolong in Lahul, as follows: (1) rDo-rje-'achang, (2) Ti-lo-pa (3) Na-ro-pa, (4) Mar-pa, (5) Mi-la-ras-pa, (6) rGam-po, (7) Thar-sab-pa, (8) gNas-phug-pa, (9) dPal-ldan-'abrug-pa.

I asked the lamas to show me the most ancient part of the monastery, and we were taken to a temple called Seng-ge-sgang, which is situated at the southern end of the

[1] *Historische Dokumente von Khalatse in West Tibet* (*Ladakh*) in *Z. D. M. G.*, Vol. LXI, pp. 583 ff.

[2] A similar legend is told about Kashmir. *Cf. Rājataraṅgiṇī* I, 25-27 transl. Stein, Vol. I, p. 5. [Ed.]

PLATE XL.

a. View of Lamayuru.

b. View of ruined town, Bod-Kharbu.

Lamayuru rock. There we were shown a hall which reminded me strongly of Rin-chen-bzang-po's temples, especially the stucco images on the walls, which were of a style similar to those at Tabo. The entrance is towards the east. The principal image is that of 'aJam-dbyangs (Mañju-ghōsha). On his right we find the blue Tārā, and on his left, the yellow Tārā. The figure above the blue Tārā is said to represent Thse-dpag-med (Amitāyus), but the identity of the figure above the yellow Tārā cannot now be established. Garuḍa is placed above the whole group of images. Below it is a stone pedestal showing well carved relievos of elephants and lions. The frescoes in this hall are far gone and most of them can no longer be identified. I noticed a picture of a divinity with very many arms, and another fresco apparently representing the 'Wheel of Life' (*Srid-pai-'akhor-lo*) showing in its better preserved parts the torments of hell, and the gods fighting the Asuras. The lama who had taken us to this temple, said that, according to an inscription in the bCu-gcig-zhal temple at Wanla, the following four temples date from one and the same time, called the *bKā-gdams-pa* time: (1) the Seng-ge-sgang temple of Lamayuru, (2) the bCu-gcig-zhal temple at Wanla, (3) the ruined temple of Chigtan, (4) the Lha-bcu-rtse-lha-khang temple at Khanji. As regards the *bKā-gdams-pa* time, this expression seems to indicate the times of the great teacher 'aBrom-ston, the founder of the *bKā-gdams-pa* sect, who lived in the 11th century. This statement is quite in agreement with the general appearance of the Seng-ge-sgang temple. I had sent a man to the famous bCu-gcig-zhal temple of Wanla to copy any ancient inscriptions, he could discover in it. He evidently did not find that of the bKa-gdams-pa times mentioned by the lama, for what he brought me, was one of the Muhammadan period, as is evident from the occurrence of Moslem names in it. In a side chapel of the Seng-ge-sgang temple, there are three large images of terrible appearance, similar to those which we found in the mGon-khang at Leh. A female figure riding on a mule, is called dPal-ldan-lha-mo (Śrī Dēvī); and a male figure seated on a man, mGon-po (Mahākāla). The two remaining figures I cannot define, although the name of one of them was said to be Abchi.

Below the monastery of Lamayuru there is an ancient shrine which appears to be the old Bon-po temple. The roof is almost gone, and for this reason the frescoes on the walls have suffered badly. The door was also in the wall towards the east. All the divinities painted on the walls of this hall are of Buddhist type; but their complexion is either blue or black, and their dress is red. These pictures seem to represent Nāgas, similar to those we saw at Ubshi and Alchi. Those ancient gates with four doors, and this mysterious temple at Lamayuru are apparently all of Bon-po origin; but they were erected in the days when the Bon-po religion was largely influenced by Buddhism and Hinduism. Although a good number of pictures of Buddha-shaped figures have been preserved in this ruined temple, I could not discover a single one with a white, yellow, or red complexion. But there were several female figures of very unusual shape whose complexion was white. They appeared to wear ear-flaps, like the modern Ladakhi women, and were depicted on the walls as well as on the ceiling. On the latter were represented well designed rows of female musicians, alternately white and grey.

The most interesting group of frescoes is that which represents what I believe to be priests of the Bon-po religion (Plate XLI, a). One of them is represented in almost life size, whilst the others are smaller. They are all clothed in white undergarments and striped gowns. The large figure, and one of the smaller ones, show a gown with black and blue stripes, the other small figures have black and grey stripes. The large figure is shown wearing a blue hat, like a European soft felt-hat with a broad brim. The smaller figures have hats of the same shape but of black colour. There are but few early references to the dress of the Bon-po priest; but in most cases it is described as being black. There are, however, a few passages which make mention of the blue colour of their dress.[1] These relics of the Bon religion at Lamayuru are of some importance; for, as we know from Sarat Chandra Das,[2] the present day Bon-po priests of Central Tibet cannot be distinguished from Buddhist priests, their dress being exactly alike.

Above the Lamayuru Bungalow, there are several modern and two ancient gateways. They are called *Khagani* (Khanggani). As the ceilings of the old ones are painted all over with blue Buddha-like figures, we may ascribe their origin also to Bon-po times.

Moorcroft[3] in 1820 discovered in the Lamayuru monastery several letters of protection issued by Aurangzeb, Mughal officers, and even by one of the Balti kings.

On the 30th September we marched from Lamayuru to Kharbu by the ordinary trade road across the Phothola Pass, 14,000 feet high. The castle of Kharbu is situated on the top of a rocky hill above the present village of Kharbu. It is all in ruins, and rather difficult of access. Puntsog climbed up to it, but he could find neither ancient implements, nor inscriptions. One of the ruins appeared to be an ancient temple, built of sun-dried bricks. But even here no ancient remains were discovered, nor any traces of raised medallions on the walls.

The old town of Kharbu lies on the rocky plateau above the present village, but below the castle (Plate XL, b). It is easier of access than the latter, and was probably deserted, between circa 1620 and 1630 A.D., when King bDe-ldan-rnam-rgyal wrested it from the Khri Sultan of dKar-rtse. According to the chronicles, the conqueror carried all women and children away into captivity, so after this war it was probably never reoccupied. Captain Oliver, the present Joint Commissioner of Ladakh, informed me that a man at Dras who is now one hundred and eight years old, told him that the fort or ancient town of Kharbu was taken by storm in the Ḍōgrā war. But I feel very doubtful with regard to this statement which is not confirmed by the Ladakhi chronicles, nor by Basti Ram's account. Moreover, Moorcroft in 1820 A.D. found the old town in ruins. At the eastern end of the old town, not far from two small whitewashed *mchod-rten*, there is an inscription of the times of King Seng-ge-rnam-rgyal carved on the rock.[4] It is very indistinct, and extremely difficult to decipher. The rough surface of

[1] Cf. *J. A. S. B.*, Vol. L, pp. 198 and 211.

[2] *Journey to Lhasa*, p. 207.

[3] *Travels*, Vol. II, p. 14.

[4] I discovered this inscription in 1906, and published it as No. 55 of my *First Collection of Tibetan Historical Inscriptions*. It seems to contain a reference to Shāh Jahān's attempt to conquer Ladakh.

Plate XLI.

a. Fresco in Bon-po Temple, Lamayuru.

b. Ancient wood-carving of Garuda, Chigtan.

the rock also makes it impossible to take impressions of it. I believe, however, that I have succeeded this time in getting a more correct reading of a certain passage. What had been read *Sku-med 'aJam-yang*, seems to be in reality *Sku-mkhar mkhar-bu*, and thus the name of King 'aJam-dbyang-rnam-rgyal does not occur in it after all. But there are several more passages, the reading of which is still very doubtful. This much we may, however, safely infer from the inscription, *viz.*, that the old town of Kharbu was still inhabited in King Seng-ge-rnam-rgyal's days. On the western end of the old town, there is a solid round tower with a staircase inside. These stairs lead down to a spring which used to provide the town with fresh water, even when it was besieged.

On the elevated plateau between the old town and the present village, there are a number of old *mchod-rten* and *maṇi* walls. But there are also many ancient graves, the origin of which is not known to the present inhabitants. They may be either of Dard, or of Muhammadan origin. For, when the town of Kharbu was in the hands of the *Khri* Sultans of dKar-rtse, the inhabitants were probably compelled to embrace Islām together with the other subjects of the Sultans in the Suru valley. Possibly they date from the Mug͟hal war.

A very remarkable ruin in the Kharbu valley is the castle of Stag-rtse (map Takhcha), on the opposite bank of the brook. It was built on a very steep rock, apparently also very difficult of access, and once formed part of the possessions of the chiefs of Chigtan. It was probably destroyed by bDe-ldan-rnam-rgyal of Ladakh at the same time as Kharbu.

In the Kharbu valley, between Kharbu and Stag-rtse, are the ruins of a large temple called Mun-dig-lha-khang, 'the dark temple.' It is 20 paces long and 16 paces broad. This temple had apparently two doors, one in the eastern, and one in the western wall, and there were separate doorways at some distance from the temple. In the vicinity, I noticed the ruined remains of at least two rows of one hundred and eight *mchod-rten*. A native whom we met, told us the following tale regarding this ruin: "It was built by two lamas after the model of the Chigtan temple. One of them went to Lhasa, and the other to Kashmir, to buy colours for painting frescoes. Both died in those distant countries, and the temple was never completed." There were no traces of any frescoes or raised medallions to be seen. But that is not to be wondered at, as the ruin was roofless.

On the 2nd October, we went to Chigtan, situated in a side valley, on a tributary of the Indus. The old castle of the chiefs of Chigtan, the Purig Sultans, is very picturesquely situated on a steep cliff (Plate XLII, a). Below the castle are the ruins of the old town. The greater part of the rooms of the former are no longer accessible, owing to the dilapidated state of the whole building. A great number of the doors, and also several windows, were adorned with very artistic wood carvings in Tibetan style (Plate XLIII, a). Two of those in the inner court of the castle were said to be the portraits of the two architects, father and son. In one of the rooms we found a large wooden board on which is carved the figure of a Nāga-devouring Garuḍa. (Plate XLI, b) Although no document recording the erection of this castle has yet been found, the

Tibetan style of the carvings suggests that its construction took place before 1550 A.D., *i.e.*, before the chiefs of Chigtan became Muhammadan.

Among the ruins of the old town below the castle, we found two stone slabs which contained inscriptions in a very faulty form of Tibetan. One of them treated of the remission of taxes and forced labour, and gave the name of Adam Malig of Chigtan. This Adam Malig is probably identical with a chief whose name is found in the genealogical roll of the chiefs of Chigtan, and who probably reigned c. 1580 A.D. The other inscription is more fragmentary. It does not contain the name of any chief, but apparently treats of a similar subject and may be attributed to the same time.

The ancient Buddhist monastery of Chigtan is situated at the other end of the village and on the further bank of the brook, coming from the palace (Plate XLII, b). It is similar in type to the monasteries of Rin-chen-bzang-po's times and is attributed to the so-called bKā-gdams-pa epoch, judging by the Wanla inscription, mentioned above. The bKā-gdams-pa epoch probably began in the middle of the 11th century, a generation or so after Rin-chen-bzang-po's time. There are a great number of raised medallions on the wall opposite the door, and all had formerly stucco images in front of them, which were destroyed, when Chigtan adopted the Muhammadan religion. I counted the medallions and found their number to be thirty-nine. This is seven more than the usual thirty-two; but the seven additional medallions seem to belong to a special group of larger images which once occupied the central portion of the wall. We found traces of a number of inscriptions on the temple walls, the best preserved of which is the Tibetan inscription of the old Lamaist chiefs of Chigtan, which I discovered in 1906.[1] There are also traces of another Tibetan, one Arabic (or Persian), and at least five or six Śāradā inscriptions. Most of them are found on the medallions. We took photos of two of the Śāradā inscriptions, and with one of them we succeeded so well that Pandit Mukund Ram Shastri of Kashmir who examined the photo with a magnifying glass, was able to read a couple of words. The inscription was in Sanskrit, and the character a very late type of Śāradā. As the words "army" and "inflated skins" occur among the distinct portions of the inscription, it looks almost as if it had been written by a Ḍogrā Brahmin during the time of the Ḍōgrā wars. In front of the medallions has been erected an altar (*lhatho*) which is ornamented with twigs of the pencil cedar; a number of brass cups containing offerings of butter, have been placed below it. The temple hall is a square of 14 or 15 paces each side. Its height is about 24 feet. The roof which was recently renovated is supported by four high pillars of pencil cedar wood. They are quite plain, but the door of the temple is elaborately carved in Indian style (Plate XLIII, b). It shows the figures of a number of Buddhist saints, whose identity it is however impossible to ascertain, owing to the decayed state of the wood. We found the temple in charge of two Muhammadans who said that they were descended from its former Buddhist keepers. Their house name is *Lha-khang-pa* or *dGon-pa-pa*. These people still light the butter-filled lamps in the temple, and look after

[1] It is described in my *First Collection of Inscriptions* under No. 43.

a. View of castle, Chigtan.

b. View of monastery, Chigtan.

a. Wood-carving in the castle, Chigtan.

b. Door of monastery, Chigtan.

the altar. They told us that the temple was still visited by their Buddhist neighbours from Da and Hanu who pay adoration to its old deities.

On the 4th October, we marched to Mulbe, crossing the Namika Pass (13,400 feet high). On the way, Puntsog and myself visited the ruined castle of Waka which is situated at the east end of the Mulbe valley. On a steep spur, to the north of the present village of Waka, lie the ruins of the old castle and town. They are of considerable extent. Some parts of the well-built castle are now inaccessible. This fortress was probably once a stronghold of great importance, as would appear from Jōnarāja's Second Rājataraṅgiṇī,[1] where a war between two Tibetan tribes, the Vakatanyas and Kālamānyas, is described. The former name probably stands for the garrison of Waka, and the second for the Baltis of Khar-mang. Of ancient remains we found only a stone mortar, a bone tube, and several sherds of thick, hand-made pottery, but no inscriptions.

A little below the fortress, towards the east, there were traces of an ancient hermitage (*mthsams-khang*), a kind of cave dwelling. Above the caves, we noticed a smooth place on the rock surface with indistinct traces of ancient frescoes. We could only make out the outlines of the picture of a *mchod-rten*, and a few letters of an ancient inscription. On the plain beneath, a little to the west of the ruined castle, are the remains of an ancient temple called Lha-khang-gog-po (" ruined temple "), a large square hall which reminded me at once of the temples of Rin-chen-bzang-po's times. It had been lately used as a dwelling place by several Muhammadan families who had built partition walls across it. This may be the reason why nothing remains of ancient frescoes. It had its door probably in the western wall.

The most famous relic at the village of Mulbe is the huge rock sculpture of Maitrēya the Mulbe " Chamba " (Byams-pa). It was noticed by Moorcroft[2] in 1820, who has the following note on it : " Near the end of this day's journey, the road passed between the foot of the mountains on the right of the valley and an insulated pillar of rock, about fifty feet high. On the face of this was sculptured the figure of one of the Tibetan divinities named Chamba. It differed from the same representation in the temples in being decorated with the Brahminical cord, hanging from the left shoulder and over the right hip. The figure was naked, except round the waist, and was about twenty-four feet high, but the lower part was concealed by a low wall in front ; the upper had been protected by a screen projecting over it from the rock, but this was gone, leaving only the holes in which the pins that had fastened it, had been inserted."

As we see, Moorcroft noticed already the Brahminical cord among the characteristic emblems of the Maitrēya sculpture of Mulbe. The other emblems, a flask and a rosary, are of similar interest. Several students of Indo-Buddhist art feel inclined to derive the most ancient types of Bōdhisattvas from deities of the Hindu pantheon. Thus

---

[1] Jonarāja, *Rājataraṅgiṇī*, 157 ff. (Bombay Sanskrit Series, No. LIV, pp. 14 f.) *Kings of Kashmīra* (transl. J. C. Dutt), Vol. III, pp. 16 ff. The passage is not quite clear, but it seems to convey that one Vakatanya was killed by certain Tibetan (*Bhoṭṭa*) chieftains called Kālamānya, who in their turn were exterminated by Vakatanya's son Riñchana (see beneath pp. 107 ff) who had escaped the massacre. [Ed.]

[2] *Travels*, Vol. II, p. 17.

Avelōkitēśvara has been compared with Śiva, and Maitrēya with Brahmā. And in fact there are representations of Brahmā which are hardly different from some of Maitrēya. Thus, for instance, among the wood-carvings of the Śakti temple at Chhatrāṛhī in Chambā State, there is a four-armed Brahmā, carrying a rosary and a water-pot, and accompanied by a pair of geese. The Chhatrāṛhī sculptures date from about 700 A.D., and the Maitrēya of Mulbe is of the same time, approximately. Cunningham, without any foundation, assigns it to the 17th century! We visited the little temple below the huge sculpture, and found that its keepers were of an old family of On-pos (Astrologers). They said that their family had always been in charge of the sculptures, and that their family name was On-po-pa. The small temple in front of the sculpture was built by Wazīrb Sod-nams, who is the present baron of Mulbe. According to these On-pos, the sculpture is either of Rin-chen-bzang-po's time, or a little older. Rin-chen bzang-po is at any rate credited with having taken an interest in it. The On-pos say that the image was carved by "the eight great sons of Nyeba," whose figures are shown carved at the feet of Maitrēya.[1] It is particularly interesting to notice that one of these sons of Nyeba is shown wearing a round hat with a brim, as is the fashion with On-pos who probably inherited this costume from the ancient Bon-po priests of Tibet. The name *Nyeba* means "friend" (*Skr. mitra*). In the modern little temple of Wazīr bSod-nams there are fanciful fresco paintings, representing "the eight great sons of Nyeba." They are of various complexions, one has a blue, another a green face; some are even yellow black- and brown-faced. Except several repetitions of the *Oṁ maṇi padme hūṁ* formula no inscriptions are found on the sculpture.

As regards the other antiquities at Mulbe, *viz.*, a Dard castle, two monasteries, and several important rock inscriptions, they have been fully treated in my article "The rock inscriptions at Mulbe."[2]

From Mulbe we marched to Kargil by way of Shargola, on the 5th October. The name of the village of Shargola (*Shar-'ago-lha*) seems to mean "Lord of the first rising" and to refer to the morning star. This amounts almost to a certainty when we examine the "Song of the *gDung-rten* at Shargola." A *gDung-rten* is a kind of *stūpa*. The song begins with the eulogy of an ancient hero, called Agu Drumba, who is the supposed builder of the monastery as well as of the *stūpa*, and ends with a direct praise of the morning star. The morning star is called here *nam-langs-kyi-skar-chen-po*, "the great star of the rising heaven." Agu Drumba is probably a personification of the morning star, as is the case with Agu 'aBu-dmar-lam-bstan of the Kesar Saga.[3] The morning star is the herald of the sun, and therefore its personification would

---

[1] As we learn from S. Ch. Das' Dictionary, the eight great sons of Nyeba are Buddhist saints. Their names are given on p. 485 of the dictionary. But on p. 91 of the same book, we find a group of eight Bon-po deities who are called *sku-sras-brgyad*, the 'eight great sons.' It is evident that the Mulbe sculptures originally represented eight Bon-po deities who were converted into eight Buddhist deities at a later time.

The custom of representing the donors at the feet of the deity is met with both in Christian and Buddhist art. See *Note sur une statue du Gandhāra.* B. É. F. E. O. Hanoi, Vol. III, 1903, p. 149. [Ed.]

[2] *Ind. Ant.*, Vol. XXXV, pp. 72 ff.

[3] *A lower Ladakhi version of the Kesar Saga*, Bibliotheca Indica. [Can Drumba be connected with Dhruva as the Polar Star is called in Sanskrit?] [Ed.]

be the messenger of the king in the Saga. And indeed, Shargola is believed to be the home of a legendary messenger *par excellence.* Here, the house of bLon-po Rig-pa can is still shown to travellers. bLon-po Rig-pa-can is said to have acted as the measenger of King Srong-btsan-sgam-po who sent him to China to fetch a bride for the king. The tale of Rig-pa-can's journey to China is apparently indentical with the Prime minister Gar's journey to the same country. I obtained a popular Ladakhi version of the former story, which also contains the tale of the passage of an ant through a spiral labyrinth, as told by Sarat Chandra Das,[1] but the other parts of the Ladakhi tale differ from the Lhasa version. This tale of the minister's embassy is very similar to such episodes of the Kesar Saga as "Kesar's journey to China." The tale of the minister Rig-pa-can's embassy is full of nature-mythology, and may have only a very slight historical foundation. The house in which the minister Rig-pa-can is believed to have been born, is situated near the bridge of Shargola. It is very well built and looks like a nobleman's house; but only a small portion of it has preserved its original beauty. Here also, a Moslem family have taken up their abode and spoilt the old architecture.

The ancient *gdung-rten* (*stūpas*) of Shargola are painted in red, blue and yellow. They are adorned with stucco figures round the base—a feature which is quite unusual in Ladakh. The figures are very time-worn, but seem to represent Garuḍas, or similar fabulous creatures. They are, however, popularly known as Gyad-pa, "heroes," and as the word *Agu* is also used to indicate the heroes of the Kesar Saga, there may be some sort of connection between these figures and Agu Drumba, mentioned above.

The idea that the messenger *par excellence* has his home at Shargola, seems to have been accepted also by Buddhism, when it entered the village. I found here a stone with a rock carving representing Vajra-pāṇi (Phyag-rdor), the constant companion of Buddha on Gandhāra sculptures. This carving is well drenched in oil or ghee, and includes an inscription running from top to bottom which gives the name of the donor, She-rab-zang-po. It looks as if it dates from about the 15th century, to judge by the form of its characters. Vajra-pāṇi is easily confused with Vajra-sattva; in fact, Jäschkee asserts that both are generally taken for the same divinity, and thus we find an inscription *Oṁ Badzrastva* on one of the ancient *gdung-rten*. This inscription is raised in stucco and appears to be older than the Vajra-pāṇi inscription.

The convent of Shargola is a genuine cave monastery and is probably very old. Its former name was apparently *Ma-khang*, "Mother house." This name is found in the above-mentioned song of the *gdung-rten*. It may refer to Śrī-Dēvī (dPal-ldan-lha-mo) or her pre-Buddhist equivalent to whom the monastery was evidently dedicated. As it was recently renovated, no ancient wall-paintings or images were found in it; but the present frescoes were possibly painted in imitation of more ancient ones. I noticed the two following pictures: dPal-ldan-lha-mo (Śrī-Dēvī) riding on a male; and Chos-skyong Satra-pa ("Satrapa, the protector of religion"). Can this be a reminiscence of the

[1] *J. A. S. B.*, Vol. L (1881), Part I, p. 220.

famous Satraps of Buddhist India? He is shown in the dress of an ancient Tibetan knight, mounted on a horse or *rkyang*, with five arrows in his quiver. The lama said that Satrapa was the brother of Agu Drumba who himself is represented by a stucco image. The latter is depicted in the dress of a Ge-lug-pa lama the order to which the monastery now belongs. On one of the walls I noticed also a modern inscription which contained a Tibetan calendar. The people of Mulbe assert that the Shargola monastery was built by two of their ancient chiefs, Thog-lde-Jo (Tog-lde-jo?) and Yang-lde-Jo, father and son.

On the way from Shargola to Kargil, and from Kargil to Dras, I was continually on the look out for traces of Buddhism, which is said to have been the prevailing religion in Purig three or four hundred years ago. But though there were many rock carvings representing ibex, or hunting scenes, I could not, even after a long search, find a single carving representing a *stūpa* or the *Oṁ maṇi padme hūṁ* formula. Yet, I feel sure that there were many of them in the old Buddhist times. They were probably all destroyed, when Kargil became Muhammadan. Many boulders there look, indeed, as if they had been deprived of their outer coating.

People told me that there was a rock with a large Buddhist sculpture at dKar-rtse in the Suru valley, and that it also contained a Tibetan inscription. I could not, however, go there. Another sculpture from Shiṅggo is found pictured in Drew's book of travel.

The Muhammadanism of Purig (Kargil to Dras) is probably closely connected with a certain type of Balti Muhammadanism, another type of which appears to be connected with that of Kashmir, to judge from the style of its mosques. The Kashmir type is found north of Skardo; and what may be called the Purig type, south of Skardo, and in Purig. As Mr. W. M. Conway has made a thorough study of this kind of architecture we cannot do better than quote his description. He says[1]: "We were now come to a country in which the mosque type is different from that north of Skardo. The *Gol* mosque may be taken as an example of the change. It is relatively lower and flatter than the *Shigar Nagyr* mosque. Its walls are built of mud. Its roof is carried on long beams transverse to the axis of the building, and each beam is supported on a row of columns. There is no emphasized central square with four columns round it, and a lantern above, as in the other type. Here the centre is occupied by a column more ornamental than the rest, and standing right between the door and the *mihrāb*. The other columns are of all sorts, oblong and polygonal in section. Capital, column, and base are carved from one log. There is a portico along the east wall. For external finish there is a kind of double corbelled arrangement of beam ends and beams, where roof and walls join. The carving about doors, capitals, and the like, is of a style that was new to me. It affects foliation and flowers rather than geometrical designs. Outside the mosque, on the east, is *meydah*, a collection of round walled latrines — numerous, obvious and large."

On the 6th October, we marched from Kargil to Shimsha Kharbu. On a rock between Kargil and Chanigund, in the Dard district, are several rock carvings which

---

[1] *Climbing and exploration in the Karakorum*, Vol. II, p. 582.

PLATE XLIV.

a. Rock carvings at Dongga.

b. Rock carvings at Dongga.

reminded me of the pre-Buddhist religion of Western Tibet, *viz.*, a *svastika* and a *yōni*, and several ibex; a little later on, we also found a sun symbol among the carvings at Chanigund.[1]

On the road from Chanigund to Shimsha Kharbu, at a place called Dongga, there is a boulder which is covered with many carvings. (Plate XLIV.) The older ones are of a yellowish colour, the modern ones are white. Here we actually found carved representations of *stūpas*, one of the cross type. Most of the more recent carvings represent ibex, but not scenes of ibex hunting. As I have already pointed out in other articles, the ibex is a symbol of fertility according to the pre-Buddhist religion, similar to the ram of Lahul. The pre-Buddhist divinities, Kesar, 'aBruguma, etc., are invoked to grant children. When one is born, the neighbours make presents of "flour ibex" to the happy family. I am inclined to think that the many figures of ibex carved on the rocks of Ladakh, represent thank-offerings for the birth of children.

On another boulder at the same site, I found carvings, representing war-like scenes, *viz.*, the capture and slaughter of prisoners. They do not look very old and may refer to the Ḍōgrā war.

There is an extensive ruin of a castle at Shimsha Kharbu, above the bungalow. When I asked the inhabitants, if they knew who built it, they said that it had been the property of the Khri Sultans of Sod (near Kargil). The word *Khri* is not pronounced *Ṭhi* at Shimsha Kharbu, but *Khri*. The Dard women here, as well as at Dras, wear high caps. We tried to induce one of them to allow herself to be photographed, but were not successful. After the long desert journey from Leh to Purig, we hailed with delight the first appearance of occasional trees on the road side, during this day's march. The mountain sides also ceased to be entirely bare, and showed occasional patches of green pasture.

On the 7th October, we marched from Shimsha Kharbu to Dras, or Hembabs. When Moorcroft visited Dras in 1820, he found it to be the joint property of the king of Ladakh and a Kashmir Malik, both of whom extracted one rupee annually from every household in the Dras valley.[2] He does not mention the ancient Buddhist stone sculptures of Dras at all. They were, however, discovered by Vigne, twenty years later. Cunningham says that the images represent females, and that they are called *Jomo*, "nuns." Both statements are wrong. The sculptures represent Bōdhisattvas and are called *Chamba* (*Byams-pa, i.e.*, Maitrēya). Cunningham made a copy of one of the inscriptions and gives his reading of it. We managed to take Nāsik paper impressions of all three inscriptions found on the sculptures, and also photos of the stones. The sculptures may be described as follows :—

(1) The first stone which is the smallest, shows a man on horseback, his right hand on the bridle, and his left hand above his head, probably wielding a sword. This rider represents a Rāṇā (*Skr. rājānaka*), and has nothing to do with *satī*, as was supposed by Cunningham.[3] This stone has a very clear Śāradā inscription on the reverse. It is the

[1] *Cf.* my article *Historische Dokumente von Khalatse, Z. D. M. G.*, Vol. LXI, p. 583.
[2] Moorcroft, *Travels*, Vol. II, p. 41.
[3] *Cf.* J. Ph. Vogel, *The Rāṇīs of the Panjāb Hills, J. R. A. S.*, 1908, p. 539.

one which was copied by Cunningham, who was unable to translate it. Pandit Mukund Ram of Kashmir who studied our rubbing of it, had, however, no particular difficulty in reading and understanding it. The language is Sanskrit, and the inscription records the erection of two images, one of Maitreya, and another of Avalékitéśvara, evidently the two larger sculptures.

(2) The second stone is about six feet high. The carving shows a plain Maitreya. He wears a three-pointed tiara, and has a rosary in his raised right hand, and a vase in his left. Three small figures, probably human devotees who reach up to his knees, are carved below him, one on his right and the two others on his left. Below them is a lotus throne which contains the figures of two lions couchant. To the left of Maitreya's head is carved another very small human figure. To the right of his head is carved a Śāradā inscription which is, however, in a very dilapidated condition.

(3) The third stone is also six feet high, and shows a standing human figure. The right hand is raised, and the left hand is probably carrying some object. The head-dress has been destroyed. This figure apparently represents Avalōkitēśvara. On his right and left we see two female figure which are almost of the same size as the main image. They are represented in the " Indian attitude," resting on one foot, and holding one hand above their heads. They may be taken as representations of the two Tārās. Below the female on Maitreya's right, we see three small kneeling figures, with their hands raised in supplication (Skr. *añjali*). Below Avalōkitēśvara, there is lotus throne, with two miniature figures emerging from it.[1] There were probably also several small standing figures on both sides of Avalōkitēśvara, reaching up to his knees; but they cannot now be distinguished. On the reverse of this stone, there is a large and elaborate carving of a *stūpa*, with thirteen umbrellas on the top. There are also thirteen steps below it leading up to a square in the centre which contains a human figure. Above the head of the female figure to the left of Avalōkitēśvara, we discovered a much damaged inscription, partly in Tibetan. All the sculptures seem to date approximately from the 10th century A.D.

(4) The fourth sculptured stone stands on the opposite side of the road. The carving represents a full-blown lotus flower, as we often find them on the fountain tablets of Manchad. But this one was decorated with additional vases on the four cardinal points of the wheel.

According to the chronicles of Ladakh, the ancient boundary between Ladakh and Kashmir was at La-rtsa, and a "stone with holes" was the boundary stone. The people of Dras told me that their village was also known by the name of La-rtsa ('Root of the Pass'); but they did not know of such a stone. They also said that, according to their belief, the watershed on the Zo-ji Pass was the frontier between the two countries. I had to leave Pindi Lal with two assistants at Dras, to wait for better weather. He had not been successful in his first attempt at taking rubbings of the inscriptions,

[1] It seems that one of these two figures is kneeling, while the other is standing and carries a lotus-flower as an offering in his right hand. They bear a remarkable resemblance to the two Indo-Scythian donors in the Vaiśravana image of the Lahore Museum. [Ed.]

as the wind tore off the moistened paper, as soon as it was laid on the rock. He and his companions caught us up at Baltal on the other side of the pass, and the Nāsik paper impressions which he brought along with him, were excellent.

On the road between Dras and Pandras, on the Tibetan side of the pass, there is a boulder, on which a much worn inscription *Oṁ maṇi padme hūṁ* can be distinguished. This is the only inscription of that kind which I have been able to trace in the now Muhammadan territory between Shargola and Kashmir. As is the case with all ancient examples of the *Oṁ maṇi padme hūṁ* formula, the Pandras inscription also has the *d* and *m* written separately, while all the more modern inscriptions show *d* and *m* combined into one compound character.

The Zo-ji Pass is called Du-zhi-la by the Tibetans after a goddess Du-zhi-lha-mo (probably Dus-bzhi-lha-mo, "goddess of the four seasons"). The following tale is told of that deity. Du-zhi-lha-mo was the wife of Naropa. When the latter went to Ladakh, he wished to leave her behind, on account of her Kashmiri smell (*Che-ri*, in full *Kha-che-dri*). She was displeased at that, and turned her back towards Ladakh, and her face towards Kashmir. This caused Ladakh to dry up, and Kashmir to become fertile. People say: "I wish he had taken her to Ladakh, then it would be as green as Kashmir." And the sudden appearance of the luxuriant vegetation on the Kashmir side of the Zo-ji Pass is really an ever fresh and pleasant surprise to the traveller from Ladakh. Although during the last two or three days a few scattered trees have made their appearance on the roadside, a beautifully wooded mountain slope is more than he would expect to rise before his vision, and yet it is so; for on turning a corner of the excellent new road across the pass, green wooded Kashmir suddenly makes its appearance, and desert Ladakh remains behind.

The first typical Kashmiri village on the south side of the Zo-ji Pass, is Sonamarg (Golden Meadow). A short distance above the village, there are remains of ancient ramparts which were built across the valley. The Tibetans call them *La-dvags-rgyal-poi-mchibs-ra*, "the king of Ladakh's horse-enclosure." They believe that their ancient kings had their horses on this side of the pass. The Kashmiri inhabitants of Sonamarg, however, believe that these ramparts are the remains of a Qila' (fort) of a certain Ibrāhīm K͟hān of Kābul. I may add that the Tibetans call the resthouse of Baltal *Shing-khang*, and the village of Sonamarg, *bSod-nams-ma-lig*.

About a mile above the village of Gund, on the old road, is a rock covered with several ancient and crude carvings of human figures which are believed by the Tibetans to represent King Kesar. They remind one of those put up in commemoration of the dead in Manchad and Lahul. How these carvings of human beings (about eight), came to be connected with King Kesar, I do not know. On the same rock we found also sun symbols, for instance, wheels with eight spikes.

In Śrīnagar, the capital of Kashmir, I was particularly interested in all those places which are connected with Riñchan Bhōṭi, the Tibetan (Ladakhi) king of Kashmīr (circa 1319—1323 A.D.). As is stated by Sir Walter Lawrence in his book on Kashmīr,[1]

[1] *Valley of Kashmir*, p. 190.

means "Tibetan" and the Ladakhis, therefore, called Riñchan's mosque "The Tibetan Mosque."

Only a short distance from Bulbul Lankar, people showed us the "grave of Rindān Shāh." It is indicated by a plain stone without an inscription, a little larger than the tombstones of ordinary people. It is surrounded by a low stone wall on all four sides, and rose bushes have been planted inside the enclosure (Plate XLV, b).

There are many rumours among the Ladakhis about another Bodro Masjid (Tibetan Mosque) at Śrīnagar. They say that it was an old Buddhist temple which was converted into a mosque several centuries ago, and that pictures of Buddhist saints are traceable under its whitewash. Popular tradition has connected this mosque with Naropa and calls it Na-ro-pai-thsogs-khang, "Naropa's Assembly Hall." Of this Bodro Masjid, it is asserted that it is situated below the Hari Parbat or castle hill of Śrīnagar; but although we tried our best to find it, we were not successful. In the course of our researches we were taken to another very insignificant little mosque outside the town, at Idka (Īdgāh) which did not appear to be very old. This little mosque was also called Bodro Masjid by the Kashmiris. It may have been erected on the site of a former mosque which was more worthy of the name; but the real Bodro Masjid with the Buddhist pictures below its whitewash still remains to be discovered.

The Ladakhis regard the Ta<u>kh</u>t-i-Sulaimān, the hill overlooking Śrīnagar, as the former abode of Padma-sambhava, and have legends connected with him. Padma-sambhava is supposed to have lived in the present stone temple on the top of the hill, which is believed to have been his hermitage. They called the hill *Puspa ari*,[1] and say that the hermit once saw seven magicians perform miracles on the surface of the lake which then covered the Kashmīr valley. He threw a handful of barley over them and thus prevented their escape; for according to Tibetan belief, spirits can be arrested by throwing barley at them. He kept them in his service, and the present inhabitants of Kashmīr are descended from them. The works of art executed by the Kashmiris are like the work of magicians in the eyes of the Ladakhis.

At Śrīnagar I enjoyed the hospitality of the two doctors Neve, well known as medical missionaries and explorers. In their house, I also made the acquaintance of Dr. Longstaff who had just returned from a most successful expedition along the frontier of Ladakh and Turkestan. The results of this expedition, *viz.*, the discovery of the largest glacier, and of one of the highest mountain peaks in the Himālayas, are now being published in various geographical journals. It was a great treat for me to be able to discuss a number of geographical questions, regarding Tibet, with this experienced geographer. It was also encouraging to meet here with Sir Francis Younghusband's interest in our work and achievements.

As Pindi Lal belonged to Dr. Spooner's establishment we travelled first to Peshāwar, to divide our office equipment between the Peshāwar and the Simla offices. After a few ideal days, spent under the hospitable roof of the discoverer of the "Buddha's relics," we reached Simla safely on the 11th of November.

[1] The original name was *Gōpādri*. *Cf.* Stein *Rājataraṅgiṇi*, Vol. 1, p. 51, note 341.

APPENDIX A.

LIST OF ANTIQUITIES ACQUIRED BY DR. FRANCKE IN INDIAN TIBET.

I.—BRITISH GOVERNMENT COLLECTION.

(Preserved in Indian Museum, Calcutta.)

1. Tablet of unburnt clay showing a seated Buddha with two standing Bōdhisattvas, surrounded by many small *stūpas* (29). Inscription in late Gupta: *Yē dharmā.* From Khalatse, Ladakh. (6 by 4½ inches.)

2. Ditto.

3. Tablet of unburnt clay showing a Buddha in Vajrāsana, seated in an ornamental arch decorated with animals. Below him a carpet with the wheel. From Nubra, Ladakh. (2¾ by 2¼ inches.)

4. Tablet of unburnt grey clay, showing Saṁvara (bDe-mchog) standing (three or four faces, twelve arms, with his Śakti) lower portion broken. From Chang, Bashahr. (2½ by 2 inches.)

5. Tablet of unburnt grey clay, showing Saṁvara (bDe-mchog) seated. (Three faces, ten arms) with his Śakti. From Chang, Bashahr. (2½ by 2⅛ inches.)

6. Tablet of unburnt clay, showing six Buddhist deities, lower row probably Avalōkitēśvara with two Tārās, upper row Maitrēya (?) in the middle, on his right Vajrapāṇi, on his left Mañjuśrī. From Nako, Bashahr. (2½ by 2¼ inches.)

7. Ditto.

8. Ditto.

9. Tablet of unburnt clay, showing Vajrapāṇi in his wrathful form. From Nako, Bashahr. (1¾ by 1⅜ inches.)

10. Tablet of unburnt red clay, showing a Bōdhisattva seated on lotus, perhaps Padmapāṇi, four arms, one with lotus. Excellent finish. From Nubra, Ladakh. (2¼ by 2 inches.)

11. Tablet of unburnt clay, gaily coloured, showing Tārā. From Leh. (1 by ⅝ inch.)

12. Tablet of unburnt clay, showing seated Mañjuśrī. Inscription: *Yē dharmā*, in Indian characters of the 9th century. From Skara, near Leh. (2½ by 2 inches.)

13. Tablet of burnt clay, showing bTsongkhapa with book seated with three disciples, two, with books sitting to his right, and one standing to his left. Two piles of books in background. Coloured red and gold; lower part broken off. On border Tibetan inscription: *dge* "virtue." From Leh. (2 by 2¼ inches.)

14. Tablet of unburnt clay, showing a lama seated in European fashion, believed to be lama Pha-dam-pa sangs-rgyas. Possibly it is Maitrēya. From Leh. (3 by 2¼ inches.)

15. Tablet of burnt clay, showing Pehar, standing on a corpse. Gaily coloured, round shape. Said to contain a relic of Buddha. Seal on reverse. Bought in Leh, came from Lhasa. (1½ by 1½ inches.)

16. Tablet of unburnt grey clay, showing Avalōkitēśvara with eight arms and eleven heads, standing. From Li, Bashahr. (6½ by 3¼ inches.)

17. Tablet of unburnt clay, showing effigy of *stūpa.* Inscription *Yē dharmā* in Indian characters of 9th century. From Skara, near Leh. (2 by 1⅝ inches.)

18. Tablet of unburnt clay, painted white, showing *stūpa* in the centre, and an inscription in twenty-seven lines, apparently in ancient Nāgarī characters, but no longer legible. From Sabu, Ladakh. (3¼ by 3¼ inches.)

19. Same as No. 17.

20. Tablet of unburnt clay, painted white, showing Padmapāṇi. From Nako (?), Bashahr. (1⅝ by 1⅜ inches.)

21. Tablet of unburnt clay, painted white, showing Padmapāṇi. Traces of Tibetan inscription. From Rarang, Bashahr. (1⅞ by 1⅝ inches.)

22. Ditto.

23. Tablet of unburnt clay, showing Buddha seated in the earth-touching attitude (*Bhūmisparśa-mudrā*). From Nako, Bashahr. (1⅝ by 1¼ inches.)

24. Tablet of unburnt clay, showing Vajradhara (rDo-rje-'achhang) seated on a lotus. From Rarang, Bashahr. (2 by 1⅝ inches.)

25. Miniature *stūpa* of unburnt clay. From Rarang, Bashahr. (1⅝ by 1⅛ inches.)

26. Ditto.

27. Miniature *stūpa* of unburnt clay, painted white. From Nubra, Ladakh. (1⅛ by ⅞ inch.)

28. Fragment of stucco, showing central figure of Buddha (?) seated on lotus, and three smaller figures of Bōdhisattvas (?) each seated on a lotus. Coloured, badly damaged. From Nyoma, Ladakh. Dr. Shawe's collection. (5¼ by 4 inches.)

29. Wooden figure of a standing Bōdhisattva. Black wood, traces of gold bronze, five-pointed crown, lotus throne, right hand pointing to the ground, left arm bent and hand pointing upwards. Bought at Leh. (3⅝ by 1 inch.)

30. Carved piece of black wood pierced at one end. Carvings on one side. One representing a pyramidal *stūpa*, the other a seated Buddha in *Bhūmisparśamudrā*. Found at the ruined site of the *bKa-blon's* house at Leh. (2½ by 1 inch.)

31. Bronze statuette of a standing lama (?). His hands folded. The object which he held in his hands is broken off, as is his head. Purchased at Leh, and asserted to come from Khotan. (3¾ by 1½ inches.)

32. Fragment of a copper pot, ornament of double vajra. Inscription *rgyal-sras-dbang-gsing dbang-po*. Found on top of *rNamrgyal rtsemo* hill, Leh. (4 by 1⅝ inches.)

33. Hammer, used at the lama dances. Tibetan name : *rDorje thoba,* on account of the *rDorje* (*vajra*) ornaments. Bought at Leh. (24½ by 7½ inches.)

34. Hatchet, used at the lama dances. Tibetan name *Chu-srin-poi-lce.* The blade proceeding from a *makara's* mouth. Purchased at Leh. (27 by 9½ inches.)

35. Iron hook, used at the lama dances. Tibetan name *Zorba*. Purchased at Leh. (21⅜ by 5½ inches.)

36. Trumpet made of a human thigh bone, used at the lama dances. Tibetan name *rKang dung*. Purchased at Leh. (12½ by 2½ inches.)

37. Wooden mask, ancient type, used at the lama dances. Tibetan name *Baq*. Found in the godown at Nako, Bashahr, and purchased. (7½ by 7½ inches.)

38. Iron head ornament of women, ornamented with eight lotus-petals, brass-plated and set with turquoises. Tibetan name *Kyir-Kyir*. Found near ancient graves at Skara, near Leh. (3⅝ by 3⅝ inches.)

39. Ancient wooden head-ornament of females, worn on the crown of the head, as in Lahul, set with Indian seeds and turquoises, four incisions. Found at sBalu-mkhar, near Khalatse. (1¾ by 1⅝ inches.)

40. Silver head-ornament of females, worn on the crown of the head called *mchod khung*. Found in Byangthang. (1¼ by 1⅝ inches.)

41. Shell button with black incised ornament of eight forked spikes, pierced in the middle. Tibetan name *Dung char*. Said to have been worn by ancient Dards. Found at Khalatse. (1 by $1\frac{1}{8}$ inches.)

42. Ancient cross of iron and bronze, hollow inside. Ornaments of double spirals at the ends of its beams. Said to have been excavated near mThsomo Riri. (2 by $1\frac{7}{8}$ inches.)

43. String of sixteen beads, fourteen of shell, one of yellow material, and one coral, the latter broken. The shell beads cir. $\frac{1}{2}$ inch in diameter. Said to have been found in a ruined *mchod-rten* near Leh.

44. String of five beads, three of bone, excavated at Khalatse, one of mother-of-pearl coloured glass from ancient grave at Leh; one of crystal found at Skinding near Khalatse (diameter $\frac{3}{8}$ to $\frac{3}{4}$ inch.)

45. Old stone lamp, plain, without handle. Tibetan name *rKyongtse*. From Khalatse. (5 by $3\frac{1}{2}$ inches.)

46. Stone lamp, plain, with handle. Tibetan name *rKyongtse*. From Khalatse. (7 by $3\frac{1}{2}$ inches.)

47. Stone lamp, with ornaments and handle. Tibetan name *rKyongtse*. From Khalatse. ($5\frac{1}{4}$ by $2\frac{3}{8}$ inches.)

48. Old stone axe, blunt, used for breaking wood. Tibetan name *Kalam*. From Spiti. (7 by $6\frac{1}{2}$ inches.)

49. Old stone axe, blunt, used for breaking wood. Tibetan name *Kalam*. From Shibke, Tibet. (4 by $4\frac{1}{2}$ inches.)

50. Stone tobacco bowl, of a *hukka*. Tibetan name *Trob*. From Khalatse. ($2\frac{3}{4}$ by $1\frac{3}{4}$ inches)

51. Stone charm. The charm to be written on it with chalk. Hole for string. From Dard Castle, Khalatse. ($2\frac{3}{4}$ by $2\frac{1}{4}$ inches.)

52. Stone charm. The charm to be written on it with chalk. Hole for string. From sBalu-mkhar near Khalatse. ($2\frac{1}{2}$ by $2\frac{1}{2}$ inches.)

53. Stone of cylindrical shape, perhaps used as a hammer, or a handle. From Khalatse. ($2\frac{1}{2}$ by $1\frac{1}{4}$ inches.)

54. Fragment of a stone lamp (*rKyongtse*) ornamented with band of foliage. Found in a Dard grave, at Khalatse. ($5\frac{1}{4}$ by $1\frac{1}{4}$ inches.)

55. Stone axe, to be used without a handle, with a hollow for the thumb. Had a sharp edge. Found at sBalu-mkhar, near Khalatse. (5 by 4 inches.)

56. Stone knife, handle missing. Tibetan name *rDo-gri*. From Skinding, near Khalatse. ($13\frac{3}{4}$ by $1\frac{1}{4}$ inches.)

57. Ancient bone knife, without handle. Found at sBalu-mkhar, near Khalatse. ($4\frac{3}{4}$ by $1\frac{1}{8}$ inches.)

58. Two stone needles (genuineness doubtful) $4\frac{5}{8}$ and $3\frac{5}{8}$ inches long. Both broken. From Khalatse.

59. Stone inkpot, pierced in the bottom. From Khalatse. ($2\frac{3}{8}$ by 2 inches.)

60. Ammonite which was worshipped in the house of lama Ngorub Tungtog of sNam-rgya and was bathed in butter. Tibetan name *Norbu yang khyil* [*dbyang* (?) *dkyil*]. From sNamrgya, Bashahr. (3 by $2\frac{5}{8}$ inches.)

61. Spindle whorl, made of burnt clay, ornamented with impressed lines, broken. Tibetan name *Phanglo*. From Khalatse. Found at sBalu-mkhar. ($3\frac{1}{4}$ by $3\frac{1}{4}$ inches.)

62. Spindle whorl, made of stone. Tibetan name *Phanglo*. From Khalatse. Found at 'aBrogpai-mkhar. ($1\frac{3}{4}$ by $1\frac{3}{4}$ inches.)

63. Tibetan silver coin, called *Nag-tang*, coined in 1722 A.D. by Ranjit Malla Deva, of Bhatgaon, for Tibet. Purchased at Leh.

64. Three early Muhammadan coins from Turkestan. Compare Dr. Stein, *Ancient Khotan*, Plate XC, No. 45. Purchased at Leh, came from Khotan.

65. Fruit of *Trapa natans*, collected by the Tibetans in Lake Rawalsa, Mandi. They call the fruit *mThso padmacangyi sbyin rlabs*. From Rawalsar.

66. Sherd of ancient pottery with linear impressed ornaments. Found at Kalagtrung castle, Poo, Bashahr. (2⅓ by 1⅓ inches).

67. Sherd of ancient hand-made pottery with linear impressed ornament. Found at Kalagtrung castle, Poo, Bashahr. (3¼ by 2½ inches.)

68. Sherd of ancient hand-made pottery, handle, with ornament of impressed lines. From bragnag mkhar, Khalatse. (4 by 3 inches.)

69. Sherd of ancient pottery, handle, plain. From Khalatse. (5 by 3 inches.)

70. Tibetan drill, made of wood and a string, with an iron point. Tibetan name *sGiri*. From Shibke, Tibet. (16 by 7¼ by 11½ inches.)

71. Tibetan scales (for weighing) consisting of a stick with marks, a bag of cloth, and a weight of stone in a bag, Tibetan name *Nyaga phordo*. From Shibke, Tibet. Length of stick 23¼ inches.

72. Tibetan writing tablet, made of wood, consisting of two boards, one showing woodcarving of *svastika* ornament. Tibetan name *samtra*. From Khalatse. (14⅝ by 2½ inch.)

73. Tibetan cup of wood, with iron ring. Tibetan name *Kore* or *Lahorgyi Kore*, "cup of Lahore." From Khalatse. (4 by 2 inches.)

74. Tibetan lock and key, of iron. Tibetan name *Kulig*. From Leh. (1¾ by 1¾ inches and 3 inches.)

75. Iron hoe and hammer, broken. Tibetan name *Togtse*. Found at Dard castle, Skinding valley, near Khalatse. (4¼ by 1⅝ inches.)

76. Iron penholder case, with incised foliage ornaments. Tibetan name *Myug rogs*. Found in Byangthang, Tibet. (10 by ⅝ inches.)

77. Iron spoon, incised with foliage ornament. Tibetan name *Thurmangs*. Found at sLas, Skamlung, Khalatse. (5 × 1½ inches.)

78. Pills, made of the Dalai Lama's excrement. Purchased at Khalatse, Ladakh.

79. Sieve cup of copper leaf with brass trimmings, was found filled with grain. Found in ruined *stūpa*, at Skara, near Leh. (3¼ by 2 inches.)

II.—Kashmir State Collection.

(*Preserved in Pratap Singh Museum, Srinagar.*)

1. Coloured tablet figure of Mañjuśri ('aJams-dpal) seated, fragmentary (4½ inches high, 3½ inches broad). Burnt clay. From Basgo, Ladakh.

2. Coloured tablet with figure of bTsongkhapa, seated on lotus throne (3¾ inches high, 2¼ inches broad). Burnt clay. From Leh.

3. Coloured round seal (3⅝ inches diameter). Burnt clay. From Basgo, Ladakh.

4. Coloured tablet with figure of Tārā (*sGrol-ma*) seated in *varamudrā*, painted gold (4 inches high, 2¾ inches broad). Burnt clay. From Tar, Ladakh.

5. The same, a little damaged.

6. Tablet of burnt clay showing seated Buddha under arch with *stūpas*, and two monks, probably his chief disciples, Maudgalyāyana and Śāriputra, standing on his right and left (1¾ inches high, 1¾ inches broad). From Tar, Ladakh.

7. Tablet of burnt clay showing seated figure of a Bōdhisattva, probably Vajrapāṇi (Phyag-rdor) (2 inches high, 1⅞ inches broad). From Leh.

8. Tablet of black burnt clay, showing a seated Tārā (sGrol-ma) (1½ inches high, 1⅛ inches broad). Inscription in Tibetan characters, indistinct. *Oṁ dvare d .... dvare duri s.* From Leh.

9. Tablet of burnt clay, showing seated Buddha-like figure, damaged, painted white (2 inches high, 1½ inches broad). Inscription in Tibetan characters *Oṁ a hum*, on reverse. From Leh.

10. Tablet of unburnt clay, showing bTsongkhapa seated on a lotus-throne between two disciples standing on each side holding a flower with a sword and book respectively (2¾ inches high, 2¼ inches broad). From Leh.

11. Tablet of unburnt clay showing bTsongkhapa seated with book and sword as in No. 10 (2 inches high, 1¾ inches broad). From sNyemo, Ladakh.

12. Tablet of unburnt clay showing a lama seated in European fashion; believed to be Pha dam-pa-sangs-rgyas. Possibly Maitrēya. (3 inches high, 2¼ inches broad.) From Leh.

13. Tablet of unburnt clay showing a four-armed, seated Maitrēya (Byams-pa) with lotus and bowl and with a *stūpa* on his head. Inscription in Tibetan characters: first *Oṁ maṇi padme hūṁ*; then the *Yē dharmā* formula, rest indistinct, then *Oṁ a huṁ.* (2¾ inches high, 2¼ inches broad.) From *Likir*,

14. Head of a stucco figurine of a Bōdhisattva coloured. Traces of colour. From Leh. (1½ by 2 inches.)

15. Tablet of unburnt clay, showing Tārā (sGrol-ma) seated. From Thugsrje chenpo in Rubshu. (2 by 2 inches).

16. Same as No. 11, but showing traces of a Tibetan inscription. Inscription... ... ...*brang po la namo.* From sNyemo, Ladakh.

17. Tablet of unburnt clay, showing Saṁvara (bDe-mchog) with his Śakti (three or four faces, twelve arms). From Leh. (3½ by 2½ inches.)

18. Tablet of unburnt clay, showing Vajrapāṇi (Phyag-dor), in his wrathful form, with six arms three faces, trampling on two corpses. From Leh. (3¾ by 2¾ inches.)

19. Tablet of unburnt clay, showing Mañjuśrī. Inscription in Tibetan characters indistinct. From Leh. (2½ by 2 inches.)

20. Tablet of unburnt clay, painted yellow, showing Buddha seated in *bhūmisparśa.* From Leh. (1¼ by 1 inch.)

21. Tablet of unburnt clay, showing Tārā, same as No. 15. From Rubshu.

22. Tablet of unburnt clay, showing indistinct Bōdhisattva, probably Avalōkitēśvara with two lotus flowers. Tibetan inscription. *Oṁ a hum.* From *Thugsrje chenpo, Rubshu.* (1½ by 1¼ inches.)

23. Ditto.

24. Ditto.

25. Miniature *stūpa* of unburnt clay with eight little *stūpas* in relief. Inscription *Yē dharmā* in Nāgarī characters of 11th century. From Spithug, Ladakh. (4 by 3 inches.)

26. Miniature *stūpa* of unburnt red clay. Inscription *Yē dharmā* in Tibetan characters. From *rGya*, Ladakh. (3½ by 2½ inches.)

27. Miniature *stūpa* of unburnt clay. Inscription in unknown characters, possibly kind of ancient Nāgarī. From Leh. (2 by 1½ inches.)

28. Miniature *stūpa* of unburnt red clay with eight little *stūpas* in relief. Inscription indistinct, apparently the *Yē dharmā* formula, in Tibetan or Gupta characters. From rGya, Ladakh. (1½ by 1 inch.)

29. Ditto.

30. Ditto.

31. Tablet of unburnt clay, showing Mañjuśrī ('aJams-dpal) seated with sword and book. Inscription *Yē dharmā* in Indian characters of circa 800-900 A.D. From rGya. (2¼ by 2 inches.)

32. Ditto.

33. Tablet of unburnt clay showing Bōdhisattva (Maitrēya?) seated with lotus, book and *stūpa.* Inscription *Yē dharmā* in ancient Tibetan characters. From rGya, Ladakh. (2¼ by 2 inches)

34. Ditto.

35. Ditto. Red clay tablet, similar to Nos. 33 and 34, but book omitted.

36. Tablet of unburnt red clay, showing **Vajradhara** (rDo-rje-'achang) seated. Tibetan inscription *Om a hūm*. From rGya, Ladakh. (1¼ by 1½ inches.)

37. Tablet of unburnt red clay, showing Buddha seated in *bhūmisparśa*. From rGya, Ladakh. (1¾ by 1½ inches.)

38. Tablet of unburnt red clay, showing wrathful form of Vajrapāṇi (Phyag-rdor) (two arms only). From rGya, Ladakh. (1¾ by 1½ inches.)

39. Tablet of unburnt clay coloured red, showing two small and one large *stūpa*, the latter of the ladder type. Inscription indistinct. Apparently the *Yē dharmā* formula in old Tibetan or Gupta characters. From Staglung, Ladakh. (2¾ × 2¾ inches.)

40. Tablet of unburnt clay painted red, showing two small and one larger *stūpa*, the latter of the ladder type. Inscription quite indistinct. From Staglung, Ladakh. (2¾ by 2¼ inches.)

41. Tablet of unburnt clay, painted red showing nine *stūpas* in two rows. Inscription quite indistinct. From Staglung, Ladakh. (3 by 3 inches.)

42. Tablet of unburnt clay, painted red, showing two small and one large *stūpa*, the latter of the ladder type. Inscription: The *Yē dharmā* formula in ancient Tibetan characters. From Staglung, Ladakh. (3½ by 3¾ inches.)

43. Tablet of unburnt clay, showing five *stūpas*, below them inscription of the *Yē dharmā* formula in ancient Tibetan characters. From Skara, near Leh. (3 by 2 inches.)

44. Tablet of unburnt clay, showing two small and one large *stūpa*, the latter of the ladder type. Inscription of the *Yē dharmā* formula in ancient Śāradā, circa 10th century. From Skara, near Leh. 2¾ by 2¾ inches.)

45. Tablet of unburnt clay, showing one *stūpa* of the ladder type. Inscription *Yē dharmā* formula in ancient Śāradā. From Skara, near Leh. (2½ by 2½ inches.)

46. Tablet of unburnt clay, showing one *stūpa*. Inscription very indistinct, probably the *Yē dharmā* formula. From Skara, near Leh. (2¼ by 2¼ inches.)

47. Tablet of unburnt clay, showing ten *stūpas*. Inscription *Yē dharmā* in ancient Tibetan characters. From Skara, near Leh. (2½ × 2½ inches.)

48. Tablet of unburnt clay, showing one *stūpa*. Inscription *Yē dharmā* in Śāradā characters. From Skara near Leh. (3¾ by 2½ inches.)

49. Tablet of unburnt clay, showing eleven *stūpas*. Inscription indistinct, probably the *Yē dharmā* formula. From Skara near Leh. (1¾ by 2 inches.)

50. Tablet of unburnt clay showing one *stūpa* of the ladder type. Inscription *Yē dharmā* in Śāradā of about the 11th century. From rGyamthsa, near Leh. (1½ by 1¼ inches.)

51. Tablet of unburnt red clay showing two small and one large *stūpa*, the latter of the ladder type and two lotus flowers. Inscription the *Yē dharmā* formula in Śāradā. From Basgo, Ladakh. (3 by 2½ inches.)

52. Ditto.

53. Tablet of unburnt clay showing two small and one large *stūpa*. Inscription *Yē dharmā* in ancient Tibetan characters. From rGya (?). (1¾ by 1¾ inches.)

54. Tablet of unburnt red clay showing one *stūpa*. Inscription *Yē dharmā* in ancient Nāgarī of about the 9th century. From rGya, Ladakh. (3¾ by 1½ inches.)

55. Tablet of unburnt red clay, showing two smaller and one larger *stūpa*. Inscription *Yē dharmā* in early Nāgarī of about the 9th century. From rGya. (1½ by 1½ inches.)

56. Tablet of unburnt clay, painted red, showing one *stūpa*. Inscription *Yē dharmā* in late Gupta. Half broken off. From Phuga, Rubshu. (2 by 1½ inches.)

57. Tablet of unburnt red clay showing three *stūpas*. Inscription *Yē dharmā* in ancient Tibetan characters. Broken. From rGya, Ladakh. (1¾ by 1½ inches.)

57*a*. Tablet of unburnt clay, showing effigy of *stūpa*. Inscription *Yē dharmā* in Indian characters of the 9th century. From Skara, near Leh. (2 by $1\frac{3}{4}$ inches.)

58. Ancient sherd of pottery from Alchi mkhar-gog with dark red designs. (4 by $2\frac{1}{2}$ inches.)

59. Ditto. ditto. ($3\frac{1}{4}$ by $1\frac{1}{2}$ inches.)

60. Ditto. ditto. ($2\frac{1}{2}$ by $1\frac{1}{2}$ inches.)

61. Ditto. ditto. ($2\frac{3}{4}$ by $2\frac{3}{4}$ inches.)

62. Ditto. ditto. ($2\frac{3}{4}$ by $1\frac{3}{4}$ inches.)

63. Ditto. ditto. ($1\frac{3}{4}$ by $1\frac{1}{2}$ inches.)

64. Ditto. ditto. ($2\frac{1}{2}$ by $1\frac{3}{4}$ inches.)

65. Ditto. ditto. ($2\frac{3}{4}$ by $1\frac{3}{4}$ inches.)

66. Ditto. ditto. ($2\frac{1}{4}$ by $1\frac{1}{4}$ inches.)

67. Ditto. ditto. (2 by $1\frac{1}{2}$ inches.)

68. Ditto. ditto. ($1\frac{1}{3}$ by $\frac{3}{4}$ inch.)

69. Bronze button from ancient grave, Leh, spiral ornament. (2 by $2\frac{1}{4}$ inches.)

70. Bronze pendant from same place, circular ornament. ($2\frac{1}{4}$ by $7\frac{3}{4}$ inches.)

71. Bronze buttons, four combined, from same place, circular ornament. ($1\frac{1}{8}$ by $1\frac{1}{8}$ inches.)

72. Bronze seal (?) from same place, cross lines and dot ornament. ($1\frac{3}{8}$ by $1\frac{1}{4}$ inches.)

73. Two bronze beads, from same place. ($\frac{3}{4}$ by $\frac{1}{4}$ inch.)

74. Bell-like pendant, from same place. (1 by $\frac{5}{8}$ inch.)

75. Bone tube from Waka castle. (3 by $\frac{5}{8}$ inch.)

76. Bronze button from ancient grave, Leh, broken, flower ornament (?) ($1\frac{1}{2}$ by $1\frac{3}{8}$ inches.)

77. Bronze button, from same place, broken, star ornament. ($1\frac{1}{2}$ by $1\frac{1}{2}$ inches.)

78. Coloured glass bead from grave at Leh.

APPENDIX B.

LIST OF MANUSCRIPTS AND WOOD-PRINTS ACQUIRED BY DR. FRANCKE IN INDIAN TIBET.

I. LITERATURE.

(a) *Books obtained chiefly in Ladakh.*

1. Shar-rgan-gyi-glu-bzhugs-so, The Songs of the Shar-rgan festival, from Poo (*sPu*). Copied from a MS. at Poo by bsKal-bzang. 29 ps. 8°.

2. The same, translated into ordinary Tibetan, by bsKal-bzang.

3. Bod-rgya-nag-rgya-gar-rnams-kyi rgyal-rabs-bzhugs-so, History of Tibet, China, and India copied from the great *rGyal-rabs* of Khalatse by bZod-pa-phun-thsogs. 96 ps. foolscap.

4. Ka-dros-chos-sder (bKā-gros-chos-gter), a small tract in Skrt. and Tibetan, extracted from a mchod-rten at Chemre and sold to us. On p. 1, it is stated to be a śāstra (bstan-chos) composed by King Srong-btsan-sgam-po and two monks, *viz.*, Nam-Khai-snying-po, and Atsar (Ācārya) Nag-po, and sent to Nga-ris (Western Tibet). 14 × 3½ cm.

5. Photographic reproduction of No. Or. 6683, sheet 34 to 72 of L-MS. of the La-dvags-rgyal-rabs. From British Museum, London. 22 × 16½ cm.

6. Bod-sa-gzhi-chag-rabs, Origin of the world, from the A-MS. of the La-dvags-rgyal-rabs, copied by Joseph Thse-brtan of Leh. 13 ps. foolscap.

7. La-dvags-rgyal-rabs, Chapter VIII, (from bDe-ldan-rnam-rgyal to Thse-dpal-rnam-rgyal), copied from B-MS. in the possession of Tsandan Munshi, Leh, by Joseph Thse-brtan, Leh. 12 ps. foolscap.

8. La-dvags-rgyal-rabs, Chapter VIII, copied from C-MS. in the possession of Munshi dPal-rgyas, Leh, by Joseph Thse-brtan, Leh. 5 ps. foolscap.

9. Dzam-mu-ma-hā-rā-dzā-gu-lāb-sing-gi-dmag-mis-la-dvags-dang-bod-la-dmag-btang-bai-lo-rgyus-bzhugs-so, History of the Dogra war, copied from C-MS. of the La-dvags-rgyal-rabs in the possession of Munshi dPal-rgyas, Leh, by Joseph Thse-brtan, Leh. 7 ps. foolscap.

10. La-dvags-la-ma-hā-rā-ja-gu-lab-sing-gis-mngā-mdzad-pa-nas-phyin-gyi-lo-rgyus-bzhugs-so, History of Ladakh after the Dogra war, copied from C-MS. of the La-dvags-rgyal-rabs in the possession of Munshi dPal-rgyas, Leh, by Joseph Thse-brtan of Leh. 10 ps. foolscap.

11. bZang-Kar-chags-thsul-gyi-lo-rgyus, History of the origin of Zangs-dKar, copied from a MS in possession of the chiefs of sTista, by bZod-pa-bde-chen of Kyelang. One sheet of Tibetan paper, 62 by 58 cm. Writing on one side only.

12. gCig-tan-gyi-jo-rabs-ni, History of the chiefs of gCig-tan. The original being lost, the history was taken down according to the dictation of the present ex-chief of gCig-tan by Munshi Ye-shes-rig-'adzin of Khalatse. One sheet, 59 by 22⅔ cm.

13. Kha-la-tse-pa-me-me-thse-bstan-gyis-bshad-pai-thā-dmag-gi-lo-rgyus-bzhugs-so, Joseph Thse-brtan's history of the Dogra war. Lithographic print from Leh Mission Press, 1903. 16 ps. 8°.

14. Chronicles of the chiefs of Kolong-Lahul, in Urdu, copied from the original in the possession of Chief Amar Chand of Kolong, by bZod-pa-bde-chen, Kyelang. Small book in octavo.

15. Genealogical tree of the chiefs of Kolong, Lahul, in Tibetan, copied from a one-sheet manuscript in the possession of Chief Amar Chand of Kolong, by bZod-pa-bde-chen of Kyelang. One sheet octavo with two additions.

16. Genealogical tree of the Chiefs of Barbog, Lahul, in Tibetan, copied from a one-sheet manuscript in possession of the Barbog chiefs by bZod-pa-bde-chen of Kyelang. One sheet, 15 by 19 cm.

17. gSer-gyi-me-long-zhes-pai-rgyal-rabs-bzhugs-so, The chronicles of Tinan, in Tibetan, copied from a manuscript in possession of the chiefs of Tinan by bZod-pa-bde-chen of Kyelang. One sheet of Tibetan paper. 45 by 22½ cm.

18. Genealogical tree of the chiefs of Tinan, copied from a one-sheet manuscript in possession of the chiefs of Tinan by bZod-pa-bde-chen of Kyelang. One sheet, 26½ by 21½ cm.

19. gSar-gzugs-'agyur-thor-bu-mi-'adra-ba-yin, Introduction to the Tibeto-Mongolian alphabet, copied from a one-sheet block-print from Leh by Munshi Ye-shes-rig-'adzin of Khalatse, one-sheet foolscap.

20. Nyo-pas-sgo-la-btang-ces-kyi-glu-yin, Marriage-songs from Tagmacig, copied from an original MS. at Tagmacig by Munshi Ye-shes-rig-'adzin of Khalatse. 74 ps. 4°.

21. gSung-don-bzhin-yung-'agrung-dgon-gyi-phyag-rabs, Tibetan MS. "the mahātmya of Lamayuru," one sheet of Tibetan paper, 24½ by 26 cm. Copied by bsTan-'adzin-dpal-'abyor of Leh.

22. Om-sba-sti-siddham-dpag-kyid-chos-khor-lha-sai-zhing-mkhams-'adir, etc., Tibetan MS. "the treaty between Lhasa and Bashahr." Copied by Lobzang of Poo, from a MS. in the hands of the rDzong-dpon of Tsaparang. One sheet of Tibetan paper, 57 by 44½ cm.

23. The same, copied by Hira of sNam-rgya from a MS. in his own possession, one sheet, 55½ by 33½ cm.

24. History of Rainchan Shah, from Azmi's History of Kashmir. Copied from a Persian MS. 4 ps. foolscap. English translation appended.

25. History of Rainchan Shah, from Malvi Haider Malik's History of Kashmir. Copied from a Persian MS., foolscap. English translation appended.

26. lTang-dmag, the war against lTang, copied from MS. containing the literary version of the Kesar-saga, in the possession of the bKa-blon at Changs-pa, by Joseph Thse-brtan of Leh.

(b) *A Collection of books acquired from Lahul.*

1. gSer-'od-dam-pa, Suvarṇaprabhāsasūtra, ancient MS. in eleventh century orthography, from the Ku-ku-zhi family of Kyelang. One complete volume, with wooden boards.

2. bsKā-brdzogs-pa-chen-po, MS. in Tibetan and Sanskrit, contents of a Tantric character. Complete in 63 sheets; circa 46 by 9½ cm.

3. bSon-gyi-spar-kha-dpungs-shig, Tibetan Manuscript, of Tantric character, on "mystical marks." Complete in 4 leaves, 46 by 9½ cm.

4. rGyol-po-skyas-'adebs-bzhugs-so, Tibetan MS. of a Tantric character, treating of 'agong-po, evil spirits; 9 leaves, 46 by 9½ cm.

5. Klu-gtor, Tibetan MS., about offerings to Nāgas; 4 leaves, 42 by 7½ cm.

6. sLob-dpon-padmai-gsungs-pai gYang-sgo-bsdam-pa, Tibetan MS., "the closed door of blessing," by Padma [sambhava]; 4 leaves, 46 by 9½ cm.

7. dGu-mig-lto-cos-kyi-bzlog-thabs, Tibetan MS. "A means to avoid the nine eyes (?)," (against the evil eye ?). A work presented to Padmasambhava by the fairy 'aGro-ba-bzang-mo; 9 leaves, 46 by 9½ cm.

8. 'aDri-moi mdos, sangs-rgyas-kyis-mdzad-pao, Tibetan MS. "Cross of defilement," composed by Buddha; 5 leaves, 43½ by 8 cm.

9. rGyal-po-chen-po-rnam-mthos-sras-kyis-gYang-'agugs-'adod-dgui-gter-mdzod, Tibetan MS. "Vairochaṇa's treasury for the nine desires;" 11 leaves, 46 by 9½ cm.

10. rGyal-po-chen-po-rnam-thos-sras-la-mchod-gtor-'abul-bai-rim-pa-dngos-grub-ky-ibang-mdzod, Tibetan MS., about offerings to Vairochaṇa. Written in black and red, with yellow lines. Bu-ston is mentioned in the colophon; he may be the author; 16 leaves, 38 by 8 cm.

11. Yi-ge-drug-pai-rig-sngags-chen-moi-sgrub-thabs-gser-gyi-'aphreng-ba, Tibetan block-print, "about the magical powers of the six syllables" (*i. e.* the Om-ma-ṇi-pa-dme-hūṁ); 3 leaves, 50 by 9 cm.

12. bSrung-ma-dpal-dgon-ma-ning-nag-poi-bskang-ba, Tibetan MS., "How to satisfy the glorious black eunuch, the guardian." On the last page, a certain Chos-'aphel-bstan-'adzin (perhaps the author) is mentioned; 9 leaves, 46 by 9½ cm.

13. bsTan-bsrung-rdo-rje-dgra-'adul-kyi-sgo-kha-dang-bskang-ba-bskul-bzlog-pa-bcad, Tibetan MS., "How to feed, satisfy, and repulse rDo-rje-dgra-'adul, the guardian of the teaching;" 3 leaves, 45 by 9½ cm.

14. rNams-sras-thse-rings-mai-rKang-phrin, Tibetan MS., "The gospel of rNams-sras-thse-ringsmak," a Tantric work. Several pages are torn and incomplete. 8 leaves, 46 by 9½ cm.

15. sLob-dpon-pa-dmai-'adzad-pai-bdud-kyi-zhal-'agyur-rgyad-pa, Tibetan MS. "The eighth diabolical manifestation (zhal-'agyur) of Padma [sambhava]." Written in dbu-med character. It belongs to the so-called gTer-ma or "hidden books." 9 leaves, 46 by 9¾ cm.

16. gNas-chen-dril-bu-ri-dang-ghandholai-gnas-yig-don-gsal-bzhugs-so, Tibetan wood-print, "the māhātmya of the Gandhola-temple in Lahul." 12 leaves, 29 by 9½ cm.

17. Ras-'aphags-aphags-pai-gnas-bshad-dang-mdon-rtogs-bcas-bzhugs-so, Tibetan wood-print, "the māhātmya of Ras-'aphags" (Triloknāth, Re-'aphagin Lahul). 8 leaves, 30 by 9½ cm.

18. Shes-rab-kyi-pha-rol-tu-phyin-pa, fragment of a Tibetan MS. of the eleventh or twelfth century, containing the Prajñāpāramitā, excavated from an ancient mchod-rten at Kyelang, by Rev. G. Hettasch. Two boxes full of large leaves, more or less complete. Kept at Simla.

19. Votive book, in fragments, Tibetan MS. of the eleventh or twelfth century. It refers to the dedication of the Prajñāpāramitā, mentioned under No. 18, and also to the cremation of an Urgyanpa lama. Excavated from an ancient mchod-rten at Kyelang by Rev. G. Hettasch. About 26 sheets have been preserved, more or less complete; 18 by 9 cm.

II. Folklore.

1. Ro-ngo-rub-can-ni-sgrungs-yin, Tales of the corpse Ngo-rub-can, collected in Purig by Munshi Ye-shes-rig-'adzin of Khalatse. (These tales remind us of the Vetālapañcaviṃśatikā); 21 ps. 4°.

2. Nyo-pai-chang-glu, The Drinking-songs of Khalatse. Taken down by Munshi Ye-shes-rig-'adzin of Khalatse; 10 ps. 4°.

3. La-dvags-dang-bu-rig-yul-so-soi-glui-spre-cha-yin, a collection of songs from Ladakh and Purig taken down by Munshi Ye-shes-rig-'adzin of Khalatse; 39 ps. 4°.

4. Various songs from Ladakh, taken down by Munshi Ye-shes-rig-'adzin of Khalatse, and others 52 ps. 8°.

5. La-dvags-kyi-glu, 14 songs from Ladakh. Writer unknown. 12 ps. 8°.

6. A collection of 28 historical songs from Ladakh, taken down by Munshi Ye-shes-rig-'adzin of Khalatse; 18 ps. 8°.

7. Ke-sar-gyi-gying-glu-lnga-yod, Five songs in praise of Kesar, taken down by Ye-shes-rig-'adzin of Khalatse; 5 ps. 8°.

8. Tales from Lahul, in Bunan and Tibetan, appendix to "Die mythologischen und historischen Erinnerungen der Lahouler;" taken down by bZod-pa-bde-chen of Kyelang; 5 ps. 8°.

9. gTam-dpe-ni, a collection of Tibetan proverbs from rGya, Ladakh, collected by dGā-phun-thsogs of Kyelang; 26 ps. 8°.

10. Bag-ma-btang-za-na-nyo-pas-sgo-la-btang-cas-si-dpe-cha-yin, Marriage-songs of Khalatse, and called Lhasa-songs from Khalatse, taken down by Ye-shes-rig-'adzin of Khalatse; 19 + 7 ps. 4°.

11. sBal-yul-gyi-glu-yin, Songs from Baltistan, taken down by Ye-shes-rig-'adzin of Khalatse; 8 ps. 4°.

12. La-dvags-kyi-glu-kha-shas-bzhugs-so, 32 Historical Songs from Ladakh, written by a native of Leh; 12 ps. folio.

13. Phyi-dbang-gi-glu-kha-shas-bzhugs-so, Songs from Phyi-dbang. Taken down by a native of Phyi-dbang in Ladakh; 24 ps. 4°.

14. Phyi-dbang-gi-gling-glu-bzhugs-so, the Gling-glu of Phyi-dbang, written by Ye-shes-rig-'adzin of Khalatse; 13 ps. 4°.

15. Thsod-pa-dang-glu-dang-gtam-dpe, a collection of riddles, songs, and proverbs from Khalatse collected by Munshi Ye-shes-rig-'adzin of Khalatse; 21 ps. 4°.

16. Pa-cha-chen-mo-dang-rgyal-po-chen-poi-sgrungs-yin, Fairy tales from Purig. Taken down by Munshi Ye-shes-rig-'adzin of Khalatse; 63 ps. 4°.

17. Folklore collected on the road, taken down mostly by bZod-pa-phun-thsogs, 11 + 4 ps. 8°.

18. Short description of mTho-lding, Guge, by Lobzang of Poo. One sheet with writing on one side.

19. A Tale of Human Sacrifices at Sarahan, Bashahr, taken down by Pindi Lal; 3 ps. 8°. In Urdu.

APPENDIX C.

NOTE ON RAWĀLSAR, MAṆḌĪ STATE.

On the 22nd January 1910, I visited Rawālsar with a guide, and on the road I met with several Tibetans, all from the western British parts of Tibet, who had come here on pilgrimage. At Rawālsar, high up on the hillside, there is a little lake, about half a mile in circumference, amidst a most glorious vegetation of palm trees and other foliage. The Tibetan name of the lake is *Pa-dma-can* "lotus-possessing." This name is mentioned by K. Marx in his "three documents," in connection with a passage in the *rGyal-rabs* which he translates "to the place where the water is fiery." This rendering is, however, misleading; for the Tibetan text which he thus translates *Chu-la-me-'abar* is really the name of another lake. We must not, therefore, suppose from this rendering that the water of the Rawālsar lake is hot. Quite a different lake situated in Nepal territory is called *Chula-me-'abar* and may possess hot springs. We received this information from a Tibetan pilgrim on his way to Rawālsar who gave us the following list of Tibetan places of pilgrimage in Nepal:—(1) *Bya-lung Ka-shor.* (2) *Chu-la-me-'abar.* (3) *rDo-la-me-'abar.* (4) *Tsan-dan Phag-mo.* (5) *Shing-ldan Phag-mo.* According to Professor Grünwedel[1] *Chubar*(-*Chula mebar*) is the place where Milaraspa died in A. D. 1122. He says that it is situated near Nalan on the Tibeto-Nepalese frontier.

The lake of Rawālsar has become famous on account of its connection with the Buddhist priest Padma-sambhava who is supposed to have dwelt here. Tibetan literature connects Padma-sambhava with Zahor, the Tibetan name of Maṇḍī; but it is not clear, whether the name *Zahor* refers to the Maṇḍī State in general or to Maṇḍī town. The Tibetans believe that his spirit still dwells in the tree on the little floating island of the lake. In their view it is his initiative which moves the island about, whilst other people attribute its movement to the wind. There are many wild ducks on the lake which enjoy the safety of the sacred spot, and the waternuts (*trapa natans*) are eagerly collected by the Tibetans, who carry them to their homes as objects of sanctity.

On the shore of the lake the Tibetans have a Lamaist temple which is asserted to have been recently renovated. It was rebuilt by the father of the present owner who belongs to a Kunawar family. This temple is furnished with one or two Nepalese bells which have long inscriptions. When we were at Rawālsar, Puntsog found a bell with an inscription in Nāgarī characters. The language seems to be Nepalese, but no one has as yet been able to read it. Miss Duncan, who was here in 1906, discovered a metal prayer wheel with a Tibetan inscription in two lines from which we learn that the man who rebuilt the temple is called Thse-ring-dor-rgyas, and that the name of the shrine is Shag-thub-chen-po.

There are, however, many Tibetan inscriptions carved on rocks round the lake. They are mostly invocations and besides the *Oṁ maṇi padme huṁ*, they contain endless repetitions of the following formulæ;

Oṁ a huṁ Vadzra guru Padma siddhi huṁ.
Oṁ Vagisvari muṁ.
Oṁ Vadzrasatva huṁ

and perhaps several others. The first of them is an invocation of the famous lama Padma-sambhava under a name by which he is also known in Lahul and Rubshu, and probably in other parts of Western Tibet. The second formula is an invocation of Mañjuśrī under the name of Vāgśvara and the third is addressed to Vajra-sattva. It should be noted that the combination of the first two incantations is very frequent in Lahul. This is by no means extraordinary, for Padma-sambhava is closely connected with

[1] *Mythologie.*

the Tibetan emperor *Khri srong lde btzan* who invited him to Tibet and who is regarded as an incarnation of Mañjuśrī. But also the third invocation we find in Lahul combined with the former two; for instance on the rock at Yurnad near Kye-lang (Lahul) which was photographed by Dr. Vogel. Is it possible that Padma-sambhava who made ample use of the *vajra* (thunderbolt) was believed to be an incarnation of Vajra-sattva?

It is of great interest that the connection of the Buddhist teacher Padma-sambhava with Rawālsar is asserted not only by Tibetan Buddhists, but also by the Brāhmans of the *tirtha*. Dr. Vogel has the following note in his article on Trilōknāth[1] "Here (at Rawālsar) in an absolutely Hindū country we find Padma-sambhava, the founder of Buddhism in Tibet, worshipped not only by lamas who have their own *dgon-pa* here, but equally by Brāhmaṇs who call him Ṛishi Lomaśa and even possess a *Māhātmya*, in which the local legend is given in its Brahmanic version."

The Śiva temples make a very beautiful picture along the shore of the lake and are undoubtedly older than the present Lamaist *dgonpa*. The stone figures of the bull Nandi in front of them struck me as being particularly well modelled. The ancient dress of Maṇḍī Buddhists has been preserved in Lamaist representations of Padma-sambhava. The unusual kind of the Lama's head-dress is still known as *Zahor-ma*, Zahor being the Tibetan name of Maṇḍī. As regards the many Tibetan rock carvings on the shore of the lake, I find it impossible to assign a fixed date to them. The forms of characters employed certainly do not suggest their being contemporaneous with Padma-sambhava; but as many of them look very time-worn, they may have been carved within the last five hundred years.

One of the Tibetans I met at Rawālsar told me that he intended to travel straight to Amritsar, as this was another place connected with Padama-sambhava. I was astonished to hear such a statement, and resolved to make enquiries on the spot.

Let me now add a few notes on Maṇḍī, collected from Tibetan historical works. There can exist no reasonable doubt as regards the identification of the Tibetan *Zahor* with *Maṇḍī*; for on our visit to Rawālsar we met with numerous Tibetan pilgrims, who all said that they were travelling to Zahor, thereby indicating the Maṇḍī State, if not the town. In the biography of Padma-sambhava, and in other books referring to his time, Zahor is frequently mentioned as a place where this teacher (c. 750 A. D.) resided. The famous Buddhist teacher Santi Rakhshita, who went to Tibet, was born in Zahor. Again in the days of *Ral-pa-can* (C. 800 A. D.) we find the statement that during the reigns of his ancestors many religious books had been brought to Tibet from rGya (India or China), Li, Zahor and Kashmir. Zahor was then apparently a seat of Buddhist learning and it is even stated that under the same king Zahor was conquered by the Tibetans. But under his successor, the apostate King Langdarma, many religious books were brought to Zahor, among other places, to save them from destruction.

Among the Tibetans there still prevails a tradition regarding the existence of hidden books in Maṇḍī, and this tradition in all probability refers to the books above mentioned. Mr. Howell, Assistant Commissioner of Kulu, told me that the present Ṭhākur of Kolong, Lahoul, had once been told by a high lama from Nepal, where the books are still hidden. Unfortunately the Ṭhākur had entirely forgotten the name of the place. My enquiries on the spot were of no avail, as none of the lamas and Tibetan laymen could or would tell where the books were concealed. I can suggest only one way of finding out the truth (or otherwise) of the tradition. A reward in money might be offered to the Ṭhākurs of Kolong in order to induce them to make another attempt to find the old books. It will be remembered that the Ṭhākurs of Kolong found out among other things who were the murderers of Schlagintweit.

---

[1] *J. A. S. B.*, Vol. LXX, p. 39.

APPENDIX D.

GENEALOGY OF THE RAJAS OF BASHAHR.

Mr. H. A. Rose, I.C.S., while in charge of census operations in the Panjāb, procured a copy of the genealogical roll of the Rajas of Bashahr. It is a list of 120 names, the years of accession and death being added in each case according to "the era of Yudhishthira." As Dr. Francke has pointed out in the course of his journal (above p. 8) the use of the cognomen *Singh* throughout the pedigree, renders its authenticity highly doubtful, except for the portion dealing with the last three or four centuries. Among the ruling houses of the Panjāb Hill States the cognomen in question does not seem to have come into use until the 16th century. In Chambā it replaced the appellation of *varman* and in Kuḷū that of *Pāl.*[1] If any further proof of the absolutely unreliable character of the earlier part of the list were wanted, I need only mention that the fifth Raja (supposed to have lived 153 years after Yudhishthira!) bears the half Persian name of Gulāb Singh. A name of this kind cannot, of course, have been in use in India previous to the Moslim conquest.

I wish, therefore, to reproduce here only the concluding twelve names of the genealogy, ending with Raja Shamsher Singh, the present ruler of the State, who is mentioned in Dr. Francke's account and portrayed in Plate IV, b. I cannot, of course, vouchsafe the accuracy of the dates assigned to each Raja, but it is noteworthy that Kēhari Singh, who is said to have reigned from A.D. 1639 to 1696, is the same who concluded in A.D. 1650 the treaty with Tibet of which Dr. Francke procured copies in the course of his tour (see above p. 24). I give in each case the names both according to the spelling of the list supplied to me and in their correct form.

Hari Singh	acc.	1464	obiit	1512
Chhatar (Chhattar) Singh	"	1512	"	1574
Bhoop (Bhūp) Singh	"	1574	"	1588
Kalyan (Kalyāṇ) Singh	"	1588	"	1639
Kehari (Kēharī from Skr. Kēśari) Singh	"	1639	"	1696
Bije (from Skr. Vijaya) Singh	"	1696	"	1719
Ode (Ude from Skr. Udaya) Singh	"	1719	"	1767
Ram (Rām) Singh	"	1767	"	1799
Roodhar (Rudar) Singh	"	1799	"	1844
Oogar (Ugar) Singh	"	1844	"	1878
Mahindar (Mahīndar or Mahēndar) Singh	"	1878	"	1906
Shamsher Singh	"	1907		

[1] *Chamba State Gazetteer*, p. 84.

INDEX

H

I

List of Public Libraries, etc., to which copies of the Archæological Survey Reports, new Imperial Series, including the Director General's Annual Report, Part II, and the Provincial Annual Reports of the Superintendents are regularly supplied.

I.—COUNTRIES OUTSIDE INDIA.

United Kingdom.

British Museum Library, Great Russell Street, Bloomsbury, London.

Bodleian Library, Oxford.

London University Library, Imperial Institute, London, S.W.

Cambridge University Library, Cambridge.

Edinburgh " " Edinburgh.

Glasgow " " Glasgow.

Aberdeen " " Aberdeen.

Trinity College Library, Dublin.

Folklore Society, 11, Old Square, Lincoln's Inn, London, W.C.

National Art Library, South Kensington Museum, London.

Royal Institute of British Architects, 9, Conduit Street, Hanover Square, London, W.

Advocates' Library, Edinburgh.

The Royal " Windsor Castle, Berks.

Royal Society, Burlington House, Piccadilly, London.

Royal Society, Edinburgh.

Royal Irish Academy, 19, Dawson Street, Dublin.

National Library of Ireland, Leinster House, Kildare Street, Dublin.

Royal Asiatic Society, 22, Albemarle Street, London.

Society of Antiquaries of London, Burlington House, Piccadilly, W.

Royal Scottish Museum, Edinburgh, Scotland.

Society of Antiquaries of Scotland, National Museum of Antiquities, Queen Street, Edinburgh.

Imperial Institute, London.

Indian Institute, Oxford.

Society for Protection of Ancient Buildings, 10, Buckingham Street, Adelphi, W.C.

The Royal Academy of Arts, Burlington House, London.

Society for the Promotion of Hellenic Studies, London.

France.

Bibliothèque Nationale, Paris.

Institut de France, Paris.

Musée Guimet, 7, Place d'Iena, Paris.

I.—COUNTRIES OUTSIDE INDIA—*contd.*

Germany.

Bibliothek der Deutschen Morgenländischen Gesellschaft, Halle (Saale), Germany.

Royal Prussian Academy of Sciences, Berlin.

Austria.

Imperial Academy of Sciences, Vienna.

Hungarian Academy, Buda-Pesth.

Italy.

Biblioteca Nazionale, Vittorio Emanuele, Rome.

R. Biblioteca Nazionale Centrale di Firenze.

British School at Rome.

American School of Classical Studies at Rome.

Other Countries in Europe.

Koninklijke Akademie van Wetenschappen te Amsterdam, Holland.

Royal Institute of Netherlands, India, The Hague, Holland.

Imperial Academy of Sciences (for the Asiatic Museum), St. Petersburg, Russia.

Royal Library, Copenhagen, Denmark.

Académie Royale d'Archéologie de Belgique, Anvers.

University Library, Upsala, Sweden.

" " Christiania, Norway.

British School at Athens, Greece.

La Société Archéologique d'Athènes, Athens, Greece.

America.

American Oriental Society, 235, Bishop Street, New Haven, Conn., U.S.A.

Smithsonian Institution, Washington, D. C., U.S.A.

Secretary, National Museum, Washington, U.S.A.

British Colonies.

The Museum, Canterbury, New Zealand.

Literary and Historical Society, Quebec, Canada.

Melbourne Library, Melbourne.

University Library, Sydney, New South Wales.

Victoria Public Library, Perth, Western Australia.

Royal Asiatic Society, Ceylon Branch, Colombo.

Straits Branch, Royal Asiatic Society, Singapore.

Museum of Arabic Art, Cairo, Egypt.

I.—COUNTRIES OUTSIDE INDIA—*concld.*

Foreign Colonies.

Directeur de l'Ecole française d'extrême Orient, Hanoi.

Bataviaasch Genootschap van Kunsten en Wetenschappen, Batavia.

Institut Français D'Archéologie Orientale du Caire, Cairo, Egypt.

Ethnological Survey for the Philippine Islands, Department of Interior, Manila.

II.—INDIA.

(1) Imperial.

Imperial Library, Calcutta.

Indian Museum, Calcutta.

*Press Room, Calcutta and Simla.

(2) Provincial.

Madras.

Secretariat Library, Fort St. George.

University „ Madras.

Public „ „

Presidency College „

School of Art, „

Government Central Museum, Madras.

Christian College Library „

Bombay.

Secretariat Library, Bombay.

University „ „

Bombay Branch of the Royal Asiatic Society, Town Hall, Bombay.

School of Art, Bombay.

The College of Science, Poona.

Bengal.

Secretariat Library, Writers' Buildings, Calcutta.

University Library, the Senate House, Calcutta.

Presidency College Library, 1, College Square, Calcutta.

Sanskrit College Library, 1, College Square, Calcutta.

Asiatic Society of Bengal, 57, Park Street, Calcutta.

United Provinces.

Secretariat Library, P. W. D., Allahabad.

University „ Allahabad.

Public Library, Allahabad.

Provincial Museum Library, Lucknow.

Sanskrit College, Benares.

Thomason College, Roorkee.

---

* Director-General's Report, Part II only.

II.—INDIA—*concld.*

PUNJAB.

Secretariat Library, Public Works Department, Lahore.

Punjab Public Library, Lahore.

Museum Library, Lahore.

University Library, Lahore.

Government College Library, Lahore.

Delhi Museum and Institute, Delhi.

NORTH-WEST FRONTIER PROVINCE.

Secretariat Library, Peshawar.

BURMA.

Secretariat Library, Rangoon.

The Bernard Free Library, Rangoon.

The Phayre Museum, Rangoon.

CENTRAL PROVINCES.

Secretariat Library, Nagpur.

Museum Library, Nagpur.

ASSAM.

Secretariat Library, Shillong.

COORG.

The Chief Commissioner of Coorg's Library, Bangalore.

NATIVE STATES.

Hyderabad.

The Resident's Library, Hyderabad.

Central India.

Library of the Agent to the Governor-General, Indore.

The Librarian, Dhar Museum Library, Dhar.

Rajkumar College, Indore.

Rajputana.

Library of the Chief Commissioner and Agent to the Governor-General, Ajmer.

College Library, Ajmer.

Baroda.

Library of the Resident at Baroda.

MAP SHOWING Dr. A. H. FRANÇKE'S ROUTE THROUGH THE INDO-TIBETAN BORDERLAND.

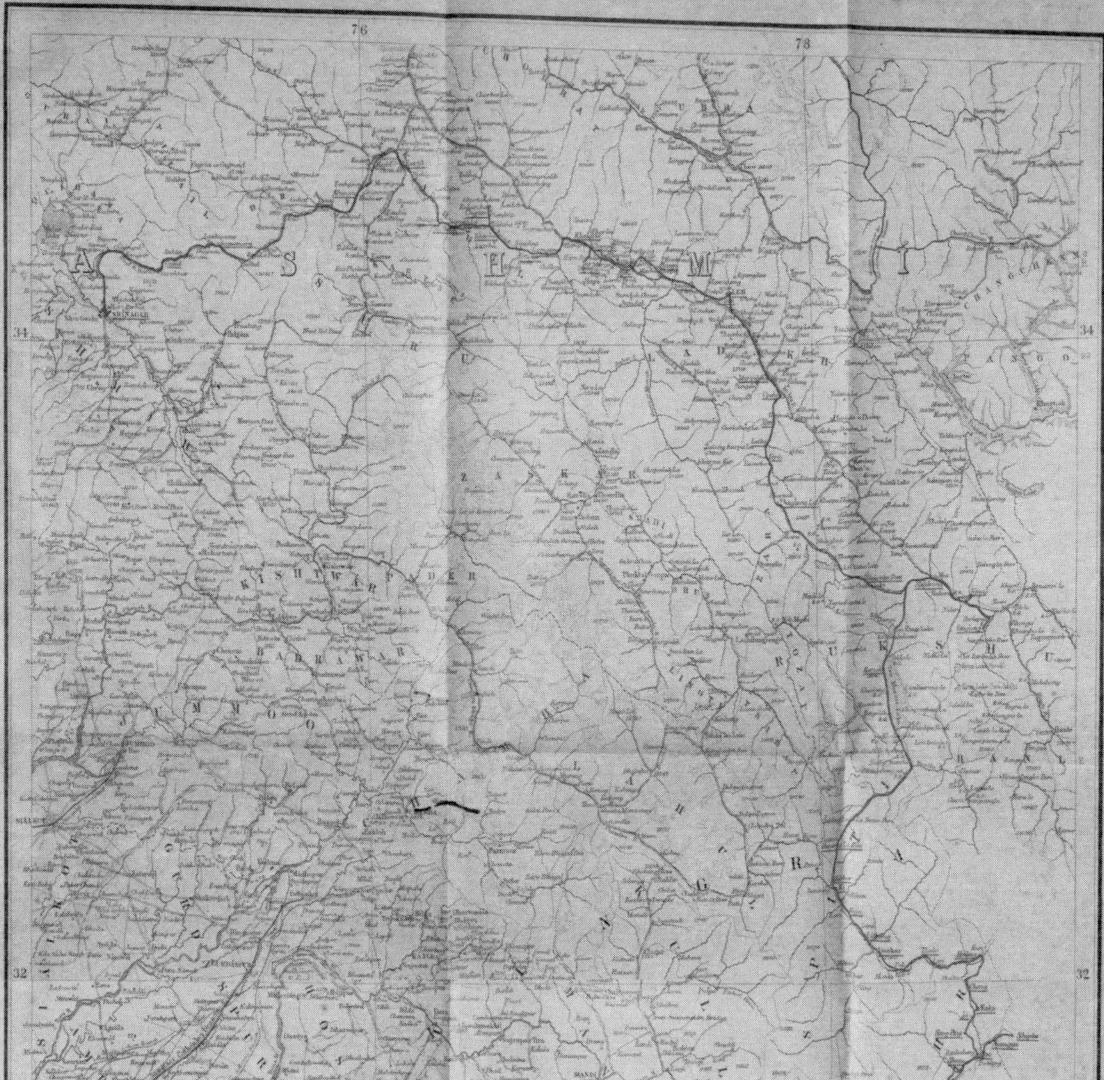

NOTE.—The route followed by Dr. Francke is shown in red, and places mentioned in his journal have been underlined in red.

Treasure of Books

Under One Roof

Demand Any Rare Book at

www.facsimilepublisher.com

Demand Any Rare Book at:

www.facsimilepublisher.com

if not available, give information,
our team will search and update you.

Promote Knowledge:

If you have any rare book
which is not available at
www.facsimilepublisher.com,
offer it to other readers so that others can also be
benefitted with your cooperation.
The book will be printed with your courtesy.

Print & Publish:

If you wish to get your book printed or published,
we have the service for you.

Customization on Demand:

We offer customization of books
as per the demand of the customer.

Published by

Facsimile Publisher
Ashok Vihar, Delhi-110052 (India)
Website: www.facsimilepublisher.com

Distributed by

Gyan Books Pvt. Ltd.
5, Ansari Road, Daryaganj, New Delhi-110002 (India)
E-mail: books@gyanbooks.com, Website: www.gyanbooks.com

2 222000 000486